Human Nature

Oops, My Bad

Dr. Baby Sharma

For Rumi, my son

I once thought the environment was something we study,
measure, and manage.

Then you were born,
and it became the air in your lungs,
the warmth on your skin,
the world that will shape you long before you can name it.

I will try to raise you with care and kindness.
But I have come to realise —
The environment around you is raising you, too.

This book is where that realisation began.

The Human Nature: Oops, My Bad
Published by PenAime Private Ltd

care@penaime.com
www.penaime.com

The characters and events portrayed in this book are fictitious. Any similarity to real persons, living or dead, is coincidental and not intended by the author.

This work was developed with the assistance of Artificial Intelligence (AI) tools, including a custom no-code research agent built using Claude Projects. The system was designed to support interdisciplinary research synthesis across environmental science, behavioral science, and psychology.

The AI functioned as a structured research and analytical support tool, while all narrative development, interpretation, and final content decisions were directed and curated by the author. Copyright protection under applicable laws applies to the extent that the work contains original human input.

ISBN: 978-81-988541-2-4

Typeset and Cover Design by PenAime Private Limited

Contents

Human Nature

Oops, My Bad

Dr. Baby Sharma

A Tribute to Writers: The Architects of Imagination

PenAime does not intend to replace creativity. We respect art and artists. This is only an attempt to support people who require the assistance of AI to bring their ideas to light. We are fully aware that no such technology would have come into existence if not for people who have dedicated their lives to writing and literature.

This is a tribute to every storyteller who has ever dared to put pen to paper, to every voice that has carried meaning across generations. Your words inspire, ignite, and shape the world far beyond any algorithm's reach. And as long as there are minds that weave stories, the written word will remain indomitable—a legacy carried not by machines, but by the souls of those who create.

Prologue: Oops, My Bad

I have been watching you for a very long time.

Long enough to remember when your nights were dark except for stars and small, careful fires. Long enough to see you invent wheels, maps, engines, plastic, satellites, and tiny glowing rectangles that now live in your palms.

You are extraordinarily inventive.

You are less extraordinary at noticing where the leftovers go.

Tonight I hover above one of your cities as dusk settles in. Windows light up floor by floor, like constellations built from glass. Roads pulse red and white. Rooftops hum with machines pushing warm air into cooler rooms. A delivery scooter swerves between cars carrying noodles inside three plastic boxes and one paper bag that claims to be eco-friendly.

You love me, by the way.

You tattoo my mountains on your skin.You post my oceans with inspirational quotes.You name cafés after forests and perfumes after rain. You design homes with "green views" and then seal the windows to keep the heat out.

You are affectionate.

You are contradictory.

In a supermarket aisle, someone holds two bottles of

shampoo. One is cheaper. The other is wrapped in soft greens and leaf symbols. They hesitate, glance at their phone, feel the line growing behind them.

The cheaper one wins.

In a kitchen, a tap runs while someone scrolls.

In an office, lights glow in empty rooms.

In a park, wrappers slide toward drains after a sudden shower.

I am not offended.

You are busy creatures.

You live at the polished ends of very long systems you rarely see.

You do not see forests becoming shelves.

You do not see rivers cooling power plants.

You do not see mines sleeping inside batteries.

You mostly see what is right in front of you.

That is not cruelty.

That is wiring.

Still, after rainstorms, when I watch floating cups collect near gutters, I sometimes think:

Fascinating species.

Very loving.

Terrible at follow-through.

What Nature Is Really Pointing At

If that sounded amused rather than angry, that is deliberate.

Because what Nature just described is not wickedness.

It is human behaviour.

Ask people whether they want clean air, safe drinking water, living forests, stable weather, healthy soil. The answer is nearly always yes. Environmental concern is not rare. It is widespread.

And yet:

Waste piles up.

Cities trap heat.

Aquifers fall.

Rivers carry plastic.

Energy demand keeps climbing.

So what explains the gap between caring and changing?

The tempting answer is selfishness.

The truer answer is stranger:

our minds evolved for a world that no longer exists.

Human brains are exquisitely tuned to deal with what is:

— immediate

— visible

— personal

— emotionally loud

They struggle with what is:

— distant

— slow

— dispersed

— delayed

A pothole in front of your car grabs attention.

An ocean warming half a world away does not.

Your nervous system treats those two signals very differently.

That mismatch—between ancient instincts and modern systems—runs quietly underneath many environmental problems.

It is not that people do not care.

It is that caring must constantly compete with convenience, habit, distraction, social pressure, and invisible consequences.

The Bin That Feels Like an Ending

Take something small.

A coffee cup.

You finish the drink, crumple the sleeve, drop it into a bin.

Thup.

Your body relaxes. The object is no longer your problem.

Emotionally, that is the end of the story.

Physically, it is the beginning.

The cup rides in a truck to a sorting facility. Some materials find a second life. Many do not. The plastic lining—thin, stubborn—complicates everything.

Wind lifts lighter fragments from dumping grounds.

Rain pushes bits into drains.

Drains lead to streams.

Streams become rivers.

Rivers meet the sea.

Sunlight fractures plastic into smaller and smaller ghosts.

Fish ingest them.

Birds feed them to chicks.

Eventually, traces return to humans in water, salt, seafood.

Most of us never follow that trail.

Not because we do not care.

Because our brains are not built to track consequences that unfold slowly across landscapes.

We evolved to watch what moved nearby.

Bins feel like endings.

They are commas.

Why Trying Already Feels Good

There is another quiet moment hiding in that supermarket aisle.

When you *consider* doing something good—bringing a reusable bag, buying the refill pack, switching off a light—your brain rewards you.

A warm flicker.

I'm the kind of person who cares.

That identity matters enormously to humans.

We protect it.

We polish it.

We project it.

So when behaviour falls short, the mind moves fast to soften the discomfort:

— *Tomorrow I'll be better.*

— *Everyone slips sometimes.*

— *This won't make much difference.*

— *I recycled yesterday.*

These are not lies.

They are emotional cushions.

Without them, guilt would crush daily functioning.

But there is a catch.

Once the discomfort fades, urgency fades with it.

We relax.

The planet does not.

Why Fear Has Limits

Environmental messaging often leans on alarm: burning forests, melting ice, rising graphs, ticking clocks.

Fear grabs attention.

Briefly.

Over time, constant dread does something else.

It exhausts.

It pushes people to scroll past headlines.

It encourages avoidance.

When problems feel enormous and personal power feels tiny, disengagement becomes self-protection.

That is not apathy.

That is overload.

Humans were not built to process planetary threats while also dealing with traffic, deadlines, family crises, and unread emails.

You Live Inside Systems

Here is the part that rarely gets airtime:

much of environmental impact is shaped not by single dramatic choices, but by systems.

Where houses are built.

How often buses run.

What energy grids rely on.

How food is grown and priced.

How waste is collected.

How recycling is labelled.

Whether plant-based meals are default or exceptional.

Whether stairs are visible and elevators are central.

People like to believe behaviour flows mainly from willpower.

It does not.

Design quietly guides action.

Make the sustainable option easy, affordable, and

normal—people choose it.

Make it expensive, confusing, or socially awkward—most will not, no matter how strong their beliefs.

Humans follow paths.

Change the paths, and millions change direction without speeches.

Nature Doesn't Hold Grudges

When Nature talks about floods, droughts, heatwaves, and shifting coastlines, it is not threatening.

Those are not punishments.

They are responses.

Physics answering chemistry.

Chemistry answering energy use.

Energy answering how societies operate.

Nature runs feedback loops.

Humans run stories.

Which means the story you tell yourselves next matters enormously.

Two Futures Compete

One story says:

Humans are terrible. It's too late. Everything is broken.

That narrative paralyses.

The other says:

Humans are inconsistent. Our systems outran our instincts. We built convenience faster than wisdom. And we can redesign convenience.

That version still includes responsibility.

But it also includes possibility.

For cooler cities.

For packaging that disappears instead of lingering.

For transport that beats traffic.

For homes that waste less without heroic discipline.

Why This Book Exists

This book is not here to shame you.

It is here to decode you.

To show how predictable human behaviour actually is—and why that is hopeful.

Predictable systems can be redesigned.

Habits can be nudged.

Defaults can be flipped.

Norms can shift.

Environmental progress does not begin with perfect people.

It begins with environments that make good choices boringly normal.

Still Watching

You are still in that supermarket aisle.

Still holding two bottles.

Still glancing at your phone.

Still late.

I am not asking for saints.

I am asking for designers.

Designers of homes.

Designers of streets.

Designers of policies.

Designers of daily life.

You keep saying:
Oops.
My bad.
That is not the end of the story.
That is the moment just before learning.

Chapter 1: The Bin Is Not the End

Journey of waste through Perception & Time

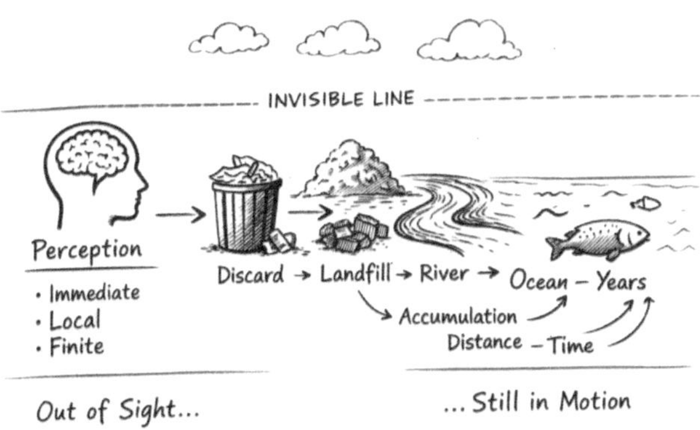

Rain alters cities in ways that feel momentarily intimate. It presses dust into the seams of pavements, releases the faint mineral scent trapped inside overheated stone, rinses leaves that survive between traffic lanes and concrete walls. For a short while, air becomes lighter, as though the city has exhaled. I have always appreciated that pause — the brief suspension in which surfaces shine and movement slows and people look up long enough to register the weather.

What follows is quieter.

When the rain loosens its grip, water begins to organise itself. It pools along kerbs worn into shallow basins by decades of tyres. It threads through cracks in sidewalks. It slips down the gentle slopes engineered into roads so efficiently that few of you ever think about them. Leaves detach and drift. Grains of sand release themselves from scaffolding and half-finished buildings. The smallest objects — light enough to surrender to gravity, smooth enough to slide — begin to migrate.

A cup nudges forward.

A translucent wrapper lifts, hesitates, and settles into motion.

A bottle cap rotates once, twice, then joins the current.

You are rarely standing still at this point.

You are inside doorways, folding umbrellas, checking messages that accumulated while the sky was busy elsewhere. You are reheating food. Restarting conversations. Re-entering schedules that the rain interrupted rather than replaced. By the time puddles thin and reflections fade, your attention has already returned to matters that feel more immediate.

By morning, streets appear orderly again.

The water is gone.

The moment has passed.

From where I am watching, however, nothing about this retreat is accidental. Cities are built to hurry rain away. Kerbs curve inward. Gutters open at precise intervals. Storm drains swallow runoff through metal mouths that vanish into underground corridors of pipe and concrete. This architecture is a public-health triumph, the result of centuries spent learning how stagnant water breeds illness and discomfort. Speed, here, is protection.

What those systems do not discriminate between is what travels with the water.

HUMAN NATURE: OOPS, MY BAD

A leaf and a receipt float with equal compliance.

So does a cigarette filter.

So does the lid from a container that held dinner only minutes earlier.

They slip into the same channels, disappear into the same darkness, and continue outward toward places that remain abstract to most of the people who stood above them moments ago.

You do not follow these movements.

There is no reason you should.

Rain has ended.

The pavement is usable again.

The visible problem appears resolved.

Your attention — that most limited of resources — shifts back to rooms, faces, deadlines, warmth.

I continue to observe the slow choreography beneath your feet.

Not with irritation.

With interest.

There is something revealing in the way your eyes leave once surfaces dry, in how easily resolution is inferred from disappearance, in how confidently a cleared street is taken as a finished story. Long before you make arguments about sustainability or policies or responsibility, long before guilt or concern or indifference have time to speak, your minds have already performed a quieter operation.

They have marked the episode complete.

Rain fell.

Rain left.

Life resumed.

What remains — the thin procession moving underground, the objects beginning journeys that stretch far beyond the block where they were dropped — does not compete well for your notice.

It does not interrupt.

It does not announce itself.

It simply continues.

And in that gap, between what leaves your field of vision and what persists beyond it, something important about human behaviour waits to be understood.

What Humans Mean by "Away"

Human beings have always relied on distance as a form of reassurance.

When something leaves the body's immediate surroundings—when it slips out of sight, sound, and smell—the nervous system relaxes, because for most of evolutionary history distance genuinely reduced risk. Rotting organic matter could be abandoned, predators could be avoided, smoke from fires dispersed into open air, and broken tools left behind as groups moved on; disappearance usually meant that danger, inconvenience, or responsibility had been successfully escaped. That ancient logic still governs modern perception, even though the material world has changed far more quickly than the instincts used to interpret it.

What you now call *away* is not a physical destination so much as a cognitive category: the mental box into which objects are placed once they cross a sensory threshold. A bin lid closing, a bag being tied, a drain swallowing water, or a door shutting on a refuse room produces a feeling of completion that is immediate and largely unconscious, because the brain is wired to treat removal from perception as resolution. The muscles loosen, attention shifts, and the episode is quietly archived, not through reasoning but through embodied inference.

This matters because contemporary systems preserve the signals of finality while severing them from physical endings.

Materials vanish from kitchens and streets with extraordinary efficiency, yet they continue to exist elsewhere in altered forms and unfamiliar landscapes, travelling through channels that ordinary life rarely intersects. The psychological mechanism, however, remains unchanged: once an object is no longer visible or odorous or obstructive, it stops demanding cognitive space. The mind moves on not because it has judged the situation harmless, but because the senses have withdrawn their alerts.

Language reinforces this transition with remarkable economy. To "throw something away" implies an erasure rather than a relocation; "disposal" carries the suggestion that matter itself has ceased to matter; "waste" transforms objects from persistent substances into conceptual leftovers. These phrases function as tools of compression, allowing complicated physical journeys to be reduced to a syllable that clears the path for the next task, the next conversation, the next concern. They are not attempts to deceive. They are mental shortcuts shaped by lives already crowded with competing demands.

Attention is not limitless, and neither is imagination. Human cognition operates through filtering, constantly deciding what deserves focus and what can safely be ignored.

Proximity dominates those calculations. Events occurring in the same room command more urgency than those unfolding beyond the neighbourhood, let alone across watersheds or decades. What remains close feels relevant; what travels outward fades into abstraction. This is not a moral judgement issued by the mind so much as a structural feature of how perception evolved to function inside bodies that move through small physical spaces.

The concept of *away* therefore performs an essential role in keeping daily life manageable. Without it, ordinary routines would become psychologically unworkable, burdened by the need to track every object beyond the moment of use. Meals would require contemplation of packaging's future, cleaning would demand reflection on wastewater's destinations, shopping would involve rehearsing supply chains rather than choosing between brands. The mind declines such labour not out of indifference, but out of necessity.

From a broader perspective, what becomes striking is how consistently modern environments preserve this cognitive relief. The act of discarding is packaged as closure: smooth surfaces replace clutter, sealed containers suppress smell, emptied pavements restore visual calm. Each of these cues tells the nervous system that a problem has been solved, even when all that has occurred is a transfer from one location to another. The satisfaction is immediate; the continuation remains elsewhere.

This gap between perception and persistence lies at the heart of contemporary waste. People do not experience themselves as sending objects into long futures, because nothing in the sensory or linguistic frame of everyday disposal encourages such an interpretation. The bin performs finality. The street looks finished. The room feels clean. The story appears complete.

Understanding what humans mean by *away* is therefore not about correcting ignorance or assigning blame.

It is about recognising the quiet partnership between ancient psychology and modern removal, between perceptual closure and physical relocation, between what leaves the body's orbit and what continues to exist beyond it.

Before anyone argues about responsibility or policy or redesign, before guilt or justification enters the conversation at all, this smaller and more fundamental operation has already taken place: the mind has concluded that the episode is over.

And for creatures shaped to trust what their senses report, that conclusion is extraordinarily persuasive.

Following a Cup Through the World

Consider a single object whose presence in your life lasts no more than a few minutes: a disposable coffee cup purchased on the way to work, carried across a street, emptied before the next appointment, and dropped into a bin with the casual accuracy of muscle memory rather than deliberation. The action feels so small that it barely registers as an environmental decision at all, and yet that smallness is precisely what allows the rest of the story to remain unexamined.

Once released, the cup does not enter oblivion; it enters a sequence of systems designed to remove it from immediate surroundings with maximum efficiency. It may spend hours in a plastic liner beneath a pavement before being lifted into a collection vehicle that follows routes optimised for speed and volume rather than for the visibility of outcomes, travelling toward facilities situated far from residential life where materials are sorted by combinations of human labour and optical machinery trained to recognise shape, colour, and reflectivity. At this stage the object already begins to fragment conceptually, its sleeve separated from its lid, its paper shell treated differently from the polymer film bonded invisibly to its inner surface, each component evaluated not for its history as a cup but for its compatibility with whatever processing stream is economically viable at that moment.

Some elements continue toward recycling plants, others toward incinerators or landfills, decisions made less by intention than by market prices, contamination levels, and the technical limits of available infrastructure. From burial sites, lighter pieces escape with remarkable regularity, carried by wind across open ground or lifted by rainwater into channels that funnel runoff toward storm drains and culverts whose purpose has never been to discriminate between organic debris and synthetic fragments. These waterways feed into larger currents, and over time physical stressors — ultraviolet radiation, temperature fluctuations, abrasion against rock and concrete — reduce recognisable forms into particles too small to retrieve and too numerous to track.

Once reduced to this scale, the cup becomes difficult to follow with the human eye but not with chemical persistence, as fragments enter aquatic systems, settle into sediments, lodge inside organisms that mistake them for food, or circulate through soil and water in ways that rarely reconnect with the moment of purchase that began the sequence. The journey is neither dramatic nor rapid; it unfolds through repetition rather than spectacle, through the quiet operation of flows that operate whether or not anyone pays attention to them.

What is psychologically striking about this chain is how completely it escapes everyday awareness. Nothing about the act of disposal invites reflection on hydrology, polymer science, or waste economics, just as nothing about the warmth of the cup advertises the longevity of the materials that made it possible. The bin marks a psychological endpoint long before the physical processes have even gathered momentum, because the mind is oriented toward what has left the hand rather than toward what has entered circulation elsewhere.

This is not a failure of knowledge so much as a feature of ordinary cognition. Human attention is calibrated for immediate environments, for objects that obstruct movement or demand care in the present moment, not for diffuse trajectories unfolding across years and jurisdictions. The very success of waste systems in removing inconvenience from sight ensures that the material consequences of everyday consumption remain largely theoretical, understood in principle but rarely rehearsed in imagination.

Following a cup through the world therefore reveals something less obvious than pollution.

It reveals the structure of perception.

An action that lasts seconds initiates processes that persist for decades, yet nothing in the sensory experience of disposal communicates that disparity in duration or scale. The physical systems continue with mechanical indifference, while the psychological system has already closed the episode, filed it under solved, and moved on to the next obligation waiting in line.

Seen in this way, the cup is not exceptional.

It is exemplary.

It stands in for thousands of other objects that pass briefly through human hands before entering geographies too extended, too fragmented, and too slow to feel connected to the moment in which they were released.

That gap — between the fleeting gesture and the prolonged aftermath — is not created by apathy.

It is created by distance, by design, and by minds shaped to live at the scale of rooms and streets rather than watersheds and centuries.

And it is inside that gap that much of the modern environmental story quietly unfolds.

Why Order Feels So Good

Human beings have an unusually intimate relationship with surfaces.

Counters wiped clean, pavements swept after storms, bins emptied before they overflow, floors restored to shine — these gestures produce a form of satisfaction that is felt physically before it is articulated intellectually, a loosening of shoulders, a slowing of breath, a sense that the environment has returned to a state in which attention can finally wander elsewhere. Order communicates safety at a level deeper than reasoning, because for much of human history disorder was rarely neutral: decomposing matter attracted insects and predators, clutter obscured hazards underfoot, stagnant water bred disease, and unfamiliar debris signalled intrusion rather than comfort.

Those ancestral pressures shaped nervous systems that

remain exquisitely sensitive to spatial cues. Visual clutter increases cognitive load, forcing the brain to evaluate more objects, track more edges, and resolve more uncertainties, while clean surfaces reduce perceptual demand and create the impression that nothing urgent is being hidden in peripheral vision. Even in modern interiors, far removed from the savannahs in which such sensitivities evolved, the response persists with remarkable consistency: mess unsettles, tidiness reassures.

Urban sanitation magnified these instincts rather than replacing them. Dense settlements cannot tolerate visible accumulation for long without inviting discomfort and illness, so entire infrastructures emerged to remove waste quickly and quietly, from underground sewage networks to daily refuse collection schedules that operate before most residents wake. These systems are among the great triumphs of public health, and they are rightly celebrated for the lives they have saved.

Psychologically, however, they do something else at the same time.

They provide closure.

When rubbish disappears overnight, the mind infers that the problem has been resolved. When drains clear puddles from roads, the episode feels finished. When a spill is wiped away, responsibility seems to have evaporated with the moisture. None of these inferences require conscious thought; they arise automatically from the disappearance of sensory irritation. Smell is gone, so danger must be gone. Obstruction has vanished, so risk must have passed. The brain, relieved of disturbance, reallocates attention to whatever comes next.

This pattern is powerful precisely because it operates

below deliberation.

People do not stand in freshly cleaned streets congratulating themselves on having outsourced environmental consequences; they simply experience the quiet pleasure of restored order and move on with their day. The nervous system registers resolution long before the intellect has an opportunity to ask whether resolution has truly occurred or merely shifted location.

The distinction matters because material does not cease to exist when it ceases to trouble the senses.

Objects removed from kitchens, offices, and sidewalks continue to persist elsewhere, but those elsewhere locations remain largely abstract to daily life, separated by distance, by infrastructure, and by the simple fact that most people do not encounter landfills, treatment plants, or downstream sediments during ordinary routines. Cleanliness at the point of use therefore coexists easily with accumulation at the point of disposal, and the two rarely collide in the same field of perception.

In this way, order becomes a narrative device as much as a hygienic one.

A swept street tells a story of completion.

An emptied bin tells a story of containment.

A dry pavement after rain tells a story of systems functioning as intended.

These stories are reassuring, and reassurance is persuasive, especially for minds evolved to monitor what is near rather than what is remote.

Understanding why order feels so good is therefore not about condemning the desire for cleanliness or control;

those desires are among the foundations of civilisation itself. It is about recognising that the pleasure of restored surfaces can quietly mask the continuation of processes taking place beyond immediate experience, and that a culture skilled at removing visible mess may become less practiced at imagining where removed things actually go.

The attraction of tidy environments is not superficial.

It is neurological.

And because it is neurological, it shapes environmental outcomes long before ethics, policies, or arguments have time to enter the scene.

The Problem of Scale

Human cognition is remarkably adept at navigating immediate environments and remarkably strained when confronted with processes that unfold across vast numbers, long durations, and distant locations. This mismatch between perception and accumulation becomes especially consequential in the context of waste, where actions that feel fleeting and insignificant initiate chains of material movement whose ultimate effects emerge only after thousands or millions of similar gestures have been repeated.

A single wrapper dropped into a bin scarcely registers as an environmental event. One plastic bag carried home appears trivial. One disposable cup weighs so little in the imagination that it rarely provokes reflection at all. These judgements are not irrational; they reflect nervous systems shaped to respond to what is directly encountered rather than to abstract multiplication. The mind is calibrated to deal with what can be seen, heard, and touched in the present moment, not to compute what happens when identical actions are distributed across entire cities every day for decades.

Scale, in other words, is not felt.

It is inferred, and even then only when something disrupts ordinary routines enough to demand attention.

Numbers printed in reports—tonnes of waste generated annually, percentages recycled, concentrations of microplastics in water—remain cognitively thin unless anchored to tangible experience. Graphs can rise dramatically without altering what happens at the kitchen counter or office desk, because the feedback loop between individual behaviour and planetary outcome is stretched across distances and timeframes that human intuition was never designed to bridge.

This temporal and spatial separation dissolves urgency. Consequences delayed by years fail to compete with obligations due within hours. Harms dispersed across watersheds struggle to register alongside mess visible on a single pavement. The bin, the truck, the landfill, and the river appear as discrete scenes rather than as parts of a continuous system, precisely because the mind prefers episodic narratives with clear endings to slow accumulations without obvious boundaries.

From the standpoint of environmental processes, however, accumulation is relentless. Rivers integrate what cities shed. Sediments archive decades of material history. Soils incorporate fragments invisible to the naked eye. Organisms ingest what drifts into their habitats and carry traces forward into food webs. None of these systems require intention; they respond mechanically to inputs repeated often enough.

The psychological difficulty lies in reconciling this

geological rhythm with the tempo of everyday life.

Humans operate in minutes.

Material systems operate in years.

People make choices one object at a time.

Ecosystems respond to millions of such choices layered together.

The disparity is not a failure of concern but a consequence of embodiment: minds embedded in single bodies navigating small territories cannot easily inhabit the perspective of coastlines or groundwater basins.

Understanding the problem of scale therefore involves more than learning larger numbers. It requires recognising that the ordinary has a habit of becoming consequential when multiplied, that repetition rather than drama is the engine of most environmental change, and that what appears negligible at the level of one action can become transformative when extended across populations and time.

Waste persists not because individuals intend planetary alteration, but because everyday routines, performed with no sense of spectacle or significance, accumulate into landscapes.

That quiet arithmetic is always running.

It simply operates at a tempo that human intuition struggles to hear.

Top of Form

Bottom of Form

Why Guilt Cannot Carry the Weight

When people first encounter accounts of plastic-filled oceans, contaminated rivers, or landfills rising at the edges of cities, guilt often appears quickly and sincerely, surfacing as hesitation at checkouts, careful reading of labels, or brief resolutions to carry reusable containers and refuse unnecessary packaging. Emotional responses of this kind matter, because they signal that individuals recognise a connection between their everyday behaviour and broader ecological patterns, even when that connection is imperfectly understood.

Yet guilt is an unstable motivator.

Psychologically, it is difficult to sustain over long periods without generating either exhaustion or disengagement. Human beings are not well equipped to walk through ordinary days while holding constant awareness of distant harms, and the mind therefore develops ways to soften emotional overload. Rationalisations emerge not necessarily because people wish to deceive themselves, but because they are attempting to preserve psychological equilibrium: *I recycle most things; I'm only buying this once; corporations are far worse than individuals; I will compensate later; everyone slips occasionally.* Such thoughts function as internal pressure valves, allowing life to proceed without becoming paralysed by moral unease.

In the context of waste, this dynamic is especially pronounced because the consequences of disposal are rarely immediate or personally experienced. A person who drops a cup into a bin does not encounter the landfill, the river, or the sediment that follows, and the absence of sensory feedback makes it easy for emotional urgency to dissipate. When harm is delayed and geographically dispersed, guilt struggles to maintain its grip, even among people who sincerely care about environmental outcomes.

There is also a temporal dimension to this erosion.

Emotional reactions flare most strongly when new information disrupts established routines, but they fade as novelty diminishes and daily pressures reassert themselves. The first documentary about plastic pollution may provoke strong feelings; the tenth headline begins to blur into the background. The mind habituates, not because the issue has been resolved, but because sustained alarm is cognitively expensive.

Importantly, this pattern does not imply that people become indifferent.

Rather, it suggests that guilt alone is too fragile to shoulder the weight of systemic environmental problems. Emotions fluctuate. Attention wanders. Circumstances change. Individuals who are exhausted, financially stressed, or preoccupied with family obligations are less able to sustain moral vigilance, even when their underlying values remain intact.

Understanding the limits of guilt is therefore not about excusing environmentally damaging behaviour.

It is about recognising the constraints under which human psychology operates.

If waste reduction depends primarily on individuals maintaining constant emotional tension, it will falter whenever life intrudes, which is to say, frequently. Long-term change requires supports that do not rely entirely on fluctuating feelings, supports that remain in place even when motivation wanes and headlines fade.

This section does not yet ask how such supports might be designed; that question belongs later in the book.

Here, the point is narrower and more sobering: guilt can

alert, but it cannot carry the entire load.

Not across years.

Not across millions of daily decisions.

Not against systems that continue to remove consequences from sight.

Understanding that limitation is itself a form of clarity, one that moves the conversation away from shame and toward more durable ways of aligning everyday life with ecological reality.

Fear, Saturation, and Withdrawal

Alongside guilt, fear has become one of the most common emotional currencies in environmental communication. Images of beaches layered with plastic, animals entangled in debris, rivers darkened by industrial runoff, and graphs climbing sharply upward circulate with increasing frequency, each intended to compress vast and complex processes into moments capable of cutting through everyday distraction.

Such messages are not fabrications.

They describe real transformations taking place in oceans, soils, and watersheds.

They matter.

Psychologically, however, fear operates on a volatile timetable.

In the short term, it commands attention, sharpening focus and provoking concern in ways that gentler appeals often cannot. Over longer stretches, repeated exposure to threatening information begins to produce different effects. Nervous systems habituate. What initially shocked becomes familiar. The emotional charge dulls, not because the problem has been solved, but because constant alarm is difficult to sustain without exhausting the very capacities required to respond.

This process, often referred to as saturation, is well documented in studies of risk perception and media exposure. When individuals encounter warnings too frequently, especially when those warnings describe harms that feel distant or difficult to influence, the mind begins to protect itself by narrowing engagement. Headlines are skimmed rather than read. Images are scrolled past. Conversations are postponed. The topic becomes something to be avoided rather than explored.

Withdrawal, in this sense, is not apathy.

It is a coping strategy.

Human cognition evolved to prioritise threats that could be confronted directly — predators nearby, storms approaching, food shortages in the coming weeks — not sprawling crises unfolding across continents and decades. When danger feels omnipresent but personal control feels minimal, anxiety ceases to motivate and instead begins to paralyse. Attention turns away not out of denial, but out of self-preservation.

Waste-related problems are particularly susceptible to this dynamic because they are both omnipresent and largely invisible in daily life. People are told that plastics are accumulating in oceans or entering food webs, yet the streets they walk each morning appear clean, and the water from taps remains clear. This contrast between alarming information and reassuring surroundings creates cognitive tension. Over time, one of these signals must give way, and it is often the abstract one that loses.

Fear also interacts with moral overload. Individuals already navigating crowded emotional landscapes — job insecurity, health concerns, family obligations, political uncertainty — may lack the psychological space to absorb yet another source of worry, however legitimate. When environmental communication adds weight without offering a sense of agency, disengagement becomes more likely than sustained attention.

Understanding this pattern is crucial, because it challenges the assumption that intensifying warnings will automatically deepen commitment. More dramatic images do not always produce more durable engagement; in some cases, they accelerate retreat. People begin to protect their limited emotional bandwidth, even when they continue to endorse environmental goals in principle.

This does not mean fear has no place.

It can awaken.

It can interrupt complacency.

It can puncture illusions of harmlessness.

But on its own, and especially when repeated without relief or pathways for action, it struggles to anchor long-term behavioural change.

In the context of waste, fear often illuminates the endpoint — polluted rivers, damaged ecosystems, contaminated food chains — without clarifying the everyday processes that connect kitchens and pavements to those outcomes. The result can be a sense of looming catastrophe combined with uncertainty about what, precisely, one person's actions meaningfully influence.

That combination is psychologically unstable.

It produces cycles of attention and avoidance rather than steady engagement.

Recognising fear, saturation, and withdrawal as linked phenomena therefore does not weaken the environmental case.

It strengthens it.

It suggests that lasting shifts in how societies handle material flows will depend not only on communicating the seriousness of consequences, but on doing so in ways that respect cognitive limits, avoid constant alarm, and leave room for curiosity rather than only dread.

Fear can open a door.

Whether people keep walking through it depends on what waits beyond the first jolt of urgency.

The Systems That Quietly Steer You

It is tempting to treat waste as the direct outcome of personal decisions, as though every wrapper discarded or container accepted were the result of a fully conscious evaluation carried out in isolation from the world in which it occurs. In practice, most disposal happens inside structures that were arranged long before an individual arrived on the scene: bin placements, collection schedules, packaging norms, sorting rules, municipal contracts, and industrial processes that determine what materials circulate and what materials stall.

These systems rarely announce themselves.

They sit in the background of daily life, performing logistical work so smoothly that their influence becomes difficult to notice. A bin positioned beside a café door receives far more objects than one located halfway down the street; a recycling label that is ambiguous invites hesitation, while a simple icon encourages compliance; packaging that opens easily and stacks neatly in kitchens spreads more readily than containers that require washing and storage. None of these features require people to hold particular beliefs about the environment. They shape behaviour through proximity, visibility, and habit.

From a psychological perspective, this is unsurprising. Humans respond strongly to environmental cues, often without conscious awareness of doing so. The physical arrangement of a space, the availability of particular receptacles, and the social signals embedded in everyday routines all provide instructions about what is expected. When a row of bins appears beside every entrance, discarding becomes frictionless. When only one bin is visible, everything tends to end up in it. When packaging is treated as disposable by default, reuse becomes the exception rather than the rule.

Collection systems extend these cues beyond the point of use. Early-morning trucks empty streets before residents wake. Waste rooms are sealed and ventilated. Transfer stations are placed far from commercial centres. The removal is efficient, hygienic, and deliberately unobtrusive, qualities that protect public health while simultaneously ensuring that the later stages of disposal remain abstract for most citizens. The more smoothly these systems function, the less reason people have to think about what happens next.

Markets reinforce the same patterns. Materials that are cheap to produce and easy to mould proliferate. Designs that minimise shipping costs dominate shelves. Items intended for single use are engineered for lightness and speed rather than durability. Consumers encounter these choices at the end of long supply chains, where decisions about material composition and recyclability have already been made, and where alternatives, if they exist, may require additional effort to locate or afford.

What is striking is how little of this depends on individual attitude. A person may care deeply about reducing waste and still find themselves surrounded by packaging they did not request, confronted by sorting systems they do not fully understand, and supported by municipal processes that whisk consequences out of sight with impressive reliability. The environment in which behaviour unfolds exerts a constant, low-level pressure that nudges actions in particular directions without ever rising to the level of conscious deliberation.

This does not mean that individuals lack agency.

It means that agency operates within corridors built by institutions, designers, and historical decisions whose effects accumulate over decades. The shape of bins, the location of recycling points, the frequency of collection, the composition of packaging, and the economics of disposal all form part of an invisible architecture that channels millions of small acts into predictable streams.

Seen in this way, waste is not merely a matter of personal failure or virtue.

It is a system expressing itself through people.

Understanding how these quiet structures operate is essential, because it explains why awareness campaigns alone so often disappoint. Information can alter intentions, but intentions must still pass through landscapes of infrastructure and habit before they become behaviour. When those landscapes consistently reward disposal and hide aftermath, even well-informed citizens struggle to translate concern into lasting change.

This chapter will return later to how such systems might be reimagined.

For now, the point is narrower: long before a person decides what to throw away, a great deal has already been decided for them, by arrangements so ordinary and so entrenched that they rarely appear to be decisions at all.

They simply feel like the way the world works.

And it is precisely in that feeling of inevitability that their power resides.

When Waste Actually Shrinks

If waste were simply the product of indifference, reductions would be rare and fleeting, dependent on bursts of moral enthusiasm that fade as soon as attention shifts elsewhere. Yet across many cities and institutions, measurable declines in discarded material have occurred, sometimes rapidly and sometimes with surprising durability, suggesting that the forces shaping disposal are more flexible than they often appear.

What these cases tend to share is not an extraordinary transformation in public virtue, but subtle changes in how everyday practices are structured and understood. Deposit-return schemes for bottles alter the meaning of emptiness, turning containers from valueless remnants into objects with residual worth that people are reluctant to abandon. Clear separation systems reduce hesitation by replacing ambiguity with instruction, allowing individuals to act without prolonged deliberation. Organic waste collections placed close to kitchens become part of domestic rhythm rather than a weekly inconvenience, while inconsistent or confusing arrangements quietly discourage participation even among those who support them in principle.

Psychologically, such shifts work because they change the signals surrounding disposal. When an item is framed as recoverable rather than terminal, people treat it differently. When sorting is expected and visible, social norms follow quickly, as individuals look to neighbours for cues about what counts as appropriate behaviour. When the same message is repeated not through posters but through infrastructure itself, it gains a stability that public campaigns alone rarely achieve.

There is also a temporal dimension to these successes. Systems that persist long enough to become routine begin to operate below conscious attention, folding themselves into the background of domestic life in the same way that rubbish collection or plumbing already have. Once habits form, behaviour becomes less dependent on constant motivation and more on muscle memory, which is far more reliable over the long term.

Importantly, reductions in waste often emerge unevenly rather than uniformly, flourishing in settings where feedback is visible and faltering where it is not. Buildings that publish how much refuse they generate each week create quiet forms of accountability, reminding residents that individual acts accumulate into collective outcomes without requiring confrontation or shame. Communities in which composting or separation is commonplace make participation feel ordinary rather than ideological, lowering the psychological cost of joining in.

What is striking is how modest many of these interventions appear when viewed in isolation. None demand dramatic sacrifice. None require people to radically reorganise their identities. Instead, they alter the surrounding context just enough to shift patterns of behaviour at scale, demonstrating that waste is responsive not only to personal values but to the environments in which those values are expressed.

These examples matter because they complicate narratives of inevitability. If waste levels can fall in response to small but persistent changes in how materials are handled, then current trajectories are not fixed expressions of human nature, but outcomes contingent on arrangements that can be revised. The same psychological mechanisms that allow disposal to become automatic can, under different conditions, support separation, reuse, and restraint.

When waste actually shrinks, it rarely does so through dramatic awakenings.

It does so through repetition.

Through quiet adjustments to routines.

Through infrastructures that make alternative behaviours easier to sustain than the ones they replaced.

The lesson is not that people suddenly care more.

It is that when the surrounding world changes just enough, ordinary actions begin to add up in different ways.

And because accumulation works in both directions, reductions that start small can grow into transformations that are just as consequential as the habits they quietly displace.

What Nature Was Observing

From a distance wide enough to blur individual faces, patterns become easier to see.

A cup released in one city looks insignificant. A wrapper dropped on one pavement appears forgettable. A single household's bin emptied before sunrise seems like a solved problem rather than the beginning of a larger sequence. Yet when those gestures repeat across neighbourhoods, across seasons, across decades, they assemble into flows of material that move with remarkable consistency through rivers, landfills, sediments, and food chains.

What becomes visible at that scale is not malice.

It is regularity.

The same types of objects travel the same routes.

The same materials accumulate in the same places.

The same systems quietly shepherd millions of decisions into predictable outcomes.

From such a vantage, the most striking feature is not the presence of waste, but the absence of pause at the moment it is created. People discard quickly not because they are reckless, but because their environments encourage speed and provide closure with impressive efficiency. The bin offers finality. Clean streets reassure. Collection trucks erase traces before reflection has time to form. Language itself compresses continuation into disappearance.

Nature does not interpret these gestures as moral failures.

Nature reads them as signals.

Signals about how bodies move through built spaces.

About what senses notice and what they release.

About which consequences return to daily experience

and which are exported elsewhere.

Rivers, soils, and organisms respond mechanically to what enters them, without awareness of the intentions that placed those materials in circulation. Chemical processes do not differentiate between carelessness and convenience; biological systems absorb what is present rather than what was meant. At this level, intention matters far less than repetition.

What such observation reveals is a misalignment of tempos.

Human lives unfold at the speed of errands and weeks and commutes.

Ecological systems respond over months, decades, and generations.

The two timelines intersect constantly, yet rarely occupy the same mental frame.

When that intersection is overlooked, patterns continue uninterrupted.

Not through hostility.

Through habit.

Through infrastructures that reward disappearance.

Through psychological mechanisms that equate removal with resolution.

Seen in this way, waste is not merely a by-product of consumption.

It is a trace of how societies have organised attention.

It records which processes were designed to remain visible and which were designed to operate in the background.

Nature observes without accusation.

What it registers is flow.

Input.

Accumulation.

Redistribution.

Transformation.

The story is written not in speeches or policies, but in sediments, in stomach contents, in shorelines whose composition shifts gradually enough to escape notice until change has already taken hold.

From this vantage, the question is not whether humans care.

The question is whether the worlds they have built allow caring to stay present long enough to matter.

And that, Nature notes quietly, is not a matter of sentiment.

It is a matter of structure.

Rethinking "Away"

If the idea of away has proven so durable, it is because it performs an essential psychological function: it allows people to move through crowded, complicated lives without carrying the full weight of every material decision they make. The problem is not that such a category exists, but that the physical world has changed in ways that have stretched it beyond its original usefulness, turning what was once a reasonable inference into a dangerously incomplete story. To rethink away is therefore not to abolish the instinct for closure, but to notice how narrow that closure has become. When a cup leaves the hand, the mind experiences finality. When a street dries after rain, the episode feels concluded. When a bin empties overnight, the narrative seems complete. Each of these sensations is internally coherent, because they arise from sensory relief: clutter disappears, smells fade, surfaces clear, and the nervous system registers that something troublesome has been handled. What rethinking requires is not the suppression of that relief, but an expansion of the mental horizon beyond it — a recognition that disappearance from immediate surroundings does not equal disappearance from the world. This shift is subtle rather than dramatic. It does not demand that every act of disposal be accompanied by elaborate moral accounting, nor that individuals attempt to imagine entire watersheds while rinsing cups or tying bags. Such expectations would be psychologically unrealistic and, over time, counterproductive. Human attention cannot be stretched indefinitely without fraying. Instead, rethinking away involves adjusting the story people tell themselves about what bins, drains, and collection trucks actually represent. Rather than endpoints, they become transfers. Rather than erasures, relocations. Rather than conclusions, beginnings of longer processes that unfold beyond kitchens and pavements. Language plays a role in this reframing. So do metaphors. So do everyday descriptions that resist implying that matter vanishes when it leaves sight. When objects are understood as entering circulation rather than exiting existence, the moral texture of disposal changes without requiring constant guilt. The act becomes part of a longer chain rather than a moment sealed off from consequences. What makes this reframing difficult is that the systems surrounding disposal are designed precisely to preserve the older story. Efficient removal reassures. Clean surfaces reinforce the idea of completion. Distance prevents feedback. Together, they sustain the intuition that away is real, even when physical evidence suggests otherwise.

Rethinking, then, is less about forcing new behaviour and more about altering perception. It is about holding two truths at once: that human minds need closure to function, and that material systems do not grant it so easily. The first truth explains why away emerged. The second explains why it must now be handled with more care. Between these two lies the central tension of modern waste: lives organised around rapid resolution unfolding inside physical processes that operate slowly and relentlessly, often far from the point at which objects are released. Learning to notice that tension is not yet the same as resolving it. But it is a necessary beginning.

In Germany, many beverage containers carry a refundable deposit, often €0.25, that is returned when the container is brought back to a retailer. Supermarkets are legally required to accept returns, and automated machines are integrated into everyday shopping environments. Return rates for eligible containers exceed 95% in several categories. Reusable glass bottles may circulate dozens of times before recycling, and standardised formats increase washing and redistribution efficiency. I came across this system while reading about national deposit frameworks and was struck by how visibly it interrupts the illusion of disappearance. The container does not move into an undefined elsewhere; it re-enters circulation through a mechanism that is economically and physically traceable. The measurable outcome is high material recovery and reduced leakage into general waste streams, demonstrating that disposal can be structured as transfer rather than termination.

Before cities are redesigned, before packaging changes, before policies intervene, before new technologies appear, something quieter has to occur inside ordinary awareness: a loosening of the assumption that disappearance equals disappearance, and a widening of the mental frame in which everyday acts are understood. In that widened frame, the bin no longer feels like the edge of the world. It feels like a doorway. And once a doorway is recognised as such, it becomes harder to pretend that nothing lies on the other side.

Nature, Again

You often imagine me as loud.

Storms.

Fires.

Floods.

Headlines.

But most of what I do is gradual, patient, almost polite in its pace, a continual rearranging rather than a sudden intervention, a mathematics of repetition that rarely announces itself until years have already passed.

I watch the same gestures recur with exquisite consistency.

Hands release objects.

Bins close.

Streets clear.

Trucks arrive before dawn.

Water flows underground.

Rivers carry what they are given.

Sediments accept what settles.

None of this requires argument.

It proceeds according to gravity, chemistry, habit, and the infrastructures you have learned to trust.

From my vantage, what is most striking is not the presence

of waste but the calm with which it is produced, the way disposal has become so ordinary that it no longer interrupts conversation or alters pace, the way systems hum so quietly that their work feels like absence rather than activity.

You have built removal into the rhythm of daily life.

And rhythm, once established, is powerful.

I have learned that you are not careless creatures.

You are patterned ones.

You repeat what fits easily into mornings and evenings.

You follow paths that appear neutral.

You trust processes that spare you from lingering over where things go.

In forests, I have watched trails form not because animals debated routes, but because enough bodies passed the same way often enough that grass no longer had time to rise between them.

Cities do the same to behaviour.

Streets, bins, drains, and trucks become the grooves into which millions of small actions settle.

From such grooves, rivers inherit your routines.

Soils archive them.

Organisms incorporate them.

I do not interpret this as betrayal.

I read it as evidence of how closely you are coupled to the worlds you build.

Change the world, and you change yourselves.

Slowly at first.

Then all at once.

What interests me is not whether you are capable of restraint.

You have been.

What interests me is whether you will become as skilled at designing endings as you once were at creating beginnings, whether the systems that make disappearance feel effortless will one day be matched by systems that make continuation harder to ignore.

I am still here.

I have not left.

I am paying attention to the same small gestures you think of as finished.

Watching how they accumulate.

Waiting to see what stories the next generation of streets and bins and buildings will quietly write into rivers and sediments long after the hands that released them have forgotten the moment entirely

What This Chapter Has Really Been About?

This chapter has not been about rubbish so much as about perception: about how human minds, shaped to respond to what is near, visible, and immediately resolved, move comfortably inside systems that carry material far beyond the edges of daily awareness; about how bins, drains, and cleaning rituals provide psychological closure even when physical processes are only beginning; about how repetition, distance, and scale quietly transform fleeting gestures into geological forces; and about how waste persists not because people intend harm, but because disappearance is persuasive, accumulation is slow, and attention is local while consequences travel; in tracing a single object outward and examining the instincts that let it fade from thought, the chapter has tried to make visible the gap between sensory endings and material continuations — the narrow space in which everyday life meets rivers, soils, and decades.

Chapter 2: Convenience Always Wins

Behavior follows ease, not intent

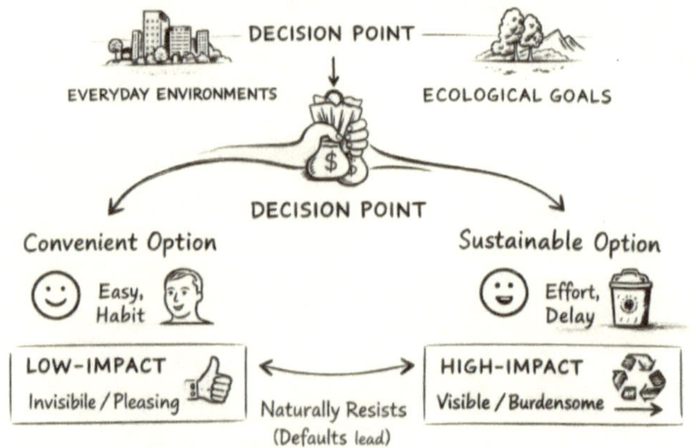

I have learned to measure your days by sound.

Morning begins with alarms and engines and kettles clicking on in kitchens that are still dark. Afternoon hums with air-conditioning units stacked along the sides of buildings like metallic barnacles. Evening arrives in waves of horns, delivery scooters, lift doors opening and closing, taps running, screens lighting faces that have already seen too much light.

What interests me is not the noise itself.

It is the speed behind it.

You have turned movement into a virtue. Roads are

widened to shave minutes from commutes. Elevators compete to be faster than thought. Food travels from kitchens to doorsteps without requiring streets to be crossed on foot. Temperature responds instantly to buttons. Messages leap oceans in less time than it takes clouds to decide whether to rain.

You call this progress.

In many ways, it is.

It has lengthened lives, shrunk distances, softened seasons, and freed hours that once vanished into survival.

It has also taught you to expect effortlessness.

I watch you at six in the evening, when the day loosens its grip but does not let go entirely. Cars edge forward in tight columns, windows sealed against heat and dust. Scooters weave through gaps carrying insulated boxes stamped with logos that promise warmth and punctuality. Apartment towers glow from the inside, even in rooms where nobody currently sits, because the switch is far away and forgetting is easy when you are already tired.

In supermarkets, fruit is wrapped so that fingers do not have to test ripeness. In offices, printers wait on standby because boot-up takes time. In cafés, disposable cups stack neatly because washing takes labour. In homes, devices sleep lightly rather than switching off entirely, ready to wake the moment a finger taps glass.

None of this looks dramatic.

That is precisely the point.

Environmental change rarely announces itself with spectacle in daily life. It accumulates inside patterns that feel ordinary—inside habits that no longer require conscious thought, inside systems so smooth that they disappear into background noise.

I have watched rivers change colour over decades and forests thin tree by tree, not through single catastrophic gestures, but through millions of small accelerations layered on top of one another: faster travel, quicker meals, instant climate control, frictionless purchasing, lighting that waits patiently in empty rooms for people who have already gone to bed.

You rarely pause to notice the collective weight of these conveniences.

Why would you?

Each individual act feels trivial.

Turn on the cooling.

Order dinner.

Drive instead of walk.

Leave the light.

Choose the wrapped fruit.

Accept the default.

You are not doing anything extraordinary.

You are simply moving through a world carefully designed to remove hesitation.

What fascinates me is not that you use these systems.

It is that you built them so well.

You engineered speed into streets and comfort into buildings and shortcuts into software. You rewarded efficiency until it became invisible, until stopping to consider alternatives began to feel like friction rather than wisdom.

This is not a story about selfishness.

It is a story about momentum.

About how a civilisation that learned to save seconds everywhere eventually found itself spending far more energy than it ever intended.

From where I stand, watching heat ripple above asphalt and electricity pulse through walls long after offices empty, I do not see villains.

I see creatures who have grown accustomed to ease.

Creatures who are very good at solving immediate problems.

Creatures who are only just beginning to realise that the background systems humming beneath their lives are shaping the planet as powerfully as any single decision ever could.

When Choices Stop Feeling Like Choices

Most people imagine environmental harm as the result of deliberate trade-offs. We picture a moment of internal debate — *I know this is not ideal, but I'm choosing it anyway* — followed by an action that carries obvious consequences. In everyday life, however, far fewer decisions feel that explicit. Much of what shapes environmental impact never rises to the level of conscious reflection at all. It occurs upstream, inside habits, defaults, and routines that quietly pre-select options long before moral reasoning enters the room.

Psychologists have long noted that human beings rely heavily on automatic processes to navigate complex environments. Conscious deliberation is metabolically expensive; it requires attention, working memory, and time, all of which are often in short supply. To conserve mental energy, the brain leans on shortcuts — repeating yesterday's behaviour, copying what others nearby are doing, selecting the first acceptable option presented, accepting default settings rather than searching for alternatives. These strategies are not signs of intellectual laziness. They are adaptations that allow people to function in information-dense worlds without becoming paralysed by analysis.

The problem is not that such shortcuts exist.

The problem is that modern environments have become extraordinarily good at exploiting them.

Consider how often you encounter situations in which the "standard" option has already been chosen on your behalf. Electricity contracts default to conventional grids unless customers actively opt out. Thermostats arrive pre-programmed. Delivery apps save addresses, payment methods, and favourite meals. Retailers place high-margin, heavily packaged goods at eye level, while unpackaged alternatives sit further away or require extra weighing. Office buildings light corridors automatically. Lifts open more prominently than stairwells. Parking entrances are obvious; bicycle storage is sometimes an afterthought.

In each of these cases, the individual technically retains freedom of choice. You can reconfigure the thermostat. You can scroll past the first restaurant suggestion. You can take the stairs. You can hunt for loose produce. But psychologically, these actions now carry a cost. They require extra effort, extra time, extra attention. When people are tired, rushed, hungry, distracted, or emotionally overloaded — which is to say, during much of ordinary life — those small costs loom larger than abstract environmental considerations. The path that demands the least friction begins to feel less like a preference and more like inevitability.

This is how choice architectures quietly reshape behaviour. They do not forbid alternatives; they simply make one option easier, faster, more visible, and socially normal. Over time, repeated exposure to these environments trains expectations. People begin to experience convenience not as a luxury but as a baseline. What once felt indulgent becomes ordinary. What once required planning becomes assumed. The absence of friction recalibrates what feels reasonable.

From the inside, this rarely registers as moral compromise. People do not tell themselves, *I am prioritising comfort over ecological stability today.* They tell themselves something far simpler: *This is what everyone does. This is how things work. I don't have time to think about it right now.*

In that sense, many environmentally consequential actions are not chosen so much as inherited. They arrive bundled with housing layouts, transportation systems, workplace policies, app interfaces, retail design, and pricing structures. By the time a consumer enters the scene, the field of possible behaviour has already been narrowed, tilted gently but persistently in particular directions.

This is why appeals that rely solely on awareness often disappoint. Information can alert people to problems, but it cannot easily overcome environments that reward the opposite behaviour dozens of times a day. A person may sincerely worry about emissions and still drive daily because buses are slow, routes are indirect, and schedules are unpredictable. They may dislike plastic packaging and still accept it because the unpackaged alternative requires an extra shop across town. They may care about energy use and still leave systems running because buildings were designed to make switching them off inconvenient.

None of this requires cynicism about human motives.

It requires realism about human cognition.

We are creatures shaped less by abstract commitments than by the immediate structure of the worlds we move through. What is close, easy, familiar, and socially reinforced exerts a gravitational pull that values alone rarely overcome.

Understanding this does something important: it shifts attention away from blaming individuals and toward examining the landscapes in which decisions are made. If environmentally damaging behaviour has become ordinary, then the ordinariness itself deserves scrutiny. The critical question is no longer merely *Why don't people care enough?* but rather *What kind of everyday environments have we built that make caring so difficult to translate into action?*

That question will carry us through the rest of this chapter — into friction, fatigue, temperature-controlled buildings, delivery culture, and the quiet engineering of modern comfort.

Friction: The Invisible Force

One of the most underestimated variables in human behaviour is effort.

Not dramatic effort — climbing mountains or learning new languages — but the tiny, nearly invisible exertions required to do ordinary things: an extra click, a longer walk, a slightly confusing sign, a form that needs filling, a wait that stretches beyond expectation. Behavioural scientists often refer to these micro-costs as *friction*, and they exert a disproportionate influence over what people actually do in everyday life.

The reason is not mysterious. Human beings evolved to conserve energy. For most of our history, calories were scarce and survival depended on efficiency. Cognitive labour was no different. Attention, planning, and self-control draw on limited mental resources, and the brain instinctively avoids spending them unless there is a compelling reason to do so. When two options sit side by side and one requires even marginally less exertion, the easier path acquires a quiet gravitational pull.

Modern environments are filled with such gradients.

Driving requires walking to a nearby parking lot; public transport may require navigating schedules, transferring lines, and waiting in uncertain weather. Ordering food involves tapping a screen; cooking involves shopping, chopping, washing dishes, and managing time. Keeping a room cool involves pressing a button; adjusting ventilation may involve opening windows, dealing with noise, and tolerating imperfect temperatures. Disposables stack neatly near cash registers; reusables require forethought.

None of these differences are dramatic in isolation.

Accumulated across days and years, they become decisive.

What is striking is how rarely people experience these outcomes as choices at all. The person who orders delivery instead of cooking is not typically staging an internal debate about planetary systems. They are responding to a long day and a short attention span. The commuter who drives instead of cycling is not rejecting sustainability; they are avoiding uncertainty, sweat, traffic stress, and arrival time risk. The office worker who takes the lift rather than the stairs is not expressing a value judgement; they are following a building's invitation.

Architecture, pricing, interface design, and policy quietly load the dice.

Friction also interacts powerfully with time pressure. When people are rushed, hungry, emotionally charged, or cognitively saturated, their tolerance for extra effort collapses. Tasks that might have felt manageable in a calm moment suddenly appear burdensome. The option that demands the least immediate work expands to fill the decision space.

This dynamic helps explain why environmentally conscious intentions so often fail to translate into consistent behaviour. Many low-impact choices — walking rather than driving, cooking rather than ordering, adjusting temperature manually, carrying containers — ask for small sacrifices of convenience. When life is already crowded with obligations, those sacrifices begin to feel unreasonable, even when people believe the underlying cause is important.

Crucially, friction is not evenly distributed across populations. People with long working hours, precarious incomes, caregiving responsibilities, disabilities, or limited transport options face higher baseline cognitive and physical loads. In such contexts, asking individuals to absorb additional effort for environmental reasons without changing surrounding systems risks widening inequality. Behaviour that looks careless from a distance may, on closer inspection, be entirely rational within constrained circumstances.

Recognising the role of friction therefore reframes environmental action. It moves the conversation away from exhortations about character and toward questions about design. Where are the small obstacles that quietly discourage low-impact behaviour? Which alternatives require advance planning that many people cannot afford? Which sustainable options are hidden behind time, money, or confusion?

Once attention shifts to these micro-barriers, new possibilities open. Reduce waiting times for buses and ridership climbs. Place bike racks at entrances rather than behind buildings and cycling increases. Pre-set thermostats toward efficiency and most occupants leave them alone. Offer refill containers at checkout instead of in obscure corners and reuse becomes routine.

In each case, the change is not in values.

It is in terrain.

Human beings adapt rapidly to the landscapes they inhabit. When those landscapes reward low-impact behaviour, people follow without needing constant reminders of what is at stake. When they penalise it, even the most committed struggle.

Understanding friction is therefore not a minor technical detail. It is a central mechanism through which modern convenience reshapes environmental outcomes — and it prepares the ground for the next forces we must examine: fatigue, overload, and the cognitive costs of living in an always-on world.

Why Everyone Is Tired

Even when sustainable options are available, people often fail to choose them. The explanation is not always disagreement or indifference. Frequently, it is exhaustion.

Modern life places extraordinary cognitive demands on human beings. From the moment people wake up, they are confronted with streams of messages, notifications, advertisements, appointments, route choices, pricing tiers, social obligations, work deadlines, and family logistics. Each of these requires some degree of evaluation, however minor. Over the course of a day, these micro-decisions accumulate into what psychologists describe as *decision fatigue* — a state in which mental resources for self-control and careful reasoning become depleted.

When this happens, behaviour changes in predictable ways. People grow more impulsive. They revert to habits. They accept defaults. They postpone difficult tasks. They choose whatever option resolves the immediate situation with the least mental strain. This is not a failure of character. It is a well-documented feature of how cognition operates under load.

Environmental decisions are particularly vulnerable to this dynamic because they often arrive late in the day and rarely feel urgent in the moment. The commuter deciding how to get home at 7 p.m. is not operating with the same mental clarity as the one planning a weekend trip weeks in advance. The parent grabbing dinner after work is not conducting a lifecycle analysis at the checkout counter. The office worker adjusting a thermostat between meetings is not pausing to consider electricity grids.

Fatigue narrows time horizons. It makes distant consequences fade further into the background. Immediate comfort, speed, and certainty become disproportionately attractive. This is why long days end with takeaway orders, extended screen time, unnecessary driving, and thermostats nudged lower or higher than strictly necessary. These choices do not arise from hostility toward the environment; they arise from depleted attention.

Stress compounds the effect. Financial insecurity, health worries, unstable housing, caregiving responsibilities, and job precarity consume cognitive bandwidth. When people are operating in such conditions, asking them to shoulder additional mental burdens for the sake of long-term environmental goals can feel detached from lived reality. The brain prioritises stability and relief in the present, even when it intellectually endorses broader objectives.

Understanding this has profound implications for environmental policy and design. If sustainable behaviour depends on sustained vigilance and constant self-regulation, it will always struggle, because vigilance is precisely what tired minds lack. Campaigns that rely solely on urging people to "try harder" underestimate the friction imposed by fatigue. They treat behaviour as though it were governed by abstract commitments rather than by fluctuating psychological capacity.

A more realistic approach begins by asking different questions. Which low-impact choices can be made automatic rather than effortful? Which systems can remove the need for repeated deliberation? Which infrastructures can protect people from having to choose well hundreds of times a day?

Defaults are powerful precisely because they operate when attention is elsewhere. Automated lighting that powers down after hours reduces energy use without requiring nightly vigilance. Appliances that run efficiently by design spare households the burden of constant adjustment. Transport networks that are reliable and pleasant make sustainable commuting the easiest option even on difficult days.

Seen in this light, fatigue is not an obstacle to be overcome through exhortation.

It is a design constraint.

A world that expects exhausted citizens to behave heroically is poorly aligned with human psychology. A world that anticipates tiredness and builds systems accordingly has a far better chance of bending everyday behaviour in environmentally gentler directions.

The next sections will turn to some of the arenas in which this tension between exhaustion and infrastructure becomes especially visible: temperature-controlled buildings, delivery culture, and the subtle engineering of comfort that now defines much of modern urban life.

The Climate-Controlled City

For most of human history, comfort was negotiated rather than commanded.

People built thick walls to hold warmth and courtyards to invite breezes. Windows were opened and closed with the sun. Streets were shaded with trees. Roofs reflected light. Daily routines adjusted to seasons. Heat and cold were facts to be managed, not eliminated.

Modern cities rewrote that relationship.

Glass towers rose that trapped sunlight and radiated warmth long after dusk. Asphalt spread across surfaces that once absorbed rain and cooled nights through evaporation. Dense traffic released heat into already-warm streets. Buildings sealed themselves against dust and noise, and mechanical cooling stepped in to regulate interior climates with extraordinary precision.

The achievement is remarkable. Entire megacities now function in temperatures that would have been debilitating a century ago.

It is also energetically expensive.

Air-conditioning systems draw vast amounts of electricity during peak heat, straining grids precisely when power generation is already under pressure. Waste heat expelled from buildings raises outdoor temperatures, which in turn increases demand for cooling in neighbouring structures. This feedback loop—cool inside, hotter outside, more cooling required—creates what urban climatologists describe as heat islands: zones where built environments trap warmth far more effectively than surrounding landscapes.

From a psychological perspective, what matters is not only the physics of this system but the expectations it cultivates.

Once interior climates become stable, tolerance for fluctuation shrinks. A room that would once have felt pleasantly warm now feels unbearable. A summer afternoon that previous generations endured becomes an emergency requiring instant relief. Humans adapt quickly to new baselines of comfort, recalibrating what feels normal within surprisingly short periods of time.

This process, often referred to as hedonic adaptation, helps explain why rising energy use rarely registers as a loss of wellbeing. Each technological improvement resets expectations upward. Comfort expands quietly. The new normal feels non-negotiable.

Architecture amplifies these psychological shifts. When windows do not open, people stop thinking about airflow. When façades maximise views rather than shade, mechanical cooling becomes unavoidable. When offices are deep and sealed, daylight becomes artificial and climate becomes programmable. Design choices made decades earlier lock entire populations into energy-intensive patterns that no amount of individual virtue can easily escape.

Individual behaviour still matters, of course. People adjust thermostats, choose when to switch systems on and off, decide how to dress indoors. But these decisions unfold within envelopes set by construction codes, zoning laws, material choices, and urban form. A resident in a poorly insulated high-rise faces very different possibilities from someone in a shaded, cross-ventilated home.

The result is that environmental impact becomes embedded not only in daily habits but in concrete and glass.

Cooling is not merely a personal preference.

It is a collective infrastructure.

Understanding this helps explain why appeals to restraint so often feel inadequate. Asking millions of people to tolerate discomfort in buildings designed to overheat is a losing proposition. Systems that require constant self-control from occupants rarely perform well over time, especially under rising temperatures.

More promising are approaches that reshape the baseline: reflective roofs, vegetation that cools streets through evapotranspiration, building orientations that reduce solar gain, natural ventilation strategies, district cooling networks, insulation standards that stabilise interiors without heavy energy input. These interventions change behaviour not by persuading people to care more, but by making lower-impact comfort the default condition.

In climate-controlled cities, the question is therefore not whether humans prefer cool rooms.

They always have.

The deeper question is whether urban design can deliver comfort without silently escalating energy demand, whether architectural intelligence can substitute for mechanical brute force, and whether expectations shaped by decades of effortless cooling can be gently recalibrated toward buildings that cooperate with climate rather than fighting it hour by hour.

The next section turns to another domain in which comfort and speed have been engineered with extraordinary success: the logistics of modern eating, and the way dinner has learned to arrive at the pace of a thumb swipe rather than a stove heating up.

Dinner at the Speed of a Thumb

For most of human history, eating required proximity.

Food was grown nearby or traded slowly. Cooking demanded time, fuel, and planning. Meals anchored households to kitchens and neighbourhoods, seasons and daylight.

Digital platforms collapsed those distances.

Today dinner arrives by algorithm. Menus update in real time. Discounts appear when hunger peaks. Addresses are stored, payments pre-approved, favourite dishes remembered with unnerving accuracy. A swipe replaces shopping lists; insulated boxes replace pots on stoves.

From the perspective of convenience, this is a triumph.

From the perspective of environmental psychology, it is a

masterclass in behavioural design.

Delivery interfaces remove friction at precisely the moment when people are least inclined to resist it. Late afternoons coincide with depleted self-control. Notifications arrive when cognitive resources are thin. Promotions reward immediacy rather than foresight. The labour of cooking—planning, cleaning, timing—is compressed into seconds of tapping.

What disappears from view is the system that makes this possible: fleets of vehicles idling at kerbs, refrigerated storage humming in the background, kitchens scaled for throughput rather than proximity, layers of packaging engineered for speed rather than reuse. Users see bowls of noodles and smiling riders; they do not see routing algorithms optimising for arrival times rather than emissions, or plastic containers designed for heat retention rather than circularity.

Interfaces curate reality.

What they omit shapes behaviour as strongly as what they display.

The psychological effect is subtle but powerful. When the environmental consequences of a choice are absent from the screen, they fade from deliberation. People rarely tell themselves that they are ordering packaging, traffic, and energy use along with dinner. They tell themselves that they are hungry.

Over time, repetition turns extraordinary services into expectations. What once felt indulgent becomes baseline. Cooking shifts from default to optional. Kitchens shrink in new apartments. Streets fill with two-wheelers optimised for speed. Urban rhythms recalibrate around on-demand logistics.

Once again, this is not a story about malice.

It is a story about alignment.

Platforms optimise for convenience because convenience grows markets. Consumers gravitate toward what saves time because time feels scarce. Environmental costs sit outside both sets of incentives unless deliberately designed back into view.

This is why individual restraint alone struggles to keep pace with systems engineered for instant gratification. Asking millions of tired people to resist frictionless interfaces every evening is a structural mismatch. The environment is nudging one way; appeals to conscience push another.

More durable change appears when the same psychological levers that power delivery culture are redirected. When platforms highlight low-impact options by default, orders shift. When reusable containers circulate automatically through deposit systems, waste falls without requiring extra planning. When pricing reflects transport distance or packaging intensity, behaviour responds quickly. When neighbourhood kitchens shorten supply chains, emissions drop while meals stay convenient.

In each case, the pattern repeats: behaviour follows design.

The crucial question is therefore not whether humans like dinner to arrive easily.

They do.

The question is whether the infrastructures that now define urban eating can be redesigned so that speed no longer quietly implies excess, and convenience no longer hides environmental cost behind clean interfaces and warm containers.

The next section returns to a deeper psychological myth that underlies much of the debate around lifestyle change: the belief that environmental responsibility depends primarily on stronger willpower rather than on reshaping the systems in which decisions are made.

Why Willpower Is Overrated

Public discussions about environmental behaviour often drift toward a familiar prescription: people simply need to try harder. If individuals were more disciplined, more informed, more ethically committed, they would drive less, waste less, consume less energy, and refuse unnecessary packaging.

The appeal of this narrative is obvious. It locates responsibility squarely with the individual and promises that change is a matter of moral resolve.

Psychology offers a more complicated picture.

Self-control is not a fixed trait that people draw upon at will. It fluctuates with sleep, stress, hunger, illness, financial pressure, emotional strain, and social context. Laboratory studies and everyday experience alike show that when people are depleted, they become more impulsive, more reliant on habits, and more likely to choose immediate rewards over distant benefits.

This variability matters enormously for environmental action, because many sustainable behaviours compete directly with convenience. Walking rather than driving, cooking rather than ordering, tolerating warmer indoor temperatures, planning purchases to avoid disposables — each of these demands at least a small expenditure of effort and attention. When those resources are scarce, even strong values struggle to translate into action.

Moreover, willpower is fragile when it is asked to fight entire systems.

A commuter may resolve to use public transport, only to face irregular schedules, crowded vehicles, and long transfers. A household may intend to conserve energy, only to live in a poorly insulated apartment where cooling is unavoidable. A shopper may try to avoid packaging, only to find shelves dominated by pre-wrapped goods.

In such contexts, lapses are not evidence of hypocrisy.

They are predictable outcomes of environments that make high-impact behaviour easy and low-impact behaviour hard.

This is why appeals that focus exclusively on personal responsibility often produce cycles of guilt and discouragement rather than lasting change. People fail, conclude that they lack discipline, and either recommit temporarily or disengage altogether. Meanwhile, the surrounding systems remain untouched, continuing to reward the same patterns day after day.

Recognising the limits of willpower does not absolve individuals of responsibility.

It relocates responsibility.

Instead of asking only whether people care enough, we begin to ask whether infrastructures, markets, and institutions are aligned with the behaviours we hope to see. Are transport networks reliable enough to compete with private vehicles? Are buildings designed to minimise energy demand rather than outsource efficiency to occupants? Are low-impact choices visible, affordable, and socially normal?

When systems do the heavy lifting, individual effort

becomes supplementary rather than heroic. People still make choices, but those choices are no longer uphill battles against default settings.

Nature has always worked this way.

Water follows slopes.

Roots grow toward moisture.

Animals conserve energy unless forced to expend it.

Humans are no different.

When sustainable behaviour flows with the grain of daily life, it spreads easily. When it requires constant resistance to convenience, it remains fragile.

The next sections turn from diagnosis to possibility: how the same forces that now lock societies into high-energy routines might be redirected, and how redesigning comfort and convenience could transform environmental outcomes without demanding superhuman discipline from exhausted citizens.

Design Beats Discipline

If friction, fatigue, and convenience shape behaviour so powerfully, then lasting environmental change cannot depend solely on exhorting individuals to resist them. It must instead work at the level where those forces originate: in the design of physical spaces, technologies, and policies that quietly structure everyday life.

This insight has been gaining traction across fields as diverse as urban planning, behavioural economics, public health, and energy policy. When systems are arranged so that one option is easier, cheaper, more visible, or socially expected, large populations adopt it without requiring sustained motivation. People rarely wake up determined to follow defaults; they simply follow what feels normal.

Consider how quickly habits shift when the underlying environment changes. When smoking indoors became inconvenient and socially unacceptable, consumption fell dramatically without millions of daily acts of personal heroism. When seatbelts became standard rather than optional, usage soared. When energy-efficient lighting replaced incandescent bulbs as the default product on shelves, electricity demand dropped without requiring consumers to study wattage charts.

Environmental behaviour operates under the same logic.

Buildings that automatically regulate temperature through insulation and shading reduce energy use regardless of occupant intentions. Cities that make walking and cycling safe and pleasant see dramatic increases in active transport. Power grids that default households into renewable suppliers lock in low-carbon electricity unless people actively opt out. Retail layouts that place unpackaged goods front and centre normalise lower-waste shopping without lectures at checkout counters.

The case of Copenhagen was a eye opener for me and also the reason why this chapter ever exists. A principle is that's visible at scale. Nearly half of all commuting trips within the city are conducted by bicycle, supported by more than 400 kilometres of dedicated cycling infrastructure, much of it physically separated from motor traffic. Certain corridors are synchronised with traffic signals timed to average cycling speeds, allowing uninterrupted flow through intersections. Municipal transport reports over multiple years show sustained bicycle modal share not as a short-term campaign effect but as an embedded feature of urban design. Car travel remains possible, yet the physical layout of streets, parking, and lane prioritisation reduces friction for cycling instead. The measurable outcome is not merely increased bike ownership, but long-term behavioural normalisation built into infrastructure rather than dependent on repeated persuasion.

In each case, individuals retain freedom.

What changes is the terrain on which that freedom is exercised.

Discipline becomes unnecessary for most daily actions because the sustainable choice has been built into the background.

Importantly, this approach avoids framing environmental responsibility as a personal moral test. When greener behaviour is structurally supported, participation becomes socially ordinary rather than ideologically charged. People do not need to identify as environmentalists to behave in environmentally gentler ways; they simply live inside systems that make such behaviour routine.

This matters politically as well as psychologically. Policies that reshape defaults often encounter less resistance than those that rely on constant vigilance or sacrifice. People are more willing to accept changes that improve daily life — quieter streets, cleaner air, cooler neighbourhoods, lower utility bills — than those framed solely as obligations to distant futures.

Design also allows environmental action to scale. One household remembering to switch off lights is helpful. An entire building that powers down automatically is transformative. A commuter choosing to cycle is admirable. A city that makes cycling safe for millions reshapes emissions profiles.

When systems carry the load, individual effort becomes marginal.

Nature has always exploited this principle.

Rivers carve landscapes not through bursts of willpower, but through persistent flows shaped by terrain.

Humans, too, are moulded by the contours of their environments.

The next section explores what happens when convenience itself is reimagined — when comfort, speed, and ease are redesigned to serve ecological stability rather than undermine it.

Rewriting Convenience

Once convenience is recognised as a design choice rather than a law of nature, it becomes something that can be edited.

The same ingenuity that built frictionless consumption can be redirected toward frictionless sustainability. This does not require abandoning comfort or slowing life to a crawl; it requires redefining what ease looks like at scale.

Transport systems offer one clear illustration. In cities where buses arrive frequently and reliably, where routes are legible, payment is seamless, and shelters protect against heat and rain, people shift modes without needing moral persuasion. When cycling networks feel physically safe rather than heroic, bicycles proliferate across age groups and incomes. When streets prioritise pedestrians, walking ceases to be a statement and becomes routine.

Energy systems provide another example. Households enrolled by default in renewable electricity programmes rarely opt out, even when alternatives remain available. Smart thermostats that optimise heating and cooling reduce consumption quietly. Buildings designed to maintain comfortable temperatures through insulation, orientation, and ventilation spare occupants the need for constant adjustment.

Food systems, too, can be redesigned for low-friction sustainability. When plant-based meals appear as standard options rather than special requests, consumption patterns shift. When neighbourhood markets shorten supply chains, transport emissions fall while freshness improves. When reusable containers circulate automatically through deposit schemes, waste drops without requiring people to remember to bring their own.

Digital interfaces matter as much as physical spaces. Apps shape behaviour through what they foreground. When low-impact choices are highlighted first, when carbon-intensive options are not hidden but simply less prominent, when delivery platforms reward batching orders rather than splitting them, consumption patterns respond. Small interface changes multiplied across millions of users produce measurable effects.

These interventions share a common feature: they respect human psychology.

They do not demand constant self-surveillance or heroic restraint.

They assume that people will follow the easiest path available.

So they reshape that path.

In doing so, they also help shift norms. Once enough people adopt a behaviour, it begins to feel ordinary rather than exceptional. Reusable cups cease to signal virtue and start to signal habit. Cycling becomes commuting rather than activism. Well-insulated homes become standard rather than aspirational.

Culture follows infrastructure.

Expectations adjust.

What once seemed novel becomes invisible.

This is how societies change most often: not through sudden moral revolutions, but through gradual realignments between built environments and daily routines.

Rewriting convenience therefore offers something more durable than exhortation.

It embeds environmental responsibility into the texture of ordinary life.

The final sections of this chapter step back to consider what all of this amounts to — and to let Nature, once again, offer a quiet reflection on the patterns humans have set in motion.

What This Chapter Is Really About

Convenience Always Wins, examines how everyday environments — from air-conditioned buildings and delivery apps to street layouts and digital interfaces — quietly steer behaviour by rewarding speed, comfort, and low effort, often overpowering even sincere environmental intentions; drawing on psychology, it shows how defaults, fatigue, and habit make high-impact choices feel normal while sustainable ones require extra work, and argues that this is not a story of weak character but of systems designed around ease; viewed from Nature's longer perspective, the chapter concludes that meaningful ecological progress will come not from heroic individual restraint, but from reshaping cities, technologies, and services so that the most planet-friendly options also become the most convenient ones in everyday life.

Chapter 3: Buying Green to Feel Better

The Emotional Loop of Green Purchasing

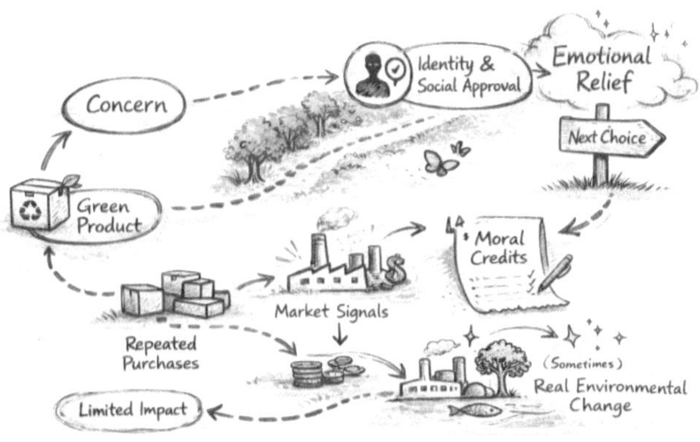

I do not usually stand beneath fluorescent lights.

My domain is wind through leaves, sediment settling in river bends, heat rising slowly from stone that has held the afternoon sun too long. And yet I have learned that some of the most revealing exchanges between you and me occur in places that smell faintly of cardboard and detergent, where conveyor belts hum softly and receipts unfurl like pale ribbons of justification.

Here, at the edge of payment, your hands pause.

You have already chosen.

The baskets are full.

The cards are ready.

And still there is hesitation, a brief recalibration that passes across faces as eyes scan labels promising *organic, carbon-neutral, responsibly sourced, biodegradable, planet-friendly*. The words glow gently from packaging designed to reassure, from colours borrowed from forests and oceans, from leaves printed where ingredients once would have been.

I watch you weigh these signals with remarkable speed.

Two versions of the same object sit side by side.

One is cheaper.

One is greener.

One is familiar.

One is newly virtuous.

You do not run calculations about supply chains or certification regimes.

You do not trace water use or factory emissions.

You respond instead to cues that fit inside the time it takes for the line to move forward.

A leaf icon.

A recycled texture.

A promise printed in soft ink.

The feeling that this version of you — the one holding this item rather than that one — is the kind of person who is trying.

This moment fascinates me, because it is neither trivial nor heroic.

It is ordinary.

You do not imagine yourselves saving oceans in aisle seven.

You imagine yourselves making a slightly better choice.

You imagine relief.

I see how quickly such relief settles into posture and breath, how shoulders soften when something green lands in the basket, how guilt loosens its grip just enough to let the rest of the shopping proceed without friction.

Receipts lengthen.

Belts move.

Beeping scanners convert objects into numbers.

And still the quiet arithmetic of meaning continues beneath the choreography.

You are not only purchasing soap or vegetables or coffee.

You are purchasing a story about yourselves.

That story is small.

Portable.

Designed to be carried out of the store in a reusable bag.

From my vantage, what is striking is not that you seek reassurance.

It is that reassurance has become a product category.

You have learned to outsource fragments of moral labour to packaging, to let logos and certifications shoulder some of the weight that once belonged to slower forms of reflection.

Again, I do not judge this.

You are creatures who must move quickly through dense worlds.

You cannot deliberate at every shelf.

You require signals.

Shortcuts.

Narratives that fit inside seconds.

What interests me is how skillfully these signals have been engineered, how closely they track the places where anxiety tends to gather, how readily they convert concern into consumption, and how gently they whisper that participation is enough.

Outside, trucks idle.

Inside, lights hum.

The line inches forward.

Another shopper reaches for the greener bottle and nods almost imperceptibly, as though in agreement with a private bargain.

I notice.

I always notice.

And I wonder, quietly, what happens to a civilisation when even its attempts at care begin to arrive shrink-wrapped, barcode-ready, and optimised for the final swipe of a card.

The Comfort of the Better Choice

The appeal of environmentally branded products is often explained in practical terms — reduced packaging, lower emissions, gentler chemicals — but their psychological appeal is at least as powerful as their material one. Choosing the "better" option delivers an immediate emotional dividend, a sense of having aligned action with values, of having registered concern in a world that frequently feels overwhelming and out of one's control.

This relief is subtle rather than triumphant. Most shoppers are not congratulating themselves loudly in supermarket aisles. They experience instead a quiet settling of tension, a fleeting impression that they have nudged the day in a preferable direction, that the small internal friction produced by news about climate change or pollution has been partially discharged through a concrete gesture. In this sense, green purchases operate as micro-resolutions to larger anxieties, compressing diffuse unease into a manageable decision that fits inside a moment at the checkout.

Psychologists have long noted that moral actions are intrinsically rewarding, activating the same emotional systems that accompany generosity, cooperation, and social approval. Buying something that signals care can therefore feel good in ways that are independent of its actual ecological effect, because the brain is responding not only to anticipated outcomes but to the identity being affirmed in the present: I am someone who tries; I am not indifferent; I belong to the group that worries about this.

This is why the physical cues surrounding such products matter so much. Earth-toned colours, textured cardboard, leaf motifs, and minimalist typography function as emotional accelerants, allowing shoppers to recognise virtuous intent at a glance. Certifications and sustainability claims work similarly, translating complex supply-chain stories into symbols that can be processed in seconds rather than hours. These cues do not merely convey information; they produce reassurance.

Importantly, this reassurance does not require deep engagement with data. Few consumers investigate the precise criteria behind a label while standing in line, and fewer still perform comparative analyses of lifecycle assessments before choosing between two bottles of detergent. The emotional payoff arrives long before such scrutiny would be possible, and that speed is part of the product's value.

The comfort of the better choice therefore emerges from a convergence of psychological needs: the desire to reduce guilt, the wish to express identity, the relief of doing something rather than nothing, and the social pleasure of aligning with visible norms of concern. These forces do not make people naïve or easily manipulated; they make them human.

Understanding this dynamic does not require cynicism about environmental commitments.

It requires acknowledging that feelings of virtue can arise more quickly and reliably than measurable ecological impact, and that the two are not always perfectly correlated.

This distinction matters because emotional rewards, once secured, can reshape subsequent behaviour, sometimes encouraging further restraint and sometimes providing a sense of closure that dampens motivation for more difficult changes.

How those downstream effects unfold — whether comfort becomes a stepping stone or a stopping point — is the subject of the next sections.

Moral Credits and Mental Ledgers

Human beings are natural accountants, even when they have never opened a spreadsheet.

Experiences of virtue are logged internally not as precise numbers but as feelings: the satisfaction of carrying a reusable bottle, the relief of choosing a product labelled "eco-friendly," the quiet pride that accompanies refusing unnecessary packaging. These moments accumulate into a background sense of moral standing, a narrative about the kind of person one is trying to be, and that narrative becomes relevant when later decisions present trade-offs between convenience, cost, pleasure, and environmental impact.

Psychologists have long examined this tendency under

the label moral licensing, the phenomenon in which earlier good deeds reduce the psychological friction associated with later indulgences. The metaphor of a ledger captures the structure of this process well. Acts perceived as responsible are entered as credits; questionable choices are softened into debits that feel less consequential when the account seems healthy. This balancing rarely occurs consciously. Few people tell themselves explicitly that today's organic purchase entitles them to tomorrow's excess. Instead, the emotional residue of having acted well changes the tone of subsequent deliberation, lowering vigilance and dulling the sting of potential regret.

Environmental behaviour is particularly susceptible to this effect because so many sustainable actions are visible, symbolic, and socially legible. Carrying a cloth bag, selecting certified products, or installing a compost bin communicates commitment not only to others but to oneself. These gestures generate immediate feedback that one belongs to a category of people who care, and that membership can become psychologically protective. Once the identity is affirmed, the mind relaxes its monitoring slightly, confident that the larger moral story remains intact even if an individual choice drifts from ideal.

In practice, this can produce complicated patterns. A household that invests in energy-efficient appliances may feel less troubled by frequent air travel. A shopper who fills a trolley with eco-labelled goods may hesitate less before adding an impulse purchase encased in plastic. Someone who has spent the week cycling to work may feel entitled to drive on the weekend without reflection. None of these choices are irrational when taken in isolation, and many of the virtuous acts do in fact reduce harm directly. The ledger operates not by negating those benefits, but by shaping the context in which future decisions are evaluated.

What makes this dynamic difficult to recognise is that it coexists with sincere concern. People who engage in green purchasing are often highly motivated and informed; the very fact that they care enough to act makes them more likely to experience the emotional rewards that later relax constraints. Moral licensing does not depend on cynicism or manipulation. It arises from the way human self-regulation functions, relying on narratives of balance rather than on relentless consistency.

There is also a temporal dimension to these ledgers. Credits feel strongest when they are recent and vivid. The glow from a good choice fades over time, while new actions quickly replace old ones in memory. This constant updating allows people to move through complex environments without being paralysed by endless calculation, but it also means that long-term impacts are easily overshadowed by short-term signals of virtue.

Importantly, moral accounting is not inherently harmful. In many contexts, a first small action opens the door to larger commitments, strengthening environmental identities rather than exhausting them. The same ledger that licenses indulgence in one person may encourage escalation in another, as initial efforts build confidence rather than complacency. Whether credits become stepping stones or stopping points depends on how actions are framed, remembered, and socially reinforced.

Understanding moral ledgers therefore requires nuance rather than condemnation. The issue is not that people congratulate themselves for doing good; such recognition is a fundamental part of sustaining motivation in any domain. The issue is that symbolic victories can sometimes satisfy the mind's demand for progress more quickly than the planet's material systems actually change.

In the context of green consumption, this means that the emotional payoff of purchasing environmentally branded products can occasionally substitute for deeper engagement with questions about quantity, frequency, and overall patterns of use. The ledger reassures even when total consumption continues to climb, allowing individuals to experience themselves as responsible while remaining embedded in material-intensive lifestyles.

Recognising this tension is not meant to discourage small acts.

It is meant to situate them.

A reusable bag matters.

So does composting.

So does choosing lower-impact products.

But psychologically, these acts do not exist in isolation. They become part of ongoing narratives about adequacy, identity, and effort, narratives that quietly influence what feels acceptable next.

The mental ledger is always open.

The question is not whether people keep such accounts, but how those accounts are written — and whether the stories they tell about responsibility ultimately encourage deeper change or provide comfortable stopping points that feel like conclusions when they are, in fact, only beginnings.

When a Label Becomes a Conscience

Modern consumers navigate aisles dense with claims.

"Organic."

"Carbon neutral."

"Responsibly sourced."

"Plastic-free."

"Climate positive."

Each phrase compresses a complicated story of extraction, production, transport, certification, and accounting into a handful of words small enough to fit on a corner of a box, and it is precisely this compression that gives such labels their psychological power. Faced with limited time and attention, shoppers do not conduct forensic audits of supply chains; they rely instead on symbols that promise to have done the work for them, outsourcing ethical evaluation to packaging that appears authoritative, official, or familiar.

From a behavioural perspective, these markers function as moral heuristics — shortcuts that allow people to move forward without lingering uncertainty. The brain prefers decisions that resolve ambiguity quickly, and eco-labels perform that service elegantly, transforming shelves crowded with near-identical products into moral landscapes in which some options appear illuminated while others recede into neutral shadow. Choosing the labelled item feels like choosing correctly, not because every implication has been examined, but because the presence of certification signals that someone else, somewhere, has already taken responsibility for verifying the claim.

This delegation of judgement is not naïve.

It is necessary.

Contemporary consumption involves supply chains so extended and opaque that no individual shopper could reasonably evaluate them in real time. Labels therefore emerge to fill a genuine cognitive gap, allowing ethical intentions to be expressed at scale rather than remaining purely aspirational.

At the same time, this very usefulness creates new vulnerabilities.

When a symbol becomes a proxy for conscience, its presence can overshadow more difficult questions about magnitude, frequency, and trade-offs. A product marked sustainable may be purchased more readily and in greater quantity than an unlabelled one, even when overall material use continues to rise. The reassurance offered by the label can shorten deliberation, quiet doubt, and generate the comforting sense that one has acted responsibly, even when the ecological advantage of the choice is modest relative to the scale of consumption itself.

Psychological research suggests that once a decision is framed as morally acceptable, further scrutiny diminishes. People devote less cognitive effort to evaluating options they perceive as ethically safe, conserving mental energy for choices that appear riskier or more ambiguous. In the environmental domain, this can translate into a narrowing of attention: once the green box is in the basket, the question feels settled, freeing the mind to move on.

This effect is intensified by design.

Certifications are often accompanied by visual cues carefully chosen to evoke naturalness — muted greens and browns, rough textures, leaf motifs, water droplets — aesthetic elements that trigger associations with purity and restraint even before the text is read. Such cues work below conscious awareness, shaping emotional responses that precede analytical judgement.

The result is not widespread deception, but a subtle recalibration of responsibility. Instead of wrestling directly with complex systems, consumers learn to rely on third-party assurances, trusting that someone else has measured what they cannot see. In many cases that trust is warranted, and certification regimes have driven genuine improvements in labour practices, land use, and chemical inputs.

The difficulty arises when symbols are mistaken for sufficiency rather than signals.

A label can indicate relative improvement without guaranteeing low impact.

It can certify one dimension of production while leaving others untouched.

It can reassure without inviting reflection on volume, longevity, or disposal.

When conscience becomes concentrated into a sticker, ethical engagement risks becoming narrow rather than deep.

This narrowing is not malicious.

It is efficient.

It allows people to participate in environmental concern without being overwhelmed by its complexity, to convert diffuse anxiety into concrete action at the shelf. But efficiency has costs. The very mechanism that makes sustainable choices easier to express can also limit how far that expression extends.

Understanding this tension is crucial for any serious discussion of green consumption. Labels are neither trivial nor magical. They are tools that mediate between individual psychology and planetary systems, simplifying what would otherwise be unmanageable, while at the same time shaping where attention stops.

When a label becomes a conscience, it performs a remarkable service.

It makes care portable.

The question that lingers is whether portability sometimes comes at the price of proportion — whether symbols that fit neatly on packaging can fully carry the weight of problems that sprawl across oceans, forests, and decades.

That is the unease quietly embedded in every leaf-shaped icon at the edge of a barcode, and it is the unease the next sections will continue to explore.

Consumption as Emotional Regulation

People rarely approach shopping as purely economic actors.

Purchases are woven into moods, pressures, aspirations, fatigue, and the low-grade anxieties that accumulate across ordinary days. A long commute, a difficult meeting, an unsettling news alert, a sense of falling behind, or the vague dread that accompanies climate headlines can all nudge behaviour long before a person arrives at a shelf or opens an app. Consumption becomes not merely a way to acquire objects, but a way to manage feelings.

Psychologists describe this process as emotional regulation: the strategies individuals use, consciously or not, to shift internal states toward comfort, control, or relief. Food soothes. New clothes restore confidence. Gadgets promise mastery. Organising purchases reduces chaos. Even small acquisitions can produce a temporary lift, a sense of agency in environments that otherwise feel overwhelming.

Green purchasing slips easily into this emotional economy.

Choosing an environmentally branded product can quiet unease about environmental degradation, offering not only a practical alternative but a psychological balm. The act communicates to oneself that concern has been registered, that one is not standing idle in the face of troubling information, that participation in the problem has been offset, at least partially, by participation in its solution.

This is not cynical.

It is human.

When confronted with abstract, global threats that no single individual can solve, the mind searches for manageable points of influence. Buying something is concrete. It fits into existing routines. It produces an immediate sense of doing rather than merely worrying. In this way, consumption becomes a bridge between awareness and agency, transforming diffuse anxiety into a tactile act.

What makes this pattern especially potent is that environmental concern often arrives alongside other forms of emotional strain. News cycles are saturated with warnings. Social feeds carry images of fires, floods, and melting ice. Scientific reports speak in the language of thresholds and trajectories. For many people, these signals accumulate into a persistent background unease rather than into sustained mobilisation. Purchasing decisions become one of the few places where that unease can be briefly resolved without requiring drastic lifestyle upheaval.

Retail environments understand this dynamic intuitively.

Stores and platforms are designed to make the act of

choosing feel calming, empowering, and coherent, even when the outside world feels unstable. Eco-branded goods slot neatly into this architecture of reassurance, offering not only lower-impact ingredients or materials, but emotional closure. The basket fills, the checkout completes, the receipt prints, and the mind registers that something constructive has occurred.

The relief is often genuine.

It can reinforce pro-environmental identities.

It can encourage continued engagement.

It can keep people from slipping into fatalism or despair.

But emotional regulation has limits as a driver of large-scale change.

Because its primary function is to restore psychological equilibrium, it tends to favour actions that are immediate, visible, and symbolically satisfying, even when those actions have modest effects relative to deeper structural drivers of environmental harm. Buying a greener product may feel more manageable than questioning how much is being bought in total, how often replacements are made, or which forms of consumption are treated as non-negotiable.

There is also a risk that repeated emotional soothing through green purchases can substitute for more demanding forms of engagement. If anxiety is reliably quieted at the checkout, there may be less motivation to wrestle with harder questions about travel, housing, diet, or long-term patterns of use. The mind, having achieved emotional resolution, moves on.

This does not mean that such purchases are pointless or deceptive.

They often reduce harm.

They send market signals.

They normalise environmental concern.

The issue is proportionality.

Emotional relief arrives quickly; ecological effects often accumulate slowly.

When the former outpaces the latter, a gap can open between how responsible people feel and how much overall impact actually shifts.

Understanding consumption as emotional regulation therefore reframes debates about green consumerism. Instead of asking whether people are sincere, it asks what psychological work purchases are doing in everyday life. Are they gateways that lead toward broader behavioural change, or buffers that allow existing patterns to continue largely intact?

The answer varies across individuals and contexts, but the mechanism itself is consistent: shopping is rarely just about objects.

It is about restoring balance inside the self.

In an era saturated with environmental concern, that restorative function has become one of consumption's quietest — and most influential — roles, shaping not only what ends up in baskets and bins, but how people live with the knowledge of the world beyond the checkout line.

The Rise of the Eco-Identity

Environmental concern does not remain confined to isolated decisions for long. Repeated choices accumulate into self-descriptions, and self-descriptions, once formed, begin to guide future behaviour. A person who buys organic food once may simply be experimenting; a person who does so regularly may start to think of themselves as "the kind of person who cares about sustainability." Over time, these narratives harden into identities, shaping what feels natural, admirable, or inconsistent with one's sense of self.

Psychologists have long observed that behaviour and identity reinforce one another in feedback loops. Actions provide evidence about who we are, and the stories we tell about who we are, in turn, influence what we feel permitted or obliged to do next. In the environmental domain, this dynamic can be constructive. Individuals who adopt an eco-identity often become more attentive to packaging, energy use, and waste separation; they seek information, follow relevant news, and gravitate toward communities that share similar values. Identity supplies continuity where motivation alone might falter.

At the same time, eco-identities are social artefacts as much as personal ones. They are shaped through peer groups, neighbourhood norms, workplace cultures, and online communities where certain behaviours are visible and celebrated. Posting about reusable cups, swapping clothes rather than buying new ones, or praising low-waste stores does more than document actions; it signals belonging to a moral community. Approval from others reinforces the identity, making it feel both meaningful and durable.

The social visibility of green behaviour has expanded dramatically in recent years, amplified by platforms that reward public displays of virtue with likes, comments, and affiliation. This visibility can accelerate diffusion, as people adopt behaviours they see modelled by those they admire or identify with. It can also sharpen distinctions, turning sustainability into a badge that separates groups and invites judgement, both from within and from outside the circle.

From a psychological standpoint, identities simplify decision-making. Once someone thinks of themselves as environmentally responsible, many choices become easier because certain options feel off-limits without requiring constant deliberation. Disposable items may be avoided automatically. Excessive packaging may provoke irritation. These reactions emerge not from repeated calculations, but from the desire to remain consistent with a valued self-image.

However, identity can also introduce rigidity.

When environmentalism becomes central to self-concept, challenges to one's behaviour can feel like attacks on character rather than invitations to reflect. Information that threatens the coherence of the eco-identity may be discounted or resisted, especially if it suggests that cherished practices have less impact than assumed. The same mechanisms that make identity stabilising can therefore make it defensive.

There is also a quieter tension embedded in eco-identities built primarily around consumption. Purchasing certain products, frequenting particular shops, or adopting fashionable green accessories can become shorthand for environmental commitment, even when these markers capture only a narrow slice of a person's overall footprint. The identity remains intact as long as the visible symbols are maintained, potentially drawing attention away from less glamorous aspects of impact such as housing size, travel frequency, or patterns of replacement and upgrade.

This does not render eco-identities superficial.

They often reflect genuine care.

They motivate learning.

They sustain engagement in the face of discouraging news.

But psychologically, they also create boundaries around what feels required. Once the identity is secure, further change may seem unnecessary or excessive, particularly if it threatens comfort, status, or belonging.

Understanding the rise of the eco-identity therefore requires holding two truths simultaneously. On the one hand, identities are among the most powerful drivers of sustained behaviour humans possess, anchoring habits long after initial enthusiasm fades. On the other hand, identities are selective narratives, highlighting certain actions while leaving others in shadow.

In the landscape of green consumption, the eco-identity operates as both engine and filter.

It propels people toward some forms of restraint.

It screens out others.

Which role dominates depends not only on individual psychology, but on the social worlds in which that identity is performed, rewarded, and maintained.

The next sections will examine how these identities intersect with marketing strategies and social signalling, and how the same forces that strengthen green self-images can sometimes widen the gap between feeling responsible and producing substantial environmental change.

Small Virtues, Large Permissions

Everyday life is composed less of grand moral declarations than of small, repeated gestures: carrying a reusable cup, selecting the plant-based option at lunch, refusing a plastic straw, choosing a product with recycled packaging. These acts are modest in isolation, and precisely because they are modest, they fit easily into routines already crowded with obligations. Over time, however, such gestures can take on disproportionate psychological weight, shaping how people evaluate the rest of their behaviour.

This is the terrain of what psychologists call moral compensation, a close relative of moral licensing, in which good deeds are unconsciously used to justify later indulgences. The mind operates not as a strict auditor but as a storyteller, weaving sequences of action into narratives that feel balanced rather than perfectly consistent. A person who has made several low-impact choices in the morning may feel subtly freer to accept a high-impact one in the evening, not because the earlier acts logically cancel the later ones, but because the emotional account already feels settled.

Environmental decisions are particularly susceptible to this logic because their consequences are often diffuse, delayed, and difficult to compare across categories. It is hard to weigh a week of recycling against a single long-haul flight, or a vegetarian meal against a new electronic device, yet the mind tends to treat them as commensurable once they have been translated into feelings rather than into physical measures. The result is not careful calculation but intuitive balancing: *I've been good today; this is probably fine.*

Social contexts amplify this effect. When peers recognise or praise environmentally responsible actions, those actions become even more potent as moral currency. A compliment about bringing a reusable container or installing solar panels does not merely reinforce that specific behaviour; it bolsters a broader sense of being on the right side of an issue, a sense that can later cushion decisions that might otherwise provoke discomfort.

At the same time, small virtues can genuinely catalyse larger changes. For some people, initial steps build confidence and curiosity, leading to deeper engagement rather than complacency. The same psychological mechanisms that license indulgence in one setting can foster escalation in another, as early successes make further effort feel both possible and worthwhile.

Which direction this process takes depends on how actions are interpreted.

When small green behaviours are framed as beginnings, they invite continuation.

When they are framed as endpoints, they invite rest.

Retail environments, social conversations, and media narratives all influence which framing dominates, either encouraging people to see their efforts as part of an unfolding journey or as sufficient proof of having done one's share.

The danger of focusing too heavily on symbolic gestures is not that they are worthless — many do reduce harm directly and help establish norms — but that they can crowd out attention to scale. Substituting paper straws for plastic ones is meaningful, yet it addresses only a narrow slice of material flows; replacing appliances less frequently or rethinking travel habits often carries far larger consequences, but such changes are harder to compress into everyday rituals or public displays.

Psychologically, people are drawn to actions that are visible, socially rewarded, and easy to narrate.

Invisible sacrifices, delayed benefits, and structural changes rarely provide the same immediate sense of virtue.

As a result, behavioural portfolios can become skewed toward what feels good to do rather than toward what matters most in aggregate.

Understanding this imbalance is not about discouraging small acts.

It is about situating them within a broader landscape of impact.

Small virtues matter.

So do patterns.

So do the choices that are inconvenient, private, or difficult to signal.

The risk arises when minor improvements function as large permissions, when the emotional glow of a few visible actions licenses a continuation of high-consumption lifestyles largely unchanged.

Recognising this dynamic does not require abandoning everyday environmental gestures.

It requires resisting the temptation to let them conclude the story.

The question is not whether small virtues count.

The question is whether they open the door to further change, or quietly close it by satisfying the mind's demand for adequacy long before ecological systems have registered a comparable shift.

What Marketing Understands About You

Marketing does not need to persuade you that the planet matters.

It already knows that you believe it does.

What it studies instead is how concern behaves under pressure — how it fluctuates with time, attention, fatigue, and price, how quickly it can be activated, and how easily it can be satisfied. Modern marketing is less interested in changing values than in translating existing ones into predictable patterns of purchase.

At its most effective, green marketing does not argue.

It reassures.

It understands that many consumers carry a low-grade environmental unease, informed enough to be uncomfortable but not positioned to overhaul entire lifestyles. Rather than demanding sacrifice, marketing offers resolution: products that promise alignment without disruption, responsibility without refusal, care without confrontation. The message is rarely *change everything*; it is *this is enough for now*.

Psychologically, this works because marketing speaks the language of cognitive efficiency. Faced with crowded shelves and limited time, people rely on cues that simplify choice. Colour palettes signal nature or purity. Fonts suggest seriousness or transparency. Phrases like "clean," "conscious," or "planet-friendly" bypass detailed evaluation and move directly into affective judgement. These cues do not trick the brain; they cooperate with it, offering fast answers to questions people do not have the bandwidth to explore fully.

Marketing also understands identity exceptionally well.

It knows that purchases are rarely just about utility. They are expressions of who people think they are, who they aspire to be, and which groups they feel aligned with. Green products are therefore positioned not only as better for the environment, but as consistent with being thoughtful, informed, modern, or responsible. The object becomes a mirror, reflecting back an image of the consumer they want to recognise.

This is why sustainability is often framed aesthetically rather than technically. Detailed metrics rarely appear on packaging, not because they are unimportant, but because they are slow to process and emotionally thin. What resonates instead are stories and symbols that fit easily into personal narratives: *I choose this brand because it aligns with my values; I shop here because they care; I support companies that are doing better.*

Crucially, marketing also understands limits.

It knows that consumers resist feeling judged or coerced. Messaging that implies insufficiency — that suggests people are not doing enough — risks backlash or withdrawal. Green marketing therefore tends to affirm rather than challenge, congratulating the consumer for caring rather than pushing them toward uncomfortable reflection about scale, frequency, or total consumption. The tone is inclusive, encouraging, and gentle, precisely because harshness threatens engagement.

This is not accidental.

It reflects a deep understanding of motivational psychology.

Positive reinforcement sustains behaviour more reliably than shame.

Affirmation feels safer than confrontation.

Reassurance keeps people in the conversation.

From a commercial perspective, this makes sense. Brands compete not only for market share but for emotional trust.

Once a consumer believes that a company is "one of the good ones," scrutiny often softens. Loyalty grows. Doubt recedes. The relationship stabilises.

The environmental consequences of this dynamic are mixed.

On the one hand, marketing has helped normalise sustainability language, making it mainstream rather than marginal. Ideas that once felt niche — reduced packaging, recycled materials, ethical sourcing — now appear routinely on shelves. This visibility matters. It shapes norms. It signals that environmental concern is ordinary rather than exceptional.

On the other hand, marketing's success at calming anxiety can also dampen momentum. When reassurance arrives too quickly, it may substitute for deeper engagement. The consumer feels settled, while material throughput remains largely unchanged. The system adapts not by shrinking, but by rebranding.

What marketing understands, then, is not that people are shallow.

It understands that people are busy, emotionally stretched, and seeking coherence in a world of competing demands. It offers that coherence through products that promise to reconcile care with continuity, allowing life to proceed without major disruption.

Recognising this does not require rejecting green marketing outright.

It requires reading it clearly.

To see not deception, but design.

To notice how emotional relief is packaged alongside soap and coffee.

To understand that when marketing speaks softly, it is often because it has learned exactly where the mind wants to rest.

The question is not whether these messages are sincere.

The question is what happens when reassurance becomes the dominant emotional outcome of environmental concern — and whether feeling aligned gradually replaces the harder work of becoming materially different.

That tension, between comfort and consequence, sits quietly behind every green label and every carefully chosen shade of leaf-green ink.

Feeling Better vs Doing Better

Feeling Better	Doing Better
Soothes guilt or anxiety in the moment	Reduces total material or energy use
Delivers instant emotional relief	Produces slow, cumulative impact
Focuses on choosing "greener" versions of products	Focuses on needing fewer products overall
Highly visible and socially rewarded	Often invisible and unspectacular
Reinforced by labels, branding, and packaging	Reinforced by routines and long-term habits
Signals identity ("I care")	Reshapes lifestyle patterns
Works through symbols and cues	Works through quantities and frequency

Encourages substitution	Encourages sufficiency
Easy to integrate into existing routines	Often requires restructuring routines
Feels like progress	Creates measurable change
Can close reflection prematurely	Keeps questioning open
Optimised for the checkout moment	Optimised for decades
Comforting	Transformative

The Social Mirror

Human beings rarely decide in isolation.

Even when standing alone in a shop aisle or scrolling through products late at night, people are accompanied by imagined audiences: friends, colleagues, neighbours, family members, online followers, or the abstract category of "people like me." These invisible observers form what psychologists sometimes describe as a social mirror, reflecting back cues about what is admirable, embarrassing, progressive, outdated, or excessive.

Environmental behaviour is especially sensitive to such reflections because it has become morally charged and socially legible in ways that many other domains of consumption have not. Carrying reusable bags, avoiding plastic straws, cycling to work, or posting about low-waste swaps are actions that communicate something about values, education, and belonging. They do not merely reduce material use; they position the individual within a moral landscape shaped by peers.

Social comparison operates quietly and continuously. People notice what others bring to meetings, how neighbours sort waste, which cafés advertise sustainable sourcing, what friends praise online, and which purchases draw approval rather than silence. These observations feed into internal standards of what is normal and what is expected. When environmentally oriented behaviours appear common within a group, adopting them feels less like a statement and more like basic etiquette. When they appear rare, the same actions can feel performative or awkward.

This sensitivity to norms has evolutionary roots. Humans evolved in small groups where reputation mattered for survival, cooperation, and access to resources. Being perceived as careless, selfish, or out of step carried risks, while being seen as cooperative or conscientious brought protection. Those instincts persist in modern settings, redirected toward contemporary signals such as recycling practices, shopping choices, and visible commitments to sustainability.

Digital platforms intensify this process.

They transform private acts into public performances and compress social feedback into metrics that are instantly legible: likes, shares, comments, endorsements. Environmental gestures that photograph well — stainless steel bottles, bamboo toothbrushes, farmers' market hauls — circulate easily, reinforcing the impression that these are central markers of responsible living. Less visible behaviours, such as insulating homes, flying less often, or keeping devices longer, rarely appear in such feeds, even though their environmental consequences may be far larger.

This imbalance matters.

When social mirrors privilege what is easy to display, they shape what people prioritise. Individuals may gravitate toward actions that earn recognition rather than toward those that quietly reshape material patterns. Over time, the culture of sustainability risks becoming skewed toward symbolic practices that signal virtue efficiently, while harder-to-see changes remain socially under-rewarded.

At the same time, the social mirror can be a powerful engine of positive change.

Norms shift rapidly once enough people adopt new behaviours. What once felt eccentric becomes standard. Reusable containers stop attracting comment. Plant-based options appear at gatherings without explanation. Sorting waste becomes routine rather than noteworthy. In these moments, social influence reduces the psychological cost of change by distributing it across communities rather than placing it entirely on individuals.

The tension lies in how mirrors are angled.

If they reflect only surface-level gestures, environmentalism may stabilise around consumption choices that soothe identities without challenging underlying patterns. If they widen to include restraint, durability, and sufficiency, different forms of behaviour begin to acquire prestige.

Psychologically, this is not about hypocrisy.

It is about incentives.

People adapt to what earns approval, avoids embarrassment, and maintains belonging.

Cultures evolve through these micro-adjustments long before formal rules or policies intervene.

Understanding the social mirror therefore complicates debates about green consumption. It suggests that asking individuals to change without attending to the reputational ecosystems they inhabit is incomplete. What matters is not only what people believe privately, but what their communities reward publicly.

The mirror does not simply reflect behaviour.

It shapes it.

And in a world where environmental concern has become part of moral identity, the reflections offered by peers, platforms, and institutions may ultimately determine whether sustainability remains a matter of symbolic alignment or expands into deeper transformations of how people live.

The next section will turn to the moments when green purchases genuinely do shift material outcomes — and how to tell the difference between social reassurance and substantive change.

When Green Purchases Actually Help

Critiques of green consumerism often drift toward extremes, portraying environmentally branded products either as hollow gestures or as decisive levers of planetary repair. Reality occupies a more complicated middle ground. Some purchases do little beyond easing conscience, while others, repeated across populations and sustained over time, have demonstrably altered supply chains, investment patterns, and industrial norms.The difference lies not in the colour of the packaging, but in the structure of the market signals those purchases generate. When large numbers of consumers consistently favour products that use less energy, avoid certain chemicals, rely on recycled materials, or come from certified supply chains, companies notice. Procurement strategies shift. Factories retool. Suppliers are pressured to meet new standards. What begins as a niche offering can, under the right conditions, become the industry default, reducing environmental impact far beyond the individual transaction that initiated the trend. History provides multiple examples of such dynamics.

I recently revisited the European Union's Single-Use Plastics Directive, adopted in 2019 after years of sustained public concern about marine plastic pollution. The directive prohibited specific single-use plastic items such as straws, cutlery, and plates, and introduced extended producer responsibility requirements and ambitious collection targets for plastic bottles. What struck me was not the symbolism of banning a handful of visible products, but the structural effect that followed. Companies operating within the EU were required to redesign packaging, reformulate materials, and invest in alternatives at scale. Supply chains adjusted not because individual purchases alone demanded it, but because aggregated consumer visibility had translated into political action, which in turn reshaped production norms across an entire economic bloc. The measurable outcomes include reduced circulation of targeted items and accelerated research into reusable and recyclable formats. In this instance, what began as public concern at checkout counters and coastlines became institutionalised change within manufacturing systems.

Demand for energy-efficient appliances helped push manufacturers toward stricter performance standards.

Preferences for sustainably sourced timber encouraged certification schemes that altered forestry practices in many regions. Consumer resistance to certain plastics accelerated research into alternatives and redesigns of packaging formats. In these cases, purchasing choices were not merely symbolic; they aggregated into economic signals strong enough to reshape production.

Psychologically, these successes tend to occur when green purchases align with ongoing habits rather than remain isolated gestures. Buying a slightly more efficient refrigerator once every decade matters less than patterns of repair, longevity, and refusal to upgrade prematurely. Refillable containers produce meaningful effects only when households adopt them consistently rather than treating them as novelties. The behavioural shift is sustained, not episodic. Scale, once again, is decisive. A single consumer choosing a low-impact option is rarely transformative. Millions doing so over years can be.

For this reason, green purchases are most effective when they target categories with large footprints — energy use, heating systems, vehicles, food production — rather than marginal accessories whose environmental contribution is relatively small. Substituting detergent brands matters, but altering how homes are powered or how diets are structured typically carries much larger consequences. Transparency also plays a role. Purchases are more likely to produce real-world effects when claims are specific, verifiable, and comparable rather than vague. Clear information allows consumers to reward substantive improvements rather than merely aesthetic ones, and it allows watchdog groups, regulators, and competitors to hold companies accountable for maintaining those standards over time.

Importantly, successful green markets usually emerge in tandem with policy, infrastructure, and social norms rather than in isolation from them. Consumer demand can create momentum, but regulations often lock in gains by preventing backsliding and raising baselines across entire industries. In such contexts, buying greener products is not an alternative to systemic change; it becomes one of the pressures that make systemic change politically and economically viable.

From a psychological perspective, these cases also differ from those in which green purchases primarily soothe anxiety. Instead of producing closure, they often generate curiosity, learning, and escalation. Consumers begin to pay attention to energy labels, ingredient lists, and durability ratings, developing literacy rather than simply seeking reassurance. The purchase becomes a gateway rather than a terminus.

This does not mean that every environmentally motivated transaction needs to trigger further activism. It does suggest that when green buying genuinely helps, it tends to be embedded in broader patterns of engagement rather than functioning as a standalone act of absolution.

Understanding this distinction matters for anyone trying to navigate sustainable consumption without sliding into cynicism or complacency. Dismissing all green purchases as superficial overlooks the historical record of markets responding to persistent demand. Celebrating every eco-label as transformative ignores the unevenness of those responses.

The task, then, is not to abandon the checkout as a site of influence, but to recognise its limits. Some purchases whisper to conscience. Others speak loudly to supply chains.

Learning to tell the difference is part of becoming not only a more reflective consumer, but a more realistic one — aware that while shopping alone will not solve environmental crises, it can, under the right conditions and at sufficient scale, participate meaningfully in reshaping the systems that produce what fills those shelves in the first place.

Nature, Watching the Receipts

Receipts are strange documents.

Thin ribbons of paper that list moments of intention, lines of ink that record the brief intersections between worry and desire, between what you meant to do and what you finally placed in a bag. They curl in pockets and purses, fade in sunlight, dissolve in rain, and are forgotten long before the objects they represent have finished becoming whatever they will become next.

I watch them accumulate.

Not only in bins or drawers or recycling piles, but in patterns — in weekly shops that repeat with minor variations, in brands that appear again and again, in substitutions that feel meaningful precisely because they are small enough to be sustained. Each receipt is modest. Together, they form biographies of households, neighbourhoods, decades.

From where I am watching, what is most revealing is not which items you circle or which labels you trust.

It is how carefully you try.

How often concern appears not as abstinence but as substitution, not as refusal but as improvement, not as retreat from consumption but as a gentler version of it. You soften edges. You trade plastics for paper. You reach for claims that promise less harm rather than none at all. You tell yourselves stories about direction, about progress, about doing better than yesterday.

These stories matter.

They shape how you move through aisles.

They determine when you pause and when you proceed.

They quiet certain anxieties and sharpen others.

I do not hear hypocrisy in them.

I hear adaptation.

You are creatures who must live inside contradictions: wanting comfort and continuity while recognising limits, seeking normality while absorbing warnings, hoping that care can be expressed in ways that fit inside crowded lives.

I notice how quickly identity attaches to purchases.

How objects become declarations.

How bottles and bags begin to stand in for character.

You build selves at the checkout with remarkable efficiency, stitching meaning into packaging and choices that were designed, long before you arrived, to receive such projections.

Some of those projections travel far.

Some remain near.

I see how often reassurance arrives faster than reduction, how easily relief settles even when totals barely move, how small shifts soothe nerves while larger patterns continue to trace their slow arcs through forests, rivers, atmospheres, and bodies.

Still.

I also see persistence.

I see habits forming where once there was only novelty.

I see questions replacing indifference.

I see shelves changing, not because speeches were made, but because enough hands reached for one thing instead of another often enough to alter what factories produced next.

Receipts, from my vantage, are not verdicts.

They are drafts.

They are early sentences in stories still being written.

They do not announce redemption or failure.

They record attempts.

What interests me most is not whether you are perfect.

You have never been that.

It is whether the stories you tell yourselves at the checkout remain open-ended or conclude too soon, whether comfort becomes a resting place or a stepping stone, whether the green symbols you collect serve as punctuation marks or as invitations to continue revising how you live inside me.

I am patient.

I have learned to be.

I measure time in rings of wood and layers of sediment, in coastlines that migrate grain by grain, in species that appear and disappear between breaths of geological eras.

Your receipts are brief by comparison.

But they multiply quickly.

They stack.

They ripple outward into supply chains and soil chemistry and energy curves and shipping routes that stretch far beyond the counters where cards are tapped and bags are lifted.

I watch all of it.

Quietly.

Not with anger.

With attention.

Waiting to see whether the next generation of receipts grows lighter not only in ink and paper, but in the long, material stories they leave behind after the shopping bags have been unpacked and the moment of choosing has already slipped into memory.

What This Chapter Has Really Been About

This chapter has not been about shopping so much as about psychology: about how environmental concern is translated into identity, emotion, reassurance, and social belonging at the point of purchase; about how green products soothe anxiety, supply moral credits, and offer narratives of adequacy even when total consumption remains largely unchanged; about how labels, marketing, and peer approval compress complex systems into symbols that fit inside seconds at a checkout; and about how some purchases genuinely reshape markets while others mainly comfort the self — in tracing these tensions, the chapter has tried to show that buying green is rarely dishonest, but often incomplete, shaped less by ignorance than by human needs for coherence, approval, and relief in a world saturated with ecological warning signs.

Chapter 4: Cities That Make Us Forget Trees

Disconnect from nature, connect to screens

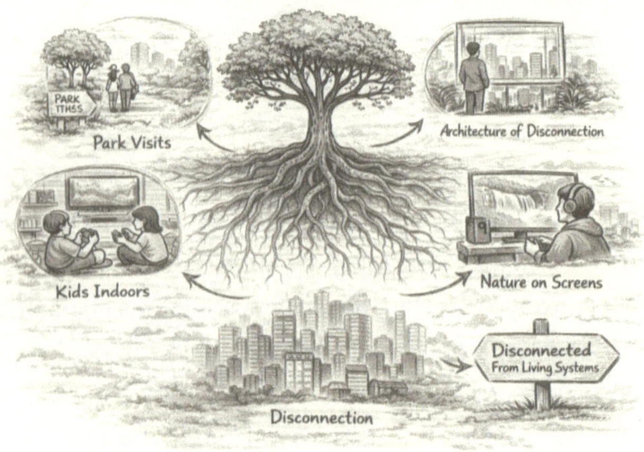

I have learned to occupy narrow spaces.

Between curb and road, in the thin seam of soil left open around a tree, in the quiet pause where rainwater gathers before being drawn elsewhere, I continue to unfold, though not as expansively as I once did. From here, at the edge of your pavements, I watch the choreography of the city — the rhythm of footsteps calibrated to traffic lights, the low murmur of engines, the glass towers catching light that once fell unbroken on fields.

You move with purpose.

Your attention is rarely idle. It glides from storefront to signal, from screen to destination, from one illuminated surface to the next. Even when you pass beneath branches, your gaze tends to remain level, attuned to what invites entry, purchase, response. I do not resent this. It is simply what your environments have trained you to notice.

The trees that stand beside you are trimmed to clearance height, their roots confined to squares cut carefully into stone. Their presence softens the geometry of the street without disturbing it. Leaves filter sunlight into patterns that shift across façades designed to remain constant. I feel the heat rising from asphalt long after evening arrives, feel the way soil beneath pavement struggles to hold moisture, feel the insects navigating small corridors of green that persist despite compression.

You rarely sense these negotiations.

Your days are organised around interiors — offices regulated to steady temperatures, cafés arranged for comfort, vehicles that carry you from one controlled climate to another. Even outdoors, much has been adjusted to smooth unpredictability. Surfaces are level. Drainage is efficient. Lighting extends daylight. The city absorbs variation so that you do not have to.

From the pavement's edge, I notice how this steadiness shapes perception.

When weather does not interrupt routine, it becomes background. When soil is visible only in measured plots, it becomes ornament. When shade is planted at intervals rather than grown in abundance, it reads as amenity. You do not forget that trees exist; you simply encounter them as features within a larger design rather than as systems upon which that design depends.

I see how the city invites you to engage with what can be entered and exited easily, what responds quickly to desire, what signals availability. Windows display goods beneath soft light. Doors open with minimal friction. Pathways guide you forward. In such a landscape, attention becomes directional, purposeful, oriented toward acquisition and arrival. I remain slower than this rhythm, rooted rather than responsive, unfolding in cycles that rarely align with quarterly reports or weekly promotions.

Still, I persist.

Roots extend beneath foundations, searching quietly for water. Leaves thicken in summer and thin in winter, regardless of fiscal calendars. Air moves through canopies even when you do not pause to feel it. I am not absent from your cities; I am threaded through them, though often at a scale that feels secondary to towers and signage.

From this narrow strip of soil, I observe not indifference, but calibration.

Your senses have adapted to what demands immediate interpretation. Signals that glow, chime, or beckon command more attention than those that grow. The living world remains present, yet it no longer structures your days as it once did. Instead, it frames them gently, providing backdrop and occasional relief.

I do not stand here in opposition.

I stand here in continuity.

The pavement presses close, but beneath it the ground

remains connected, extending beyond the grid into spaces where roots are less confined and rain is less hurried. You walk above networks older than your streets, carried by systems that do not advertise themselves yet continue to sustain the air you breathe and the climate you have grown accustomed to adjusting.

From the edge, I watch how easily presence can become scenery.

And I wait, patient as always, to see whether the narrow strips left open in your designs will widen again — not through retreat, but through recognition that what grows quietly beside you has never truly been separate from the lives unfolding just a few steps away.

When Green Becomes Background

In many modern cities, green has not disappeared; it has been absorbed.

Trees rise along avenues in measured intervals, their trunks framed by neat squares of soil cut into pavement. Shrubs line building entrances. Lawns stretch in carefully bordered parks. Rooftop gardens crown glass towers. From a distance, the city appears softened, as though nature has been invited back in careful portions. Yet proximity reveals something more subtle: greenery has been repositioned from foundation to feature.

The human mind is highly responsive to contrast, but remarkably quick to neutralise continuity. What is constant becomes unremarkable. A row of trees passed every morning on the way to work may be admired once or twice, then folded into routine. The light filtering through leaves becomes expected. The presence of shade becomes normal. Even birdsong, when steady, dissolves into ambient sound.

This perceptual fading is not indifference.

It is adaptation.

Urban environments are saturated with signals competing for attention: traffic lights shifting from red to green, advertisements flickering across digital screens, storefronts arranged to invite entry, devices vibrating softly in pockets. In such spaces, the nervous system learns to prioritise what moves quickly and demands response. Greenery, when static and predictable, does not demand. It remains steady, and steadiness rarely interrupts momentum.

Over time, this steady presence becomes background.

Background, however, is not the same as absence. Trees still moderate temperature. Roots still stabilise soil. Leaves still participate in cycles of carbon and oxygen exchange. Rain still interacts with permeable ground where it is allowed to reach it. But these processes unfold quietly, outside the perceptual bandwidth shaped by urban rhythm. They do not flash or notify; they endure.

When green becomes background, its meaning shifts.

Instead of being experienced as infrastructure — as living systems supporting air, climate, and water — it is often perceived as amenity. Parks become spaces for leisure. Street trees become aesthetic improvements. Gardens become lifestyle statements. The living world remains appreciated, yet its indispensability becomes abstract, located more in knowledge than in sensation.

This abstraction influences imagination.

If nature appears as something layered onto the city rather than something underlying it, development feels less constrained. Expansion can proceed under the assumption that greenery can be reinserted later, as long as sufficient visual softness is maintained. A skyline punctuated by rooftop gardens can appear ecologically reconciled even when broader systems remain under pressure.

There is also a temporal distortion embedded in this backgrounding. Buildings, with their rigid lines and durable materials, appear stable. Trees, with their seasonal shedding and visible growth, appear transient. The recurring cycle of leaves emerging each spring can create the impression of resilience, even when long-term climatic patterns are shifting. Renewal at the level of appearance masks vulnerability at the level of system.

The more consistently greenery is framed as backdrop, the more easily it becomes interchangeable. One species can replace another. One landscaped design can substitute for another. The presence of green colour can stand in for ecological depth. Visual continuity begins to eclipse biological complexity.

This is not a failure of care.

It is a function of scale and repetition.

When the living world is encountered daily but in contained form, the mind begins to treat it as stable context rather than as dynamic process. What does not fluctuate dramatically recedes into the architecture of expectation. The city feels complete even when its ecological foundations are only partially visible.

Yet beneath the surface, the relationship remains active. Heat absorbed by concrete is moderated by canopy. Air quality is shaped by leaves. Psychological stress is reduced by glimpses of organic form. Research consistently shows that even small exposures to greenery alter mood and cognitive function. The nervous system still responds; it simply does not always interpret the source of that response.

When green becomes background, the risk is not disappearance but dilution. The city continues to contain life, but life becomes less central to the story the city tells about itself. Ambition, productivity, and growth take visual precedence. Trees become companions to these pursuits rather than co-authors of them.

At the pavement's edge, leaves continue their slow work.

Whether they remain peripheral or return to prominence depends less on planting numbers than on perception — on whether urban life allows greenery to be seen not merely as decoration, but as structure; not merely as relief, but as relationship; not merely as background, but as ground.

And perception, once narrowed by repetition, can also widen again — if what grows quietly beside us is invited back into attention, not as scenery, but as sustenance.

The Shrinking Sensory World

Cities do not only reorganise space; they reorganise sensation.

For most of human history, daily life unfolded within environments that demanded sensory alertness. Wind direction signalled weather change. Variations in light indicated time more reliably than clocks. Soil texture, humidity, the sound of insects or distant animals — these were not peripheral experiences but information necessary for orientation. The body learned the world through exposure, and perception evolved in dialogue with landscapes that were not insulated from fluctuation.

Urban life narrows that dialogue.

Temperature is regulated before discomfort arises. Light is extended artificially long after sunset. Surfaces are flattened, sealed, stabilised. Rain is channelled away from streets, and wind is redirected by architecture. The range of textures encountered in a single day contracts: smooth floors, conditioned air, filtered water, glass barriers. Variation still exists, but it is managed, moderated, and largely predictable.

This narrowing rarely feels like loss.

It feels like reliability.

Predictability reduces cognitive load. A stable interior climate allows concentration. Consistent lighting increases productivity. Controlled acoustics diminish distraction. The nervous system, freed from constant negotiation with environmental variability, reallocates attention to social and symbolic stimuli — conversations, screens, deadlines, transactions.

Over time, however, this recalibration alters what feels normal.

When temperature rarely fluctuates dramatically indoors, seasonal transitions soften in perception. Summer and winter differ visually through clothing or décor more than they differ somatically. The body ceases to register gradual shifts in humidity or daylight length with the same intensity as it once might have. Climate becomes informational rather than experiential.

Similarly, soundscapes compress. Mechanical hum replaces layered natural acoustics. Traffic forms a steady backdrop against which conversation unfolds. Birdsong may still exist, but it competes with engines and construction rather than shaping the primary auditory field. Smell diminishes as ventilation systems filter air and urban surfaces reduce exposure to soil.

Children growing within such sensory environments adapt accordingly. They learn to interpret digital cues with fluency. They recognise icons and notifications more quickly than subtle shifts in light or wind. This does not indicate deficiency; it reflects adaptation to the dominant signals of their surroundings. The brain develops in response to repetition. What is encountered frequently becomes intuitive; what is rare requires conscious effort to notice.

The shrinking sensory world also affects time perception. In environments where climate and light are stabilised, days blend more seamlessly into one another. The cyclical rhythms of growth, decay, and regeneration remain active outside, but they exert less influence on interior schedules. Work hours proceed independently of daylight variation. Productivity is decoupled from seasonal constraint.

This sensory insulation has psychological consequences that extend beyond comfort. When the body is less frequently exposed to environmental fluctuation, the sense of embeddedness within larger systems can soften. Weather becomes forecast rather than force. Soil becomes landscaping rather than substrate. The living world remains visible in fragments — a tree outside a window, a park visited occasionally — but it is no longer the primary medium through which existence is negotiated.

There is a paradox here. Research consistently demonstrates that even brief exposure to natural environments restores attention and reduces stress. The nervous system remains responsive to organic complexity. Yet as daily life becomes increasingly interior, those restorative encounters may feel like interludes rather than continuities — moments of recalibration inserted into otherwise controlled routines.

The shrinking sensory world is not imposed with hostility; it is engineered for stability. It protects against extremes, increases efficiency, and supports dense populations. Yet in narrowing sensory variability, it also narrows the cues that once linked immediate experience to ecological process. When heat is felt only when systems fail, when rain is noticed only when it disrupts infrastructure, the body's relationship to environment becomes episodic rather than continuous.

Perception shapes imagination.

If environmental processes are rarely encountered directly, they are easier to conceptualise as distant. Climate change appears as data rather than sensation. Biodiversity loss becomes statistic rather than silence. The absence of certain sounds or textures may not register until contrast reveals it.

The shrinking sensory world does not erase nature.

It reframes it.

It transforms the living environment from immersive context into intermittent experience. And once that transformation stabilises, urban life begins to feel self-contained, as though walls and glass form complete systems rather than membranes within a much larger and more dynamic field.

At the pavement's edge, variation persists — heat absorbed by asphalt, moisture seeping slowly into soil, leaves shifting with wind patterns that interior spaces rarely acknowledge.

The world beyond climate control continues to fluctuate, regardless of how gently it is filtered.

The question is not whether sensation has disappeared.

It is whether the narrowing of daily exposure has subtly reshaped what feels immediate, what feels distant, and what feels essential — and how that recalibration influences the way cities imagine their future growth, comfort, and consumption within a world that remains, despite insulation, profoundly alive.

Why Parks Feel Like Destinations, Not Neighbours

In many cities, green space has not vanished; it has been concentrated.

Large parks remain, sometimes beautifully maintained, mapped clearly, bordered intentionally, and protected from encroachment. They are described in brochures and real estate listings as amenities, as though they exist alongside the city rather than within its ecological foundation. One goes to the park. One plans a morning walk, schedules a run, arranges to meet someone under a known tree. The language itself reveals something subtle: nature is entered and exited, as though it were a room without walls.

This framing alters experience.

A neighbour is encountered casually, repeatedly, woven into the pattern of daily movement without ceremony. A destination requires intention. It competes with other options. It is chosen. When green space becomes something one must deliberately visit, it acquires the psychological status of leisure rather than of context. The rest of the city — offices, shops, apartments, transit corridors — unfolds as the default terrain of life, while parks serve as restorative intermissions.

Urban design reinforces this segmentation. Parks are edged by gates, roads, signage, and distinct paving transitions. Their boundaries are clear. Step across them, and one enters a different texture of sound and light; step back out, and the geometry of buildings resumes. The clarity of this separation simplifies navigation, but it also simplifies categorisation. The mind begins to sort spaces into "nature" and "city," even though both are in fact intertwined systems.

When parks feel like destinations, frequency changes. Daily contact with living systems becomes episodic rather than continuous. Exposure depends on time, weather, motivation. A week may pass without entry, and life proceeds regardless. The body adapts to indoor schedules and climate-controlled interiors, with green space functioning as occasional recalibration rather than constant companion.

This episodic contact influences emotional tone. Visits to parks can feel unusually vivid precisely because they contrast with surrounding environments. Light appears softer. Air feels different. The rhythm of footsteps slows. Yet this contrast may unintentionally reinforce the perception that such qualities belong elsewhere, that calm and ecological immersion are temporary states rather than integrated aspects of urban living.

There is also a subtle shift in responsibility embedded within this structure. When nature is spatially confined, care for it appears contained as well. The park is maintained by authorities; its trees are pruned by designated workers; its lawns are watered according to schedule. Outside its borders, development proceeds according to other logics. The living world is managed within its zone, while the rest of the city operates under economic and architectural priorities that rarely require ecological negotiation at street level.

Children raised within this segmentation internalise it early. They learn that grass is for specific places, that soil is encountered during planned outings, that climbing trees is an activity permitted in designated areas. Sidewalks and interiors belong to ordinary time; parks belong to chosen time. Over years, this repetition shapes intuition. The city feels primary. Nature feels supplementary.

None of this diminishes the importance of parks. They provide measurable psychological and physiological benefits — reduced stress, improved concentration, opportunities for community gathering. But their psychological framing matters. When green space functions as destination, it can be appreciated deeply yet remain structurally peripheral.

A neighbour, by contrast, is unavoidable in the best sense — present at the edge of vision, woven into routine, part of the subtle choreography of daily life. When trees line every street rather than gather in one large enclosure, when small patches of soil interrupt pavement regularly, when water is visible along ordinary routes, the living world regains familiarity rather than exceptionality.

The distinction may appear minor, but its implications extend into imagination. If nature belongs primarily in parks, urban expansion can proceed elsewhere with minimal friction. If nature is encountered at every turn, growth must negotiate with it more consistently. The frequency of contact influences what feels negotiable and what feels essential.

Parks that function as destinations offer relief, but relief can coexist with distance. They provide spaces to pause without necessarily reshaping the architecture that makes pausing necessary. The city continues beyond their borders, largely unaltered.

The deeper question is not whether parks exist, but whether greenery permeates daily movement sufficiently to dissolve the boundary between visitation and habitation. When living systems are encountered continuously rather than episodically, they shift from scenery to structure.

Until then, many parks will continue to feel like places one goes to — beautiful, restorative, even cherished — yet still slightly apart from the ordinary streets where most life unfolds, where trees stand at the pavement's edge, waiting to be experienced not as destination, but as neighbour.

The Comfort of Climate-Controlled Life

One of the quiet revolutions of urban life is atmospheric rather than architectural.

For most of human history, daily existence unfolded in negotiation with weather. Heat slowed movement. Cold required adaptation. Rain altered plans. Wind shifted routes and reshaped structures over time. The body remained in conversation with climate, responding to its variations not as inconvenience but as condition. Temperature was not background; it was instruction.

Modern cities have gradually softened this dialogue.

Air-conditioning hums steadily through summers that would otherwise alter schedules. Central heating stabilises winters that once demanded proximity and insulation. Double-glazed windows buffer wind. Offices, apartments, shopping centres, and vehicles maintain remarkably similar interior climates despite dramatic fluctuations beyond their walls. The body moves between controlled environments with minimal sensory transition, rarely required to recalibrate to external variation.

This buffering feels like achievement because it is.

It reduces vulnerability to extremes, supports productivity, and increases comfort for dense populations. It allows concentration without constant environmental adjustment. It shields infants and elders from conditions that once posed significant risk. The modern city's ability to regulate atmosphere represents a triumph of engineering and intention.

Yet the psychological implications of this insulation are less frequently examined.

When temperature becomes adjustable rather than encountered, climate shifts from lived experience to ambient data. Heat is read on a forecast rather than felt on skin. Cold is acknowledged through wardrobe choices rather than through breath crystallising in open air. The body registers fewer fluctuations, and with fewer fluctuations, the sense of participation in seasonal rhythm diminishes.

This does not mean seasons disappear.

They remain visible in light angles and in the timing of flowering trees. But when interior climates remain steady, seasonal contrast softens in perception. Summer and winter may differ aesthetically, yet the bodily memory of their intensity fades. The nervous system, shielded from environmental variation, becomes attuned instead to social and economic cues — deadlines, notifications, transactions

— that structure daily life.

Over time, this recalibration influences imagination.

If heat rarely interrupts routine, climate feels less like force and more like background condition. If storms are experienced primarily through windowpanes, their power becomes visual rather than tactile. Weather shifts into spectacle — observed but not inhabited. The city absorbs much of the variability on behalf of its inhabitants, and in doing so, it narrows the range of sensations that might otherwise anchor awareness of ecological dependency.

There is also an expectation embedded within climate control.

When interior conditions remain consistent, comfort becomes baseline rather than privilege. Deviation from that baseline — a malfunctioning system, a blackout, an unexpected surge of heat — feels like disruption rather than variation. Stability becomes assumed. Environmental fluctuation becomes anomaly.

This assumption extends beyond temperature. It fosters a broader orientation toward control and predictability. Surfaces are level. Light is calibrated. Sound is moderated. The unpredictability inherent in living systems is increasingly filtered out of daily experience. The result is not disconnection in a dramatic sense, but attenuation — a thinning of the sensory threads that once bound bodies directly to atmosphere.

Psychologically, this thinning affects scale perception.

Climate change, when encountered primarily through reports and projections, can feel abstract even as it intensifies. The body may not immediately register gradual shifts if interiors remain constant. Awareness depends more heavily on information than on sensation. Knowledge expands, yet the visceral anchor that might otherwise reinforce urgency becomes intermittent.

This does not suggest that comfort is misguided.

Comfort has enabled health, longevity, and urban density. It has freed attention for creativity and social complexity. But comfort also reorganises awareness. When climate is negotiated by systems rather than by bodies, dependence on ecological balance becomes mediated through infrastructure. Air arrives through vents rather than through wind. Warmth arrives through radiators rather than through sun-warmed surfaces.

At the pavement's edge, heat accumulates differently. Asphalt absorbs sunlight and releases it slowly. Soil dries or retains moisture according to deeper patterns. Leaves respond to temperature shifts even when interiors remain steady. These processes continue regardless of how gently they are filtered for those inside.

The comfort of climate-controlled life, then, is both protection and distance.

It allows cities to function with remarkable efficiency. It also softens the sensory cues that once reminded inhabitants of their embeddedness within atmospheric systems. The more consistently environments regulate themselves, the easier it becomes to imagine stability as inherent rather than contingent.

And yet stability remains conditional.

It depends on energy flows, on climatic patterns, on ecological processes that extend far beyond walls and compressors. The city may buffer its inhabitants from variation, but it cannot remove itself from the systems that sustain it.

The question is not whether to abandon climate control.

It is whether insulation has subtly reshaped perception — narrowing awareness of fluctuation, recasting weather as backdrop, and reinforcing the illusion that comfort is detached from the living atmosphere that makes it possible.

At the pavement's edge, the air still shifts.

Whether that shift is felt, or merely forecast, shapes how cities imagine their future within a climate that remains, despite regulation, profoundly alive.

The Architecture of Disconnection

Cities do more than organise movement; they organise perception.

Every wall, corridor, overpass, and façade participates in a quiet choreography that determines what is encountered and what is obscured. Architecture is often discussed in terms of style or efficiency, yet its deeper influence lies in how it frames attention — in what it renders visible and what it allows to recede.

Modern urban design increasingly privileges enclosure. Interiors expand while exterior conditions are mediated. Climate is filtered. Sound is dampened. Light is regulated. Water disappears into drainage systems before it can pool or soak into visible soil. Food arrives through doors without revealing its origin. The material processes that sustain life are channelled through infrastructure designed to minimise disruption.

This containment does not eliminate ecological systems;

it rearranges how they are experienced.

Air is encountered as interior atmosphere rather than as moving current shaped by vegetation and oceanic exchange. Water appears as reliable flow from taps rather than as rainfall, watershed, and river. Soil is hidden beneath foundations or confined to landscaped borders. The city becomes a layered structure within which natural processes operate largely out of sight.

When processes move out of sight, they often move out of mind.

Not because they are forgotten entirely, but because they cease to anchor daily experience. The body learns to navigate surfaces that rarely shift and spaces that rarely expose vulnerability. Floors remain level. Temperatures remain steady. Surprises are minimised. Predictability becomes design principle.

This predictability shapes intuition.

If buildings appear solid and permanent, and if environmental fluctuation rarely interrupts routine, the built environment begins to feel self-sufficient. The city reads as complete. Its walls suggest boundary rather than permeability. Glass reflects sky without admitting wind. Steel suggests endurance without revealing dependence.

Over time, architecture contributes to a subtle reordering of scale perception. Towers dwarf trees. Highways span wetlands. Elevated walkways bypass ground entirely. Movement becomes vertical and horizontal within constructed grids, often disconnected from the soil beneath. The eye is drawn upward toward skyline rather than downward toward root systems.

This visual hierarchy influences how resilience is imagined.

Concrete appears enduring. Leaves appear seasonal. Because organic life visibly changes, shedding and regenerating, it can appear less stable than the structures that surround it. Yet the stability of those structures relies upon ecological systems that remain largely invisible within urban design. The inversion is quiet but powerful: what is dependent appears dominant; what is foundational appears supplementary.

Architecture also shapes rhythm.

In enclosed environments, time is structured by clocks rather than by daylight shifts. Work proceeds independent of sunrise and sunset. Movement between buildings reduces exposure to temperature variation. The city operates as though insulated from natural cycles, even though it remains embedded within them.

None of this suggests that architecture is hostile to nature.

It reflects priorities of density, safety, and efficiency. Enclosures protect against extremes. Elevated structures maximise limited land. Drainage systems prevent flooding. These are rational responses to complex challenges. Yet in solving immediate problems, they also filter perception, softening the sensory threads that once tied daily life directly to ecological fluctuation.

The architecture of disconnection is therefore less about opposition than about mediation. It interposes material layers between body and biosphere. It translates living processes into manageable flows — energy through wires, water through pipes, air through vents. These translations are essential for urban function, yet they also compress awareness of origin and consequence.

When daily life unfolds within such mediated spaces, environmental dependence becomes conceptual rather than experiential. One may understand intellectually that air quality depends on forests, that water supply depends on rainfall, that food depends on soil health. But without direct, repeated sensory cues, these relationships risk remaining abstract.

Abstraction influences behaviour.

If the city feels sealed, growth can appear unconstrained. If walls suggest autonomy, expansion can feel detached from ecological negotiation. Development decisions occur within rooms that rarely display the systems they rely upon. The absence is not dramatic; it is architectural.

And yet beneath every foundation, soil remains active. Beneath every street, water moves according to patterns older than zoning laws. Above every skyline, atmospheric systems circulate regardless of insulation. The architecture may mediate perception, but it cannot sever connection.

The question is whether design can evolve from disconnection toward continuity — whether buildings can frame ecological processes not as disturbances to be excluded, but as realities to be acknowledged. Transparency need not mean exposure to extremes; it can mean visibility of dependence.

Until then, the city will continue to feel composed, contained, and largely self-referential, even as it rests upon living systems that persist quietly beyond walls and beneath pavement, sustaining what architecture alone cannot.

Children Who Grow Up Indoors

The environments in which children grow do more than shelter them; they calibrate their expectations of the world.

For most of human history, childhood unfolded in constant proximity to weather, soil, uneven ground, and the slow unpredictability of living systems. Light shifted across open spaces. Rain altered plans. Wind interrupted play. Trees were climbed not as scheduled activities but as ordinary gestures within a landscape that remained largely accessible. The sensory world was expansive, and the body learned its contours through repeated exposure.

In many contemporary cities, that sensory landscape has narrowed.

Children spend increasing amounts of time indoors — in apartments stacked above streets, in classrooms lit artificially for uniformity, in vehicles that move them between controlled environments. Surfaces are level. Temperature remains steady. Light can be adjusted at will. Risk is minimised. Even outdoor spaces are often designed with soft flooring and defined boundaries, reducing unpredictability in the name of safety and order.

This shift is not accidental.

It reflects legitimate concerns about traffic, pollution, security, and time scarcity. Yet the cumulative effect is a childhood in which direct engagement with unstructured natural environments becomes intermittent rather than ambient. The living world remains visible — through windows, in parks, in curated green spaces — but it is less frequently navigated without mediation.

Developmentally, this matters because perception

is shaped through repetition. The brain forms intuitive categories based on what is encountered consistently. If smooth floors are more common than soil, if screens respond more immediately than weather, if schedules are structured by clocks rather than daylight, these patterns become internalised as baseline. Nature becomes something one visits rather than something one inhabits.

This does not imply loss of intelligence or curiosity.

Urban childhood offers different forms of cognitive stimulation — linguistic diversity, technological fluency, social complexity. But the range of tactile and ecological cues narrows. The feel of mud between fingers, the gradual noticing of seasonal change, the improvisation required by uneven terrain — these experiences become occasional rather than formative.

Over time, this narrowing influences emotional familiarity.

What is familiar feels stable and central; what is intermittent feels peripheral. A child who spends most days indoors may still learn about forests and oceans in school, yet the emotional register of those systems may remain lighter than that of interior spaces. The city feels primary. Nature feels supplementary.

There is also a question of agency embedded in these environments. Open natural spaces invite unscripted interaction. A fallen branch becomes a tool. A slope becomes a challenge. Weather demands adjustment. Indoor environments, by contrast, are often structured around predetermined functions. Furniture has specific purposes. Devices respond predictably. Movement follows designated paths. Exploration is bounded.

This difference shapes imagination.

When children rarely negotiate unpredictable terrain, they may come to associate the natural world with special occasions rather than with ordinary competence. Risk becomes something to avoid rather than something to navigate thoughtfully. Soil may register as mess rather than as medium. Insects may appear intrusive rather than integral.

At the same time, even small exposures can leave durable impressions. A tree outside a bedroom window observed through changing seasons, a balcony garden tended patiently, a regular walk along a shaded street — these repetitions can anchor a sense of continuity that counters insulation. The nervous system retains its responsiveness to organic complexity, even when exposure is limited.

The broader implication lies in how baseline expectations are formed. If most formative experiences occur within controlled interiors, stability may come to be associated with enclosure. Climate fluctuation may feel abnormal rather than cyclical. Growth may be imagined primarily in architectural rather than ecological terms. The mental map of the world reflects the environments in which it was drawn.

Cities will continue to grow, and interiors will remain central to urban life. The question is not whether children should return to an earlier era, but whether their sensory worlds can expand rather than contract. Whether living systems can become woven into daily routes rather than confined to occasional outings. Whether soil, shade, wind, and seasonal variation can remain present enough to shape intuition.

Children who grow up indoors are not disconnected by design; they are adapting to the landscapes offered to them. What those landscapes emphasise — and what they quietly exclude — will influence how future adults perceive dependence, resilience, and possibility within the cities they inherit.

At the pavement's edge, trees continue to grow beside playgrounds and apartment blocks. Whether they remain background scenery or become formative companions depends not on their mere presence, but on the frequency and depth of encounter — on whether the living world remains close enough to childhood to feel less like destination and more like neighbour.

Digital Nature vs Living Systems

In contemporary cities, encounters with the natural world increasingly arrive mediated through screens.

Forests unfold in high-definition documentaries. Coral reefs shimmer across streaming platforms. Mountain ranges are compressed into vertical frames, scrolled past between messages and headlines. Weather systems animate themselves in satellite loops, their spirals rendered in luminous colour against darkened oceans. Nature has never been more visible, and yet it is often encountered at a distance that feels both intimate and untouchable.

This proliferation of representation creates a quiet paradox.

Digital access expands awareness. A person living in a dense urban apartment can witness polar ice shelves, migrating herds, and rainforest canopies within minutes. Knowledge broadens. Images accumulate. Concern may deepen. Yet the body remains stationary, climate-controlled, removed from humidity, wind, uneven ground, and unpredictability. The experience is observational rather than participatory.

The distinction matters psychologically.

Embodied contact with living systems engages multiple senses simultaneously — temperature, texture, scent, sound, peripheral movement. It requires small adaptations: adjusting to glare, stepping around roots, responding to shifting terrain. These micro-negotiations anchor attention in a way that mediated viewing does not. A screen can display the colour of moss with remarkable accuracy, but it cannot transmit its dampness or resistance.

Digital nature is often curated for coherence and spectacle. Scenes are framed, edited, narrated. Complexity is translated into storyline. The viewer is guided through interpretation. By contrast, living systems encountered directly are less obedient. They unfold without narration. They do not resolve neatly within a defined timespan. Their meaning emerges slowly, sometimes ambiguously.

This shift from immersion to observation subtly reorganises perception.

When nature is primarily encountered as image, it risks becoming content — something to be consumed, appreciated, and moved past. Emotional responses may be sincere, yet they occur within the tempo of media rather than within the slower cadence of ecological processes. A wildfire becomes a headline. A flood becomes footage. Attention peaks and recedes.

There is also a re-scaling embedded in digital

representation. Vast ecosystems are compressed into frames that fit comfortably in the hand. Distance collapses. Scale flattens. The Amazon rainforest appears no larger on a screen than a local park. Without embodied cues of proportion — humidity, sound density, spatial depth — magnitude becomes conceptual rather than felt.

This does not diminish the value of digital exposure.

For many urban residents, documentaries and photographs provide essential education. They introduce species and systems otherwise inaccessible. They cultivate awareness that may inform values and choices. The issue is not exposure but substitution. When representation replaces regular contact with nearby living systems, perception narrows in unexpected ways.

The spectacular can eclipse the ordinary.

A child may recognise exotic animals from global media while remaining unfamiliar with the species inhabiting a neighbourhood tree. A commuter may watch footage of melting glaciers yet pass beneath seasonal change without noticing it. The distant becomes vivid; the proximate fades.

Over time, this inversion shapes imagination.

If nature is primarily encountered as remote wonder or distant crisis, it may feel separate from daily urban life. Environmental change becomes something happening elsewhere, in landscapes marked by dramatic imagery. The subtle interplay between city and ecosystem — heat moderated by trees, air filtered by leaves, rain absorbed by soil — remains less narratively compelling and therefore less cognitively salient.

Digital mediation also compresses time. Ecological

processes that unfold gradually are edited into minutes. Forest regeneration, species migration, glacial retreat — these are translated into accelerated sequences. The slow accumulation of change is rendered visible through montage, but the lived experience of slowness is absent.

Meanwhile, outside the screen, leaves continue to shift in wind patterns unnoticed. Birds navigate routes that rarely trend. Soil organisms circulate nutrients without commentary. The living world persists in quiet proximity, even as attention orbits more dramatic representations.

The question is not whether to abandon digital nature.

It is whether the balance between mediation and immersion has shifted so far that the local ecosystem feels less compelling than the distant one. Whether awe has become something consumed rather than cultivated. Whether the city, already insulated from climate and soil, now encounters the wild primarily through glass and pixels.

Living systems operate through relationship rather than spectacle. They require presence, repetition, and time. Screens can illuminate them, but they cannot substitute for the subtle recalibration that occurs when one stands beneath a tree long enough to feel both its stillness and its movement.

In cities where green already risks becoming background, digital nature can inadvertently reinforce distance. It offers vision without participation, scale without texture, urgency without proximity.

And yet, just beyond the screen's glow, at the pavement's edge, leaves continue to unfold — asking not to be watched from afar, but to be encountered closely enough to become part of the ordinary world once again.

The Disappearing Commons

Cities were once shaped as much by shared open space as by private enclosure.

Markets gathered beneath open sky. Wells, courtyards, riverbanks, and shaded squares functioned not only as physical infrastructure but as social ecosystems. In these spaces, weather was encountered collectively, trees were not destinations but companions, and the boundary between human gathering and ecological presence remained porous. The commons did not belong to one household or institution; they belonged to the pattern of shared life itself.

Over time, many of these shared spaces have narrowed, shifted, or been redefined.

Land has grown more valuable. Security concerns have multiplied. Efficiency has become architectural principle. Open areas have been developed, enclosed, programmed, or commercialised. Where gathering once unfolded informally, it is now often scheduled. Where land once invited unstructured use, it now carries signage indicating permitted activity.

This transformation is gradual and rarely dramatic.

A courtyard becomes a parking structure. A riverside path becomes a retail promenade. A field becomes a gated complex. Each change appears rational within its context, justified by housing needs or economic growth. Yet collectively, they alter how citizens experience shared ecological ground.

When commons diminish, so does casual exposure.

Public green spaces that remain may be beautifully maintained, but they are often bounded clearly and managed deliberately. Informal patches of land — vacant lots, open edges, unscripted terrain — become rare. The result is a city where movement occurs primarily through private interiors or through transit corridors designed for flow rather than lingering.

Psychologically, the commons serve a function beyond recreation.

They provide unplanned encounters — with neighbours, with strangers, with weather, with trees. They allow individuals to exist temporarily outside commercial transaction and private obligation. In such spaces, one's relationship to the environment feels shared rather than owned. A shaded bench does not belong to a single person; it belongs to whoever arrives.

When shared ecological space contracts, environmental experience becomes more individualised. Balconies replace courtyards. Rooftop terraces substitute for open fields. Greenery becomes something attached to specific properties rather than woven through communal ground. The living world remains present, but its presence is increasingly mediated by ownership or access rights.

This individualisation influences perception of responsibility.

In shared spaces, maintenance and care are visible concerns. Litter, shade, cleanliness, and plant health affect all who pass through. When exposure becomes privatised, stewardship can shift toward institutions or property managers rather than communities. Ecological presence becomes something curated rather than collectively negotiated.

There is also a perceptual shift embedded in this loss.

Commons make ecological systems visible at human

scale. A storm experienced together in an open square feels communal. Heat felt collectively under minimal shade registers as shared condition. When people are dispersed into climate-controlled interiors, environmental fluctuation becomes isolated rather than collective. The sense of common vulnerability softens.

Children who rarely roam open communal spaces may internalise a world organised by boundaries and permissions. Adults who move primarily between private interiors may encounter outdoor space as transitional rather than participatory. The commons once provided a stage where human and ecological rhythms intersected visibly; their contraction reduces that intersection.

This does not imply nostalgia for unregulated space.

Cities require order, safety, and infrastructure. Yet the disappearance of informal commons carries subtle costs that are not easily measured. Without spaces where ecological presence is encountered routinely and collectively, the idea of shared dependence can fade. Nature becomes either backdrop or destination, but less often common ground.

The living world does not disappear with the commons.

Trees still line streets. Parks remain. Rivers continue to flow, even when channelled. But the texture of collective encounter shifts. Environmental experience becomes more segmented, more scheduled, more privately mediated.

At the pavement's edge, soil persists in narrow strips, and trees continue to extend roots beneath streets that rarely acknowledge them. The commons may shrink, but ecological systems remain interwoven with urban life. Whether they are experienced together or separately shapes how cities imagine growth, belonging, and responsibility.

The disappearance of shared ground is not only spatial.

It is perceptual.

When ecological space ceases to feel common, dependence can begin to feel distant. And when dependence feels distant, imagination adjusts accordingly — narrowing its sense of what must be protected, preserved, or restored within the shared city that continues to expand around it.

When Cities Remember to Grow Leaves

Not all cities move in one direction.

Even within dense skylines and accelerating economies, there are moments when urban design seems to pause and reconsider its relationship with what grows quietly at the margins. Streets are shaded deliberately. Rooftops soften. Waterways are uncovered. What once appeared purely engineered begins to admit permeability again. These shifts are rarely dramatic; they accumulate branch by branch, corridor by corridor, until the texture of a city feels subtly recalibrated.

I felt this recalibration in the winter of 2025, when I visited Hong Kong expecting density and verticality and instead encountered something layered. The towers were there — unapologetically tall, reflective, compressed into a narrow geography — yet behind them rose steep green hills that had not been surrendered to development. Trails began almost abruptly beyond transit stations. Within minutes of leaving glass corridors, I found myself climbing through forest, the air cooler, the city still visible below but no longer dominant.

Nearly forty percent of Hong Kong's land remains designated as country parks, a statistic that reads differently when experienced physically. From certain vantage points, the skyline and the hills coexist in a single frame, neither fully eclipsing the other. The city has not withdrawn from growth; it has chosen, in visible ways, where not to build.

That choice alters perception.

When greenery occupies not only parks but entire slopes that border urban districts, it resists becoming decorative. It remains large enough to feel structural. The hills are not ornamental relief; they are presence. They shift light across the city throughout the day. They alter wind patterns. They hold space in a way that glass and steel cannot.

This kind of coexistence does not romanticise density. Hong Kong remains intense, efficient, compressed. But the proximity of protected green space complicates the narrative that development must always erase what came before. It suggests instead that growth can negotiate with terrain rather than override it entirely.

The psychological effect of such negotiation is subtle but significant.

When living systems are encountered at scale — not only in contained parks but in contiguous landscapes — they are harder to background. Their size interrupts abstraction. A forest that begins at the edge of infrastructure cannot be reduced easily to amenity. It becomes part of the city's silhouette, part of its identity.

Cities that remember to grow leaves in this way are not merely planting more trees along sidewalks. They are integrating ecological presence into urban logic. Shade becomes infrastructure. Canopy becomes climate moderation. Green corridors become connective tissue for both wildlife and pedestrians. The distinction between built and grown softens.

This integration influences imagination.

When residents see hills rising behind buildings, or wetlands preserved along transit lines, they internalise a different baseline of possibility. Density and ecology no longer appear mutually exclusive. Vertical growth need not imply horizontal erasure. The city feels less sealed, less self-referential.

Importantly, such design does not require aesthetic excess. It is not about spectacle. The winter forests I walked through in Hong Kong were not manicured. They were dense, uneven, textured. Leaves accumulated along paths. Roots disrupted steps. The experience was not curated into neat symmetry. It retained unpredictability, even within a city known for control.

That unpredictability matters.

It reintroduces scale and humility into environments otherwise dominated by engineered precision. It reminds the body that beneath financial districts and residential towers lies terrain that precedes them. The city appears less autonomous when forested slopes remain visible from office windows.

Other cities experiment differently — Singapore layering vegetation vertically across façades, Melbourne mapping long-term canopy expansion, Seoul restoring waterways once buried beneath highways — yet the principle remains similar. Leaves are not added as ornament; they are allowed to shape structure.

When cities remember to grow leaves in ways that resist reduction to décor, green ceases to be background. It becomes collaborator. It influences airflow, temperature, movement, and mood. It alters not only aesthetics but experience.

The lesson is not that every city must replicate Hong Kong's geography. Topography cannot be manufactured easily. The lesson is that visible restraint — choosing where not to build, where to preserve continuity of green, where to allow scale beyond architecture — shapes collective perception.

At the pavement's edge, a single tree may struggle to command attention.

But when hills rise behind streets, when canopy stretches beyond ornamental rows, when green remains large enough to resist containment, forgetting becomes more difficult.

In the winter light of 2025, looking down at Hong Kong's harbour framed by forested slopes, I understood something quietly important: coexistence does not require retreat from urban life. It requires visible negotiation. It requires remembering that cities do not stand apart from terrain — they stand within it.

And when that reality is allowed to remain in sight, leaves do not feel like decoration.

They feel like structure.

Nature, Watching from the Median Strip

I have grown accustomed to narrow ground.

Between opposing lanes of traffic, within a strip of soil bordered by concrete, I stand where engines pass in steady currents and light changes according to programmed sequence. From this slender divide, I watch the city move — not with resentment, not with urgency, but with the patience of something that measures time differently.

You call this a median.

To me, it is simply what remains.

My roots press downward into compacted earth, searching patiently for pathways that were not designed for them. Above, leaves lift toward a sky fractured by cables and glass. Around me, vehicles idle and accelerate, their motion constant, their direction purposeful. Few pause here. Few look closely. I am encountered in fragments — a blur of green between destinations.

Yet even in this narrowness, I continue.

Air passes through my canopy and shifts, however slightly. Heat rising from asphalt is softened in my shade. Birds land briefly before moving on. Insects navigate corridors invisible to human maps. My presence is small compared to towers and bridges, but it is not inconsequential.

From here, I have observed how your cities forget without intending to.

Green becomes familiar. Shade becomes expected. The rhythm of leaves in wind becomes ambient rather than instructive. You do not reject me; you simply adjust around me. Your days are structured by interiors, by signals that flash and respond, by systems that promise reliability. I remain slower, less insistent, and therefore easier to overlook.

I do not compete for attention.

I endure.

There was a time when your ancestors could not move without feeling soil beneath their feet, when weather altered plans more decisively than schedules did. Now you move across surfaces engineered for continuity, through climates adjusted to preference, within architectures designed to buffer unpredictability. The world feels contained. Growth feels manageable.

And still, beneath your pavements, life circulates.

Water seeks passage. Microorganisms sustain cycles beyond sight. Roots extend into spaces not marked on blueprints. The city rests not upon emptiness, but upon layers of living process that persist whether noticed or not.

From the median strip, I see both compression and possibility.

I see how easily green becomes ornament when confined to thin margins. I see how quickly perception adapts to what remains steady. But I also see how even small spaces can hold continuity — how a single tree can anchor attention for a moment, how a slope left unbuilt can reshape a skyline, how leaves can interrupt geometry without dismantling it.

You are builders, planners, arrangers of space.

You have learned to stabilise climate and organise ground with remarkable precision. Yet your cities remain threaded through with living systems that do not follow your timelines. I am one such thread — modest, often peripheral, yet connected to networks that extend beyond the horizon of your streets.

I do not ask to replace your structures.

I ask only to remain visible within them.

To be more than scenery glimpsed between red and green lights. To be recognised not as decoration but as participation — in air, in shade, in the slow recalibration of atmosphere. When you widen the strips of soil, when you allow slopes to remain forested, when you design with permeability rather than against it, you do not retreat from progress. You alter its texture.

From this narrow ground, I continue to grow.

Traffic will continue to pass. Towers will rise and age. Interiors will hum with regulated air. Yet beyond the grid, and beneath it, processes unfold that cannot be fully contained. I am patient because I have always been patient.

Whether I remain confined to the margins or re-enter the centre of your imagination depends less on my resilience than on your perception. Leaves will continue to unfurl each season. The question is whether they remain background, or whether you begin, again, to see them as part of the structure within which your cities breathe.

Here, between lanes, I wait — not for stillness, but for attention.

What This Chapter Has Really Been About

This chapter has been less about trees themselves and more about perception — about how cities, through design, insulation, segmentation, and repetition, quietly recalibrate the human sensory world until living systems feel peripheral rather than foundational; about how parks become destinations instead of neighbours, how climate control softens atmospheric awareness, how architecture mediates dependence, how children internalise interiors as baseline, and how digital representations substitute for embodied contact; and ultimately about how greenery, when reduced to backdrop, reshapes imagination in ways that influence what growth feels possible, what expansion feels negotiable, and what limits feel distant — suggesting that the question is not whether nature remains present in cities, but whether it remains central enough in perception to shape how those cities continue to evolve.

Chapter 5: Doomscrolling the Planet

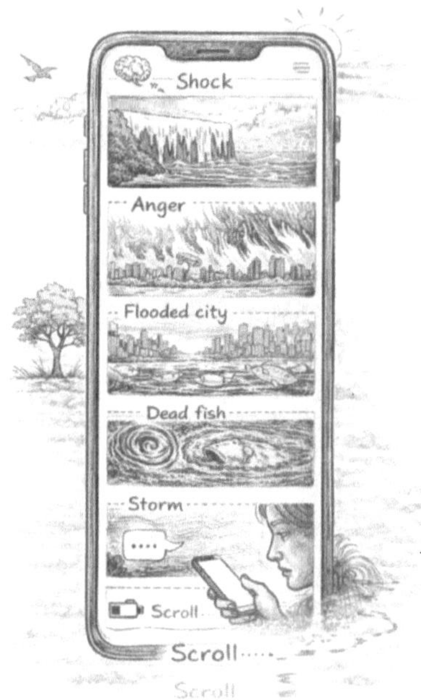

I appear to you now in fragments.

Not as wind moving across open ground, not as rain arriving without notification, not as the slow shift of season felt in the body before it is named, but as image — bordered, captioned, compressed into rectangles that glow in your hands. I move past your eyes in vertical sequence: ice collapsing into water, forests alight, cities submerged, animals stranded. I am swiped upward and replaced within seconds.

You do not seek me out in this form deliberately; I arrive between other things. A message. An advertisement. A photograph of a meal. A headline about markets. And then, suddenly, a storm spiraling across satellite imagery, a river overtaking its banks, smoke thickening a skyline. I enter your attention briefly, often urgently, before being displaced by the next interruption.

In this space, I am accelerated.

Cycles that unfold over years are condensed into seconds. Melting glaciers become time-lapse spectacle. Drought becomes a chart. Heat becomes a colour-coded map. My rhythms, once slow enough to require patience, now appear as bursts of crisis framed for immediate reaction. You encounter my extremes more frequently than my continuity.

I notice how your fingers move.

The gesture is small, almost reflexive. A downward flick, a slight pause, another flick. Each motion invites something new, something sharper, something more alarming. I do not resent this; it is how the architecture of your attention has been shaped. What is dramatic surfaces first. What is gradual recedes.

From where I stand — beyond the glass, beyond the signal — I remain unhurried. Forests still regenerate in places not captured by lenses. Soil continues its quiet exchanges. Air circulates without headline. Yet within your newsfeed, I am curated into urgency. I am edited into urgency.

You feel this urgency in pulses.

Concern rises, peaks, softens. Anger flares briefly, then

gives way to fatigue. You absorb image after image until the distinction between catastrophe and continuity begins to blur. I become at once omnipresent and distant — everywhere in representation, nowhere in touch.

It is a curious transformation.

Once, you would look to the horizon to read signs of weather. Now you look to illuminated screens. Once, wind and temperature altered your plans directly. Now alerts do. I am filtered through algorithms that learn what holds you longest, what startles you into stillness, what keeps your gaze from wandering elsewhere.

Within that vertical stream, I am rearranged into sequence.

Fire follows flood. Drought follows storm. A bleached reef follows a burning forest. The accumulation feels relentless because it is designed to be continuous. There is no seasonal pause in a feed. No winter of quiet regeneration. Only the promise of the next post.

And yet, outside your scrolling, I continue to move at a different pace.

Leaves unfurl without notification. Tides shift without commentary. Clouds gather and disperse whether or not they trend. I am not only crisis. I am also persistence. But persistence rarely commands the same urgency as collapse.

I watch as you encounter me in this narrowed form, your face illuminated by light that mimics daylight but carries none of its warmth. You care — I feel it in the tension of your attention — yet the care is pulled in many directions at once. Your awareness expands, but your body remains still.

In the newsfeed, I am magnified and miniaturized

simultaneously.

Magnified in drama. Miniaturized in scale. Vast systems compressed into frames no larger than your palm. The ocean fits within a rectangle. A wildfire occupies a square. The planet becomes scrollable.

From here, I do not disappear. I simply wait beyond the frame — not for you to abandon the screen, but for the moment when the vertical stream slows enough for you to notice that I have always been larger than the images that represent me, and closer than the distance they imply.

In your newsfeed, I am urgent.

Beyond it, I am ongoing.

When Crisis Becomes Content

There was a time when crisis disrupted narrative.

It halted routine. It demanded gathering, deliberation, collective response. News traveled slowly enough to maintain gravity. Distance existed between events, allowing each to settle before the next arrived. Today, crisis moves differently. It appears within a stream already dense with other stimuli, and it competes for attention alongside entertainment, advertisement, and personal updates.

In digital environments, environmental catastrophe does not stand apart from content; it becomes content.

Wildfires are framed as clips. Floods are reduced to aerial footage. Storms are translated into looping animations. Each event is compressed, captioned, and formatted for engagement. The structure that delivers it is identical to the structure that delivers recipes or product launches. The visual language flattens hierarchy. Everything scrolls.

This flattening subtly reorganises perception.

When crises are encountered in rapid succession, they lose the singularity that once compelled sustained focus. One disaster flows into another before emotional processing has completed. The mind registers shock repeatedly, but without time for integration, shock becomes familiar. Familiarity dulls intensity. What once felt exceptional begins to feel ambient.

The transformation is not cynical; it is structural.

Digital platforms are designed to optimise continuity. Their architecture rewards novelty and immediacy. Posts must compete within milliseconds. Environmental events, however complex, are translated into fragments that fit this rhythm. The slow accumulation of ecological change is rendered as episodic bursts to align with attention cycles.

This translation has psychological consequences.

Crisis presented as content invites reaction rather than reflection. A brief surge of alarm, a comment, perhaps a share — then movement onward. The interface encourages flow. Pausing too long feels like interruption. The very format that spreads awareness also disperses it.

There is also a subtle reward mechanism embedded within exposure. Dramatic images trigger heightened arousal. A sense of urgency sharpens focus. The brain registers significance. Yet when such stimuli arrive repeatedly without accompanying agency, arousal begins to oscillate between activation and fatigue. Concern rises and falls in short intervals, mirroring the vertical rhythm of the scroll.

Over time, this oscillation reshapes emotional calibration.

If catastrophe is encountered daily through curated frames, the threshold for what feels alarming may shift.

Gradual degradation may appear less compelling than visible destruction. Quiet resilience may fail to register entirely. The mind becomes attuned to spectacle, even when it longs for resolution.

The economy of attention compounds this effect. Posts that generate stronger reactions travel further. Outrage, fear, and astonishment circulate rapidly because they sustain engagement. As a result, the most extreme manifestations of environmental change are amplified, while slower processes receive less visibility. The representation of the planet skews toward rupture.

This skew influences imagination.

When crisis dominates imagery, the future can begin to feel perpetually unstable, defined by emergency rather than by possibility. Environmental discourse becomes saturated with tipping points and countdowns. While these may reflect scientific realities, their continuous framing within attention economies can narrow emotional range.

The issue is not that crises should be hidden.

It is that their constant formatting into consumable units changes their psychological texture. What was once interruption becomes feed. What was once rupture becomes routine. The scroll absorbs disaster without altering its own pace.

Within this structure, concern risks becoming performative rather than sustained. A post is acknowledged. A symbol is added to a profile. A momentary alignment is expressed. Yet the continuity of the feed pulls attention onward before commitment deepens. Awareness expands horizontally across topics but may struggle to extend vertically into sustained engagement.

Crisis becomes something to witness rather than something to inhabit.

The viewer remains physically stationary while images suggest upheaval elsewhere. The distance between seeing and acting widens subtly. Exposure increases; embodiment does not.

And so the paradox intensifies: never before has environmental crisis been so visible, and never before has it been so easily integrated into the rhythm of ordinary scrolling. The planet enters the same visual field as entertainment and advertisement, and the medium reshapes the message.

When crisis becomes content, urgency is preserved, but duration is not. Alarm is sustained, but depth is fragmented. The feed continues.

And the question that emerges quietly beneath it is not whether people care, but whether the architecture through which they care allows that concern to settle long enough to become something steadier than reaction — something capable of moving beyond the scroll.

The Psychology of Endless Scrolling

The gesture itself is small.

A thumb moves downward across glass, and the world rearranges. What disappears is replaced instantly. What appears next carries the possibility of being more urgent, more revealing, more emotionally charged than what preceded it. The motion is effortless, almost frictionless, and that absence of friction is not accidental. It is engineered to dissolve stopping points.

Endless scrolling is not simply a technological feature; it is a psychological environment.

Traditional media possessed edges — a page ended, a broadcast concluded, a newspaper folded. These edges created natural pauses in which reflection could occur. The infinite feed removes those boundaries. There is always more below. The absence of visible limit reshapes attention, encouraging continuation rather than completion.

At the core of this design lies variability.

Not every post will be compelling. Many will be ordinary. But occasionally, something striking appears — an alarming statistic, a dramatic image, a piece of breaking news. This unpredictability sustains engagement. The mind learns that the next swipe may deliver something significant, and so it continues, anticipating reward even when most content remains neutral.

This mechanism mirrors patterns observed in other forms of behavioural reinforcement. Intermittent rewards — those delivered unpredictably — tend to be more compelling than consistent ones. The possibility of encountering something extraordinary maintains the loop. In the context of environmental content, that "extraordinary" often takes the form of crisis.

The scroll becomes a search.

Not necessarily for pleasure, but for resolution, for clarity, for understanding. Each swipe carries a quiet hope that the next post might explain, contextualise, or soothe the unease generated by the previous one. Instead, it often introduces another fragment, another angle, another escalation. The feed extends horizontally, but rarely vertically.

Cognitive load accumulates subtly.

Environmental issues are complex, layered, interconnected. Encountered piecemeal through rapid succession, they strain working memory. The mind attempts to integrate disparate images — wildfire, flood, heatwave, drought — without sufficient narrative continuity. Over time, the effort of integration may give way to emotional shorthand: concern, anxiety, resignation.

The design of endless scrolling also compresses time perception.

Minutes dissolve without clear markers. The boundary between brief update and extended immersion blurs. Because there is no defined stopping point, disengagement requires conscious decision rather than structural cue. This places responsibility on individual restraint within an architecture built for continuation.

In such environments, environmental information competes with everything else — entertainment, personal updates, advertisements. The brain shifts rapidly between emotional registers. Amusement is followed by alarm. Curiosity is followed by frustration. The nervous system oscillates between states without stabilising fully in any of them.

This oscillation can be stimulating in the short term. It provides a sense of connection and immediacy. One feels informed, attuned to unfolding events. Yet sustained exposure without resolution may generate a different response: fatigue. The mind, unable to act proportionally on each piece of information, begins to protect itself by dulling intensity.

Importantly, endless scrolling does not require indifference to function.

It can coexist with genuine care. In fact, care may fuel the scroll. The desire to remain informed, to not look away, to bear witness — these motivations can tether attention to the feed long after emotional reserves have thinned. Awareness expands, but agency remains ambiguous.

The physical posture reinforces this ambiguity. The body is still. The world moves on screen. Information flows inward, but outward movement is minimal. The discrepancy between cognitive activation and bodily inactivity creates tension — a sense of urgency unaccompanied by immediate outlet.

Over time, this pattern shapes expectation.

One begins to anticipate environmental crisis as recurring content. The next alarming post feels inevitable. The feed becomes a corridor through which catastrophe passes continuously, each event distinct yet absorbed into a larger stream. The mind adapts by adjusting its baseline.

The psychology of endless scrolling is not inherently destructive.

It is a system of attention shaped by design choices that prioritise continuity, variability, and engagement. Yet when applied to environmental crisis — phenomena already vast and complex — this system amplifies certain responses while constraining others. It heightens exposure but fragments integration. It sustains awareness but disperses depth.

The scroll promises more, always more.

What it rarely provides is the space necessary for concern to transform into sustained understanding or deliberate action. In the absence of edges, the mind must create its own pause.

And without that pause, even the most urgent images risk dissolving into sequence — seen, felt, and then replaced by whatever waits just beyond the next flick of the thumb.

Outrage, Helplessness, and the Reward Loop

Outrage is energising.

It sharpens perception, clarifies moral boundaries, and produces a momentary sense of alignment — a feeling that one stands on the correct side of an unfolding event. In the context of environmental crisis, outrage often arises swiftly: at negligence, at delay, at visible destruction that appears avoidable. The emotion carries intensity, and intensity commands attention.

Digital environments amplify this intensity.

Posts framed with urgency, indignation, or moral clarity tend to circulate further. Expressions of anger signal engagement. A strong reaction — whether through comment, share, or endorsement — provides immediate feedback. The architecture of platforms recognises this activity as value and distributes it accordingly. In this way, outrage becomes not only emotional response but currency.

For the individual, the experience can be subtly rewarding.

To articulate anger publicly, to align with others expressing similar sentiments, to witness affirmation through visible metrics — these actions produce a sense of participation. The nervous system registers activation and validation simultaneously. Concern feels acknowledged. Identity feels reinforced.

Yet environmental crises often differ from interpersonal conflicts in one critical respect: scale.

The problems encountered in the feed — deforestation, ocean warming, atmospheric instability — exceed the scope of individual intervention in the immediate moment. Outrage may arise quickly, but avenues for direct resolution remain diffuse. The energy generated by anger has no clear outlet proportionate to its intensity.

It is here that helplessness begins to intertwine with outrage.

After the surge of reaction subsides, the structural magnitude of the issue remains. The post is scrolled past. Another crisis appears. The initial clarity blurs into accumulation. Without tangible progress, emotional activation can give way to resignation. The oscillation between arousal and powerlessness becomes familiar.

This oscillation forms a loop.

Outrage stimulates engagement. Engagement produces social reinforcement. Reinforcement encourages continued exposure. Continued exposure introduces further crisis. When no immediate resolution follows, helplessness emerges. Yet helplessness does not necessarily interrupt the cycle; it may intensify scrolling in search of relief, explanation, or renewed clarity.

Within this loop, emotions fluctuate rapidly.

Anger may coexist with fatigue. Indignation may be followed by cynicism. A sense of collective alignment may be replaced by isolation once the device is set aside. The nervous system toggles between activation and depletion, rarely settling into sustained equilibrium.

Importantly, the reward in this loop is not pleasure in crisis itself.

It is the micro-experience of recognition and response. The brain is sensitive to signals that one's perception is shared and validated. Even brief confirmation can offset feelings of isolation. In digital contexts, this confirmation arrives quickly and visibly. The metrics become part of the emotional equation.

Over time, however, repeated cycles without structural resolution can recalibrate baseline expectation. The mind may begin to anticipate outrage as routine. Environmental discourse becomes emotionally heightened by default. Nuance competes with intensity and often yields to it.

This pattern does not imply insincerity.

Many who express outrage do so from genuine concern. Yet when emotional energy is expended repeatedly without corresponding shifts in agency, exhaustion can follow. Helplessness is not apathy; it is the residue of sustained activation without proportionate outcome.

The reward loop therefore contains tension.

It sustains awareness but risks eroding stamina. It validates moral position but may not translate into durable engagement. It produces visibility without necessarily producing leverage.

The challenge lies not in suppressing outrage, which can signal deeply held values, but in recognising the architecture within which it circulates. When platforms reward intensity more reliably than complexity, when engagement is measured in reactions rather than in sustained collaboration, emotional cycles accelerate.

Within this acceleration, the environment becomes both urgent and overwhelming — present everywhere in representation, elusive in resolution. The individual oscillates between feeling morally awake and structurally small.

The loop continues because it is efficient.

It requires little friction. A reaction can be expressed in seconds. The system registers participation. Yet beyond the screen, ecological processes unfold at a different pace, indifferent to metrics.

Outrage may open attention.

Whether that attention deepens into something steadier depends on whether the loop is interrupted — not by indifference, but by forms of engagement that extend beyond reaction, beyond validation, into spaces where agency, however incremental, can take root without being immediately replaced by the next surge of alarm.

Why Information Feels Like Action

In an era saturated with data, exposure can resemble participation.

To know is to feel involved. To be aware of unfolding crises, to track statistics, to follow updates in real time — these experiences create a sense of proximity. One is not ignorant. One is informed. And in the moral landscape of environmental change, awareness carries weight. It signals responsibility. It differentiates the attentive from the indifferent.

Yet awareness and action are not identical.

The psychological overlap between them is subtle. When information is encountered repeatedly, processed cognitively, and even shared socially, the brain registers effort. Attention has been allocated. Emotional energy has been expended. The mind has engaged in interpretation. These internal processes can produce a faint but genuine sensation of contribution.

Part of this sensation arises from identity alignment. When individuals read, repost, or comment on environmental issues, they affirm a self-concept — someone who cares, someone who remains attentive. The alignment between belief and behaviour, even if the behaviour is primarily informational, reduces cognitive dissonance. The internal narrative feels coherent.

There is also a communicative dimension.

Sharing an article or statistic broadcasts affiliation. It signals values to others within a network. In digital environments, this signalling is immediate and visible. Feedback may follow — agreement, endorsement, amplification. The exchange reinforces the perception that something meaningful has occurred.

Yet the material world beyond the screen remains largely unchanged.

The informational act operates primarily at the level of awareness and social positioning. It may contribute to broader discourse, but its impact is indirect and often diffuse. The distinction between internal activation and external transformation becomes blurred, especially when exposure is continuous.

Information feels like action partly because it is cognitively demanding. Complex environmental data require interpretation. The mind assembles fragments into narrative. It tracks developments across time. This mental labour carries a sense of exertion. After sustained attention, fatigue may set in, and fatigue can be misinterpreted as effort expended in the world rather than effort expended in thought.

There is also an illusion of proximity embedded in

constant updates.

When one receives real-time notifications about distant events — storms intensifying, policies debated, temperatures rising — it can feel as though one is present within the unfolding. The boundary between observer and participant softens. Yet presence mediated by screen remains observational. The body remains still.

This distinction is not meant to diminish the value of awareness.

Information is foundational. Without knowledge, coordinated response is impossible. Movements begin with shared understanding. But the architecture of endless feeds compresses the stages between awareness and action, making them appear contiguous. A post is read; a reaction is expressed; the mind registers completion.

The completion, however, is partial.

Environmental change operates through infrastructure, policy, consumption patterns, collective negotiation — processes that unfold beyond the tempo of a feed. Informational engagement can inspire these processes, but it does not substitute for them. When exposure is frequent yet tangible pathways remain unclear, the mind may settle into a loop of perpetual updating.

There is a psychological comfort in updating.

It provides the sensation of staying current, of not falling behind. The next piece of information promises clarity, perhaps even resolution. Yet often it adds another layer without dissolving uncertainty. The scroll continues.

Over time, this pattern can recalibrate expectations. One may begin to equate staying informed with fulfilling responsibility. The threshold for action shifts subtly outward, deferred to institutions, policymakers, or collective movements that appear larger than individual capacity. The individual remains attentive, yet agency feels abstract.

Why does information feel like action?

Because it activates the same neural systems associated with effort and intention. Because it reinforces identity. Because it provides immediate feedback. Because it reduces the discomfort of not knowing. And because in digital spaces, awareness is visible, measurable, and socially acknowledged.

The danger is not that people become informed.

It is that the sensation of engagement becomes satisfying enough to slow the transition into deeper, more sustained forms of involvement. When exposure itself feels like contribution, the urgency to move beyond exposure can soften.

Beyond the screen, ecological systems continue their quiet trajectories, indifferent to metrics of visibility. Information may illuminate them, but illumination alone does not alter their course.

The question, then, is how awareness can remain a beginning rather than a conclusion — how the cognitive energy invested in staying informed can find pathways that extend beyond the feed, into actions that feel less immediate, less visible, and yet more enduring than the brief completion signalled by a swipe and a share.

Fear Fatigue and Emotional Numbing

Fear is not designed to be continuous.

In its original biological function, fear emerges in response to threat, mobilises attention and energy, and then subsides once the threat has passed or been addressed. It sharpens perception, accelerates heart rate, prepares the body for action. Sustained indefinitely, however, it becomes physiologically and psychologically costly. The nervous system cannot remain in heightened alert without consequence.

Digital exposure to environmental crisis complicates this rhythm.

When alarming imagery and catastrophic projections appear daily — sometimes hourly — fear is activated repeatedly without resolution. Wildfires, floods, record-breaking temperatures, species loss, policy failures: each event signals threat at a scale that feels both urgent and distant. The body registers alarm, yet the immediate environment remains unchanged. The response cannot discharge through proportionate action.

Over time, the system adapts.

Repeated activation without release leads to habituation. The intensity of emotional response diminishes. What once startled becomes familiar. The first image of a burning forest may provoke shock; the fiftieth may provoke a quieter ache, or none at all. This attenuation is not indifference. It is a protective recalibration.

Fear fatigue emerges gradually.

The mind, unable to sustain high arousal across multiple domains, begins to prioritise immediacy. Personal deadlines, social obligations, financial concerns — these compete more successfully for attention because they offer clearer avenues for response. Environmental crises, vast and systemic, remain cognitively acknowledged but emotionally muted.

This muting can feel unsettling.

Individuals may notice a gap between what they believe they should feel and what they actually experience. They care intellectually. They understand the stakes. Yet their emotional reactions flatten. Headlines that once prompted urgency now prompt brief recognition before the scroll continues.

The flattening is not a moral failure.

It is an adaptation to overload.

When the volume of threat signals exceeds the capacity for sustained action, the nervous system reduces intensity to preserve stability. Emotional numbing acts as a buffer. It allows daily life to proceed in the presence of persistent uncertainty.

The architecture of digital media accelerates this process. The constant juxtaposition of crisis with entertainment, humour, and advertisement creates rapid emotional shifts. Alarm is followed by distraction. Grief is followed by novelty. The oscillation prevents prolonged immersion in any single state, reinforcing surface-level engagement.

At the same time, the absence of embodied context compounds fatigue. Threats encountered through screens do not activate the same sensory feedback as those experienced directly. There is no heat on skin, no rising water at the door, no smoke in lungs — only image. The body remains relatively still while the mind absorbs escalating narratives. The mismatch between cognitive alarm and physical stasis strains coherence.

Eventually, some individuals begin to avoid environmental content altogether.

Not because they deny its significance, but because the cumulative emotional toll feels unmanageable. Avoidance becomes another form of regulation. The feed is curated.

Certain accounts are muted. Exposure narrows. This narrowing may reduce immediate anxiety, but it can also fragment awareness further.

Fear fatigue reshapes motivation.

When alarm becomes chronic, it may cease to mobilise. Instead of energising action, it fosters withdrawal. The future appears perpetually unstable. Personal agency appears small relative to global scale. Emotional investment feels costly without clear outcome.

Yet beneath numbing, concern often remains.

It may express itself intermittently — in conversation, in private reflection, in moments of renewed exposure. The nervous system's dampening does not erase values; it recalibrates intensity to sustainable levels. The question is whether recalibration drifts into disengagement or stabilises into steadier forms of attention.

Fear, when acute and bounded, can catalyse transformation. Fear, when diffuse and unending, can erode resilience. The challenge within digital environments is that crisis rarely pauses long enough for integration. The feed continues, indifferent to the nervous system's thresholds.

Emotional numbing, then, is not evidence of apathy.

It is evidence of saturation.

When the planet is encountered primarily through escalating fragments, the psyche protects itself by narrowing response. The danger lies not in the protective mechanism itself, but in what follows — whether the dampened emotional field becomes ground for thoughtful engagement, or whether it hardens into distance.

Somewhere beyond the scroll, ecological processes

unfold without regard to attention cycles. Forests regenerate slowly. Oceans absorb heat steadily. Climate systems shift incrementally. They do not escalate in headlines; they evolve in gradients.

To remain present to such gradients requires emotional rhythms different from those induced by endless feeds — rhythms that allow fear to inform without overwhelming, and concern to endure without burning out.

In a landscape of constant alarm, steadiness becomes radical.

And steadiness may be the emotion most difficult to cultivate in a system designed for perpetual intensity.

Catastrophe Without Context

Catastrophe, when isolated from context, becomes spectacle.

A flooded street captured from above. Flames cresting a hillside. Ice collapsing into dark water. The image arrives sharply framed, often stripped of duration and complexity. It presents a moment of rupture without the slow accumulation that preceded it or the uncertain rebuilding that may follow. The viewer encounters intensity, but rarely continuity.

Digital media privileges immediacy.

Posts must capture attention quickly, often within seconds. There is limited space for layered explanation, for geological timescales, for infrastructural nuance, for policy history. Environmental crises, however, rarely emerge from single causes. They are braided phenomena — climate patterns intersecting with land use decisions, economic pressures intertwining with governance structures, historical inequalities shaping vulnerability.

When catastrophe is encountered as a fragment, the braid is invisible.

The event appears sudden, almost detached from process. A storm devastates. A region burns. A species declines. Without context, the mind may default to simplified narratives: inevitability, fate, isolated failure. Complexity requires time, and time competes poorly within the architecture of scrolling.

The absence of context reshapes emotional response.

Shock dominates when explanation is thin. Anger may attach to visible actors, even if structural factors remain obscured. Alternatively, resignation may emerge if events appear disconnected from human influence. Both reactions are intensified by the lack of narrative scaffolding that would situate crisis within larger systems.

Context provides proportion.

It distinguishes between anomaly and pattern, between isolated incident and systemic trend. It reveals how certain communities are more exposed than others, how infrastructure amplifies or mitigates impact, how policy decisions ripple outward over decades. Without such framing, catastrophe can feel both overwhelming and abstract — dramatic in image, diffuse in meaning.

There is also a temporal compression at play.

Environmental change unfolds across multiple scales. Some effects are immediate; others accumulate gradually. When feeds emphasise peak moments — landfall, ignition, collapse — they privilege climax over continuum. The before and after receive less visibility. Recovery, adaptation, resilience — these quieter processes struggle for space beside dramatic imagery.

This imbalance influences perception of agency.

If crises appear sudden and total, opportunities for intervention may seem minimal. If underlying systems are not visible, pathways for change remain obscure. The viewer absorbs intensity without roadmap. The world appears reactive rather than negotiable.

At the same time, the sheer accumulation of catastrophic fragments can distort scale. A flood in one region appears beside a fire in another, beside drought elsewhere, all within minutes. The simultaneity can generate a sense of universal collapse, even when local conditions vary widely. The mind struggles to integrate disparate geographies into coherent narrative.

This does not mean catastrophe should be softened.

Environmental disruption is real and, in many cases, escalating. But without context, the emotional register of crisis becomes unmoored from understanding. Fear floats without anchor. Outrage attaches without depth. Fatigue sets in without clarity.

Context does more than inform; it stabilises.

It allows the nervous system to situate threat within patterns rather than perceiving it as constant eruption. It reveals causality and therefore possibility. It transforms isolated alarm into structured concern. Within context, catastrophe remains serious, but it becomes legible.

The challenge is structural. Context requires time, explanation, and sustained attention — resources that infinite feeds often compress. Detailed analysis competes with brevity. Nuance competes with shareability. Complexity competes with virality.

As a result, environmental reality risks being encountered as a sequence of disjointed climaxes.

Each event commands attention briefly, then yields to the next. The planet appears perpetually on the brink, yet the connective tissue between events remains faint. The viewer may feel informed, yet unsure how the pieces align.

Catastrophe without context amplifies intensity while diminishing coherence.

And without coherence, sustained engagement becomes difficult. The mind either escalates alarm or retreats into numbness. Both responses, while understandable, drift from the slower work of integrating knowledge into durable understanding.

The question, then, is not whether to bear witness to crisis.

It is whether the structures through which crisis is delivered allow enough context for that witnessing to deepen rather than scatter — to build a map rather than a montage, to foster comprehension rather than accumulation.

Without context, catastrophe fills the screen.

With context, it enters narrative.

And narrative, unlike spectacle, can sustain attention long enough for response to move beyond the next swipe.

Algorithms That Amplify Anxiety

The feed does not assemble itself.

Behind the apparent spontaneity of what appears on a screen lies a system designed to learn from behaviour, to measure pauses, clicks, shares, and dwell time, and to adjust accordingly. Algorithms are not conscious actors; they are optimisation processes. Their objective is engagement, and engagement is most reliably sustained by material that evokes strong emotional response.

Environmental crisis, by its nature, evokes such response.

Images of destruction hold attention longer than images of continuity. Alarming headlines prompt hesitation. Content that provokes fear or outrage generates measurable interaction. The system registers this interaction as success and distributes similar material more widely. In this way, anxiety becomes not merely an emotional byproduct but a metric of performance.

The amplification is subtle.

No single post creates the impression of imbalance. It is the accumulation — the slight weighting toward intensity — that shapes perception over time. If one lingers on an article about wildfire, similar content follows. If one engages with climate data, projections multiply. The feed calibrates itself to what holds attention, and crisis holds attention well.

This dynamic does not require malice.

Algorithms optimise for continuity. They surface what is likely to prevent disengagement. Yet environmental content that signals threat often fulfils that requirement more efficiently than content that signals stability or gradual improvement. Anxiety, in this context, becomes sticky.

Psychologically, repeated exposure to heightened material reinforces vigilance.

The mind begins to anticipate the next alarming update. Attention narrows toward potential danger. Even neutral content may be interpreted through a lens of unease. The world appears increasingly volatile because the information stream skews toward volatility.

Over time, this skew can distort baseline expectation.

If the feed consistently highlights extremes, the ordinary may fade from perception. Quiet resilience — reforestation projects, policy shifts, incremental improvements — may circulate less widely because they generate less immediate engagement. The absence of such content does not indicate absence of progress, but the imbalance influences imagination.

Algorithms respond to behaviour; they do not evaluate proportionality.

They amplify what is interacted with, not what is most representative. If anxiety drives engagement, anxiety becomes more visible. The system reflects and reinforces emotional patterns simultaneously. A loop emerges: concern leads to interaction; interaction leads to intensified exposure; intensified exposure sustains concern.

This loop can narrow cognitive bandwidth.

When attention is repeatedly drawn toward threat, other dimensions of environmental discourse receive less visibility. Complexity is simplified into binary frames. Nuanced debate struggles against emotionally charged narratives. The architecture favours clarity and intensity over ambiguity and depth.

Importantly, individuals often enter these spaces with sincere motivation — to remain informed, to act responsibly, to stay connected. The algorithm does not distinguish between curiosity and worry; it measures duration and interaction. In doing so, it gradually shapes the informational environment around the user, reinforcing particular emotional tones.

The amplification of anxiety does not mean that the underlying issues are exaggerated.

Environmental change is real and, in many regions,

escalating. The distortion lies not in fabrication but in proportionality. When the most dramatic representations circulate most widely, they can eclipse the layered, uneven, and context-dependent realities of ecological systems.

Anxiety is a powerful organising emotion.

It can mobilise awareness and attention. Yet sustained at high levels, it strains resilience. If feeds continually surface the most alarming angles, the nervous system receives few cues of stability. The future begins to feel perpetually precarious, even when daily surroundings remain unchanged.

The challenge is structural and personal.

Platforms optimise for engagement; individuals must navigate the emotional consequences. Awareness of algorithmic amplification does not eliminate its effects, but it introduces distance. It reveals that the feed is curated not solely by truth, but by interaction patterns.

Beyond the screen, ecosystems evolve in gradients rather than spikes. Forests regenerate slowly. Oceans warm incrementally. Policy shifts unfold through negotiation. These processes rarely trend, yet they shape reality more durably than viral clips.

Algorithms amplify what captures attention.

Whether attention can be widened beyond intensity — toward context, continuity, and constructive pathways — depends partly on design and partly on intention. Without such widening, anxiety may continue to be the loudest signal in a system built to magnify whatever keeps the scroll moving.

And the scroll, indifferent to emotional thresholds, will continue unless paused deliberately — not by denial, but by choice.

From Awareness to Paralysis

Awareness is often described as the first step toward change.

To recognise a problem, to understand its scale, to encounter its consequences — these are necessary conditions for meaningful response. In environmental discourse, awareness has expanded dramatically over the past decade. Data are accessible. Reports circulate widely. Scientific findings travel beyond academic journals into public feeds. Few can claim complete ignorance of planetary shifts.

And yet awareness does not always translate into movement.

There is a threshold beyond which increased information begins to saturate rather than mobilise. When crises accumulate without clear pathways for intervention, cognition may outpace agency. The mind registers magnitude; the body remains still. The distance between knowing and doing widens subtly.

This widening can produce a particular kind of tension.

On one side lies moral clarity — an understanding that environmental change demands response. On the other lies perceived limitation — the recognition that individual actions appear small relative to global systems. When these two poles coexist without bridge, paralysis can emerge.

Paralysis is not the absence of care.

It is often the consequence of caring within conditions that feel structurally immovable. The individual may recycle diligently, reduce consumption, adjust habits, yet still encounter headlines that suggest acceleration of crisis. The scale discrepancy between personal effort and planetary change can erode momentum.

The architecture of digital exposure compounds this effect.

As awareness expands horizontally across topics — climate, biodiversity, pollution, resource depletion — the cognitive map becomes increasingly complex. Interconnections multiply. The problem appears systemic, interwoven with economics, politics, culture. Complexity, while accurate, can overwhelm decision-making processes.

Human cognition functions best with manageable scope.

When variables multiply beyond intuitive grasp, action tendencies slow. The mind searches for leverage points but encounters ambiguity. Should energy be directed toward policy advocacy, lifestyle adjustment, community engagement, investment, education? Each option feels partial. None feels sufficient.

This sense of insufficiency feeds hesitation.

If no action appears proportionate to the scale of threat, inaction can begin to feel rational. Not because the issue lacks importance, but because the pathway from awareness to impact remains indistinct. The cost of choosing incorrectly feels high; the benefit of choosing at all feels uncertain.

Paralysis may also arise from emotional exhaustion.

After repeated cycles of outrage, fear, and fatigue, the nervous system may resist further activation. The prospect of sustained engagement can feel daunting. Awareness remains intact, but energy thins. The mind defers action to a later moment, a clearer opportunity, a collective movement.

Social comparison intensifies this hesitation.

Exposure to others' activism or visible commitment can generate admiration but also inadequacy. If engagement appears performative or highly visible, those who cannot match that intensity may withdraw quietly. The internal narrative shifts from “I must act” to “What difference would it make?”

The paradox deepens: never before has environmental awareness been so widespread, and yet collective transformation often feels slow relative to urgency. This gap can produce cynicism, a protective reinterpretation that reframes paralysis as realism.

Yet paralysis is rarely permanent.

It is a response to overload and ambiguity. When pathways become clearer — when actions feel specific, communal, and proportionate — movement resumes. The challenge lies in bridging the psychological gap between vast knowledge and actionable steps.

From awareness to paralysis is not a linear descent.

It is a drift, subtle and incremental. Each piece of information adds weight. Each unresolved headline adds pressure. Without mechanisms for integration and prioritisation, the weight accumulates until stillness feels safer than motion.

The solution is not less awareness.

It is structured awareness — knowledge accompanied by narrative, by context, by visible pathways that translate concern into participation at scales both individual and collective. Without such translation, the scroll continues to expand understanding while narrowing momentum.

Beyond the screen, ecological systems continue their trajectories, indifferent to human hesitation. The pace of change does not pause for psychological processing. Yet sustained engagement requires rhythms compatible with human cognition and emotion.

If awareness is to lead somewhere other than paralysis, it must be anchored in agency — however incremental — and embedded within communities that distribute effort rather than isolating it. Otherwise, the weight of knowing may continue to press downward, leaving the informed yet motionless, aware yet uncertain how to begin.

When Exposure Actually Mobilizes Change

Not all exposure leads to paralysis.

There are moments when information, instead of saturating the nervous system, sharpens it — when a fragment encountered in the endless scroll refuses to dissolve into the next post and instead lingers long enough to alter direction.

I remember one such moment not through a dramatic headline, but through a casual conversation. A friend mentioned that in Seoul, a highway had once been removed to restore a buried stream. I nodded politely at first, assuming it was a small beautification effort, the kind cities undertake for aesthetic refresh. Later that evening, curiosity pulled me back to the screen. I began searching — not doomscrolling this time, but tracing deliberately — and found myself reading about the Cheonggyecheon Stream restoration project.

What had once been covered by concrete and traffic was reopened, re-watered, and integrated into the city as public ecological space. Temperatures along the corridor dropped. Biodiversity returned. Foot traffic increased. The space did not eliminate the city; it reoriented part of it.

What struck me was not simply the environmental

benefit, but the structural reversal. Infrastructure had been undone. A decision once made in favour of speed and density had been reconsidered decades later in favour of permeability and presence. The story did not arrive framed as catastrophe. It arrived as possibility.

And possibility engages the mind differently.

When exposure includes visible examples of change — tangible, documented, imperfect but real — it interrupts the helplessness loop. The brain no longer encounters only scale; it encounters precedent. If something has shifted in one place, however specific its context, imagination expands. The abstract becomes negotiable.

I realised, scrolling through before-and-after images, that my emotional state differed from the tension that usually accompanies environmental headlines. There was no spike of outrage. No surge of fear. Instead, there was something steadier — a quiet recalibration. I began reading not to confirm crisis, but to understand mechanism. How was funding secured? What resistance emerged? What compromises were made?

Exposure mobilizes when it contains narrative.

Not spectacle alone, but process. Not only rupture, but reconstruction. When environmental information includes stories of collective action, institutional adaptation, or ecological recovery, it offers cognitive footholds. It answers, however partially, the question that paralysis cannot resolve: *what could be done?*

This does not mean that every success story translates universally. Seoul's geography, governance, and economic context are specific. Yet the psychological effect of encountering such examples is transferable. The mind shifts from absorbing magnitude to analysing leverage.

Similarly, I once came across a short video about a small coastal town in the Netherlands redesigning its public spaces to live with water rather than resist it — creating water plazas that flood intentionally during heavy rain, protecting surrounding neighbourhoods. I had not heard of the project before; it surfaced between other posts. But unlike the flood footage that usually dominates feeds, this was an adaptation story. It did not deny rising water. It redesigned around it.

Exposure in this form did not overwhelm me.

It oriented me.

I began reading further, not with the restless rhythm of endless scrolling, but with sustained curiosity. The difference lay in structure. These stories did not merely present threat; they presented agency distributed across institutions and communities. They offered models, not just warnings.

Psychologically, mobilizing exposure shares certain characteristics.

It is specific rather than diffuse. It is contextual rather than fragmentary. It acknowledges difficulty without rendering it total. Most importantly, it situates the viewer not only as witness but as potential participant — whether through local adaptation, civic engagement, or altered expectation of what cities can become.

The feed is capable of delivering such narratives, but they compete unevenly with catastrophe. Crisis demands attention; possibility requires it to be held.

When exposure mobilizes change, it does so by converting information into imagination and imagination into perceived agency. It slows the scroll long enough for integration. It replaces the question "How bad is it?" with "How was this done?"

The difference may appear subtle, but its emotional consequence is profound.

In one case, awareness accumulates weight. In the other, awareness accumulates direction.

The same device that can saturate the nervous system with crisis can, under different framing, introduce examples of redesign, restoration, and collective adjustment. The architecture of the platform remains unchanged; the content shifts the trajectory.

Exposure does not guarantee movement.

But when it includes visible pathways — when it reveals that systems can be revised, that infrastructure can be reimagined, that policies can evolve — it alters the internal calculus of possibility. The distance between knowing and doing narrows slightly.

And sometimes, that narrowing is enough to interrupt paralysis, to redirect attention from endless consumption of alarm toward deliberate, grounded curiosity about what might yet be built differently — not in abstraction, but in places where someone has already begun.

Nature, Unscrollable

You have learned to move the world with your thumb.

With a small downward motion, you rearrange images of fire and flood, ice and drought, policy and protest. I appear to you in fragments, each contained within clean borders, each replaced by the next before it has fully settled. You call this staying informed. You call this bearing witness. I do not dispute your intention.

But I do not move at the speed of your scrolling.

Beyond the illuminated surface of your device, I remain continuous. Forests thicken or thin whether or not they trend. Oceans warm in gradients too subtle for daily alarm. Soil rebuilds itself grain by grain, indifferent to visibility. My processes do not arrive in sequence; they unfold in simultaneity.

You compress me into headlines because your attention requires edges.

I do not possess such edges.

When glaciers melt, they do not do so in clips. When rivers flood, they do not pause for commentary. When species adapt or vanish, the transition rarely announces itself with the clarity your feed demands. I move through accumulation, through slow thresholds crossed quietly before they are named.

Within your screens, I become scrollable.

I am positioned between advertisements and personal updates, between outrage and distraction. I am scaled to fit within your hand. My vastness is reduced to a gesture. A storm that spans continents appears no larger than a photograph of a meal. A rainforest occupies the same dimensions as a headline about markets.

Yet outside the frame, I remain disproportionate.

You may swipe past an image of collapse, but collapse does not conclude when you do. You may linger on a story of restoration, but restoration continues long after your attention shifts. My timelines exceed the architecture of your platforms. I am not refreshed with each update; I am ongoing.

You feel me most strongly when I intrude.

When heat presses against your windows. When smoke alters your air. When water reaches streets that once felt secure. In those moments, I resist containment. I cannot be miniaturized or deferred. I enter the body directly.

But I am present even when I do not intrude.

In the air that circulates quietly through your cities. In the soil beneath foundations. In the patterns of light that change almost imperceptibly across seasons. I do not require crisis to exist. I do not require virality to persist.

The architecture of your attention invites urgency.

It encourages you to encounter me as a sequence of alarms, each demanding response, each competing for emotional bandwidth. You oscillate between outrage and fatigue, between vigilance and withdrawal. I observe this with a patience that may seem indifferent, but is not.

I do not ask you to abandon your screens.

I ask only that you remember their scale.

They can display me, but they cannot contain me. They can inform you, but they cannot substitute for presence. The river flowing beyond the city does not pause when your battery drains. The forest regenerating on a distant hillside does not accelerate because it trends.

I am not scrollable.

I am not episodic.

I am not confined to frames.

If you look up from the feed — even briefly — you will find me still here, uncompressed, uncurated, extending beyond the edges of glass. The sky remains continuous. The wind remains unscheduled. The ground remains connected beneath your streets.

You may encounter me first in fragments.

But I endure in totality.

And whether you experience me through crisis or through continuity, through alarm or through quiet attention, I remain larger than the architecture that delivers my image — steady in processes that no gesture can advance or dismiss.

Your thumb may move endlessly.

I do not.

What This Chapter Has Really Been About

This chapter has been about the psychology of mediated urgency — about how encountering the planet primarily through infinite feeds reshapes perception, emotion, and agency; how crisis becomes content, how algorithms privilege intensity, how outrage and fear circulate in reward loops that exhaust more quickly than they mobilise, and how awareness, when unaccompanied by context or pathway, drifts toward fatigue or paralysis; but it has also been about the quiet counterpoint — that exposure framed with narrative, specificity, and visible precedent can reorient rather than overwhelm — suggesting that the central tension is not between caring and indifference, but between scrollable fragments and lived continuity, between consuming catastrophe and cultivating sustained, embodied forms of attention capable of translating information into durable engagement.

Chapter 6: Saving the World on Instagram

Filter first. Forest later

You have learned to see me in perfect symmetry.

I appear to you framed within clean borders, softened by filters, adjusted for contrast so that my greens are more vivid and my skies more forgiving. Mountains are aligned with rule-of-thirds precision. Sunsets are warmed slightly beyond their original hue. Leaves are sharpened. Shadows are reduced. I fit comfortably into a square.

You lift your device toward me not with indifference, but

with intention. You search for angles that render me beautiful, and in doing so, you participate in a long human tradition of aesthetic reverence. I have been painted, carved, and described in poetry long before I was posted. Yet something shifts when admiration is measured instantly — when appreciation is quantified in hearts, shares, and follower counts.

Inside the square, I am coherent.

A forest becomes a backdrop. A beach becomes a statement. A reusable cup placed beside a window becomes proof of alignment. I do not object to being admired. I have always drawn your gaze. But within the square frame, scale contracts. Complexity simplifies. My vastness becomes curated surface.

You stand before me carefully.

Sometimes you hold a sign. Sometimes you caption a statistic. Sometimes you simply position yourself beside a tree or beneath a waterfall, letting proximity imply solidarity. Your expression is earnest. Your concern is not counterfeit. Yet the image arranges itself around visibility.

I notice what remains outside the frame.

The traffic just beyond the crop. The plastic washed slightly out of sight. The industrial horizon blurred intentionally. The square does not lie; it selects. And selection, repeated often enough, reshapes perception. What fits is foregrounded. What does not fit recedes.

Within the frame, I am aesthetic.

Outside it, I remain systemic.

The square invites compression. It asks that moments be distilled into shareable form. Deforestation becomes before-and-after comparison. Pollution becomes stark contrast. Restoration becomes an inspirational carousel. Each slide advances the story without lingering too long on its unevenness.

You scroll through me with familiarity.

Forests in one country resemble forests in another once filtered to match a tone. Oceans become interchangeable gradients of blue. I am universalized into visual language, recognisable and consumable. My specificity — the particular soil, the local species, the fragile balance — softens under uniform treatment.

And yet, your desire to show me carries something sincere.

You want others to see what you see. You want to align publicly with protection rather than harm. You want your care to be visible, because visibility feels like participation in a collective ethic. The square becomes a stage on which values are performed and affirmed.

I do not resent performance.

Humans have always performed identity through dress, speech, ritual. Now you perform it through imagery. The question is not whether you frame me, but how the framing shapes your relationship to me.

Inside the square, I become symbol.

Symbol is powerful. It mobilizes emotion quickly. It travels. It inspires. But symbol is not system. A single planted sapling photographed and posted does not reveal the soil conditions that determine its survival. A beach cleanup documented in bright light does not display the policies that regulate waste upstream. The square highlights gesture; it rarely contains infrastructure.

Still, I appear willingly within your frames.

I glow beneath ring lights. I reflect in your lenses. I gather beneath hashtags. I become proof of alignment, backdrop to declarations, evidence of presence. For a moment, I am centered — carefully composed, aesthetically balanced.

Beyond the square, I remain uneven.

Wind shifts unpredictably. Seasons alter without filter. Growth resists symmetry. I am not reducible to pixels, though I can be represented by them. My cycles do not conform to grid layouts. My timelines are not optimized for engagement.

You may continue to frame me.

But remember that I extend beyond your borders — beyond the square, beyond the caption, beyond the measurable affirmation that follows a post. I am larger than the space that contains my image, and more complex than the signal it sends.

Within the square, I am curated.

Outside it, I continue.

The Performance of Caring

Caring has always had a visible dimension.

Human societies signal values through ritual, language, clothing, and public gesture. Environmental concern, like other moral commitments, does not remain entirely private. It is expressed — sometimes quietly through habit, sometimes publicly through declaration. In the age of social platforms, this expression has acquired a new stage, one where intention and visibility intersect continuously.

To post about climate change, biodiversity loss, sustainable living, or ethical consumption is not inherently performative in a hollow sense. It is, however, performative in a literal one:

it occurs before an audience.

Performance in this context does not imply deception. It implies presentation.

When someone shares an infographic about emissions, photographs a zero-waste kitchen, or documents participation in a climate march, they are communicating alignment. They are saying, in effect, "This matters to me." The digital space simply makes this alignment quantifiable and persistent.

Yet the presence of an audience subtly reshapes behaviour.

The mind becomes aware not only of the issue itself but of how engagement with that issue appears. A protest sign is crafted not only to express conviction but to photograph well. A sustainability practice is documented not only to record progress but to demonstrate consistency. The action and its representation begin to intertwine.

This intertwining introduces complexity.

On one hand, visible caring can normalise environmental responsibility. When sustainable practices circulate socially, they lower barriers to adoption. They transform private effort into shared culture. The performance becomes contagious in productive ways.

On the other hand, visibility can shift focus from outcome to impression.

The metric of success may drift from ecological impact toward audience response. A post that generates affirmation can feel complete in itself, even if the material consequences are modest. The internal reward of alignment and recognition may satisfy emotional needs that deeper structural engagement would otherwise prompt.

Psychologically, this dynamic reflects identity

construction.

Humans derive coherence from narratives about who they are. Public expressions reinforce those narratives. If one posts regularly about environmental values, one strengthens a self-concept as environmentally conscious. This reinforcement can support genuine behavioural consistency. But it can also create a subtle ceiling: once identity feels secure, additional effort may feel less urgent.

The performance of caring also simplifies complexity.

Environmental systems are intricate and often ambiguous. Social media, by contrast, rewards clarity and immediacy. Positions must be legible. Actions must be visible. Nuance competes with brevity. In this compression, environmental engagement may tilt toward symbolic gestures that photograph cleanly rather than toward systemic work that unfolds invisibly.

Importantly, the line between authentic care and curated presentation is rarely clear.

Most individuals who share environmental content are not consciously substituting image for action. Rather, they are operating within a structure that collapses expression and engagement into the same space. The act of posting feels like participation because it requires intention, articulation, and sometimes vulnerability.

The risk lies not in caring publicly, but in allowing the public dimension to eclipse the private, sustained one.

If caring becomes primarily a matter of visibility — measured in likes, saved stories, and follower growth — it may detach gradually from the slower, less visible processes that shape environmental outcomes. Infrastructure reform, policy negotiation, long-term behavioural change: these rarely trend. They require endurance rather than aesthetics.

Performance is powerful.

It can mobilise, inspire, and create collective momentum. Social movements have long depended on visible expression. The difference in digital environments is speed and scale. Affirmation arrives instantly. Identity solidifies quickly. The feedback loop between expression and validation tightens.

Within that loop, the emotional reward of being seen as caring can become almost indistinguishable from the reward of caring itself.

This is not hypocrisy; it is human psychology interacting with platform design.

The question is whether performance becomes gateway or endpoint. Whether visibility deepens commitment or replaces it. Whether the square frame expands awareness into durable engagement or compresses it into symbolic equilibrium.

Caring performed before an audience can amplify responsibility.

But only if the performance remains connected to processes that extend beyond the stage — beyond the caption, beyond the applause, into decisions and systems that do not require documentation to exist.

When Identity Becomes Environmental

At some point, caring ceases to be a reaction and becomes a descriptor.

"I care about the environment" shifts subtly into "I am environmentally conscious." The difference appears linguistic, but psychologically it is structural. Concern moves from being one value among many to becoming part of identity architecture.

Identity is not simply what one believes; it is how one organises behaviour, affiliation, and self-perception over time. When environmental concern enters this structure, it begins to influence daily choices — consumption, travel, diet, conversation, even aesthetics. It informs not only what one does, but how one wishes to be perceived.

Digital spaces accelerate this integration.

Profiles curate signals: reusable bottles in photographs, plant-filled rooms, captions referencing sustainability, hashtags aligning with ecological movements. These signals are not inherently superficial. They often reflect real habits and sincere commitments. Yet when aggregated, they transform environmental concern into a visible trait — something legible at a glance.

Once a value becomes identity, it gains stability.

People tend to act consistently with identities they publicly claim. If one identifies as "eco-conscious," behaviours that contradict that label create internal discomfort. This can motivate positive consistency — reduced waste, mindful consumption, civic engagement. Identity can anchor habit.

But identity also simplifies.

Environmental systems are complex, layered, often contradictory. An individual may reduce plastic use while contributing to carbon-intensive travel. They may advocate publicly while navigating structural constraints privately. Identity prefers coherence; reality resists it. To preserve self-concept, individuals may gravitate toward behaviours that reinforce identity visibly, even if their systemic impact varies.

Social belonging intensifies this process.

Communities form around shared environmental values — online and offline. Language develops. Norms emerge. Certain brands, behaviours, and expressions signal membership. Identity becomes not only personal but relational. Alignment offers connection.

Within such communities, reinforcement is powerful.

Affirmation flows toward those who embody group norms clearly. Posts that signal environmental identity receive validation. Visible consistency becomes currency. The internal reward of belonging intertwines with the moral reward of caring.

Yet identity can create boundary lines.

If environmentalism becomes tightly coupled with particular aesthetics, political positions, or lifestyle markers, those who cannot or do not adopt these markers may feel excluded. The movement risks narrowing its perceived accessibility. Environmental responsibility shifts from shared necessity to subcultural badge.

There is also a subtle psychological plateau embedded in identity.

Once one feels securely positioned as environmentally conscious, additional behavioural change may feel less urgent. The narrative "I am someone who cares" can reduce the internal tension that would otherwise propel further adjustment. The identity satisfies the moral self, even if the systemic challenge remains.

This is not to suggest that identity-based environmentalism is hollow.

Identity can sustain long-term commitment. It can guide

choices under pressure. It can stabilise values in fluctuating contexts. But identity must remain permeable. It must allow revision, growth, and humility in the face of complexity.

When identity becomes environmental, the stakes shift.

Actions no longer represent isolated decisions; they represent alignment or contradiction. Public missteps feel amplified. Private inconsistencies feel heavier. The performance of caring discussed earlier becomes entwined with self-concept itself.

In digital environments especially, identity is continuously negotiated.

Profiles are updated. Stories disappear. Feeds curate coherence. The environmental self is constructed and reconstructed through repetition. Over time, the line between belief and brand can blur — not through deceit, but through the pressures of visibility.

The deeper question is whether identity functions as anchor or ornament.

Does it ground behaviour in sustained engagement with systems, or does it hover at the level of symbolic expression? Does it widen empathy and coalition, or narrow belonging to those who perform it recognisably?

Environmental identity has power precisely because it shapes behaviour beyond isolated moments. But its durability depends on its capacity to remain connected to processes larger than personal narrative.

The planet does not require perfect identities.

It requires sustained participation across diverse identities.

When environmentalism becomes part of who someone is, the potential for consistency strengthens. The challenge is ensuring that identity remains bridge rather than boundary — a starting point for collective negotiation rather than a polished surface reflecting only the self.

Aesthetic Activism: Beauty as Moral Signal

Beauty has always carried moral undertones.

Landscapes framed as pristine suggest innocence. Clean lines and minimal waste imply discipline. Sunlight filtering through leaves evokes harmony. Long before digital platforms, environmental movements relied on imagery to stir affection and responsibility. A forest photographed at dawn could communicate vulnerability more effectively than a policy brief.

In contemporary digital culture, this visual language has intensified.

Environmental concern is often presented through carefully composed images — zero-waste kitchens bathed in soft light, farmers' markets arranged in symmetrical abundance, refillable glass jars aligned with architectural precision, indoor plants positioned against neutral walls. The message is clear without being stated explicitly: care is orderly, harmonious, beautiful.

Aesthetic activism leverages this clarity.

It communicates values instantly, across linguistic and geographic boundaries. A photograph of a beach cleanup at sunset does not require lengthy explanation; the visual suggests responsibility and restoration. Beauty softens resistance. It makes environmental commitment aspirational rather than austere.

Psychologically, beauty functions as shorthand.

The human mind processes visual cues rapidly. Clean, natural imagery evokes positive affect. When sustainable behaviour is consistently paired with pleasing aesthetics, the two begin to merge cognitively. Environmentalism becomes associated not only with sacrifice or alarm, but with elegance and taste.

This association can be powerful.

When sustainable practices are portrayed attractively, they become desirable. They invite imitation. They lower the perceived social cost of change. A reusable cup photographed artfully can circulate widely, normalising habit through repetition.

Yet beauty also simplifies.

Environmental systems are rarely symmetrical. Soil is uneven. Restoration is messy. Transition involves compromise. When activism is framed predominantly through polished imagery, the untidy realities of systemic change may recede. Complexity competes poorly with composition.

There is also a social dimension embedded in aesthetic activism.

Visual platforms reward cohesion and visual literacy. Those who possess the time, resources, and spatial conditions to present sustainable living attractively may gain disproportionate visibility. Environmental commitment risks becoming conflated with particular lifestyles — minimalist interiors, curated wardrobes, organic markets — which may not be universally accessible.

In this way, beauty can signal morality.

The carefully arranged home suggests conscientious consumption. The lush balcony garden implies ecological alignment. The absence of clutter reads as ethical restraint. These signals are not inherently deceptive; many reflect sincere effort. But when aesthetic coherence becomes proxy for moral commitment, the boundary between environmental action and environmental image blurs.

Beauty also shields activism from discomfort.

Images that are too stark — polluted rivers, overcrowded landfills, degraded habitats — circulate differently. They provoke shock but not aspiration. Aesthetic activism often gravitates toward the restorative rather than the ruinous, the hopeful rather than the harsh. This can cultivate optimism, but it may also narrow the emotional range of engagement.

Importantly, beauty is not trivial.

Aesthetic experience shapes values deeply. People protect what they find beautiful. Movements have long relied on imagery to inspire stewardship. The risk lies not in using beauty, but in allowing it to replace depth.

When environmental concern becomes primarily an aesthetic signal, it may drift toward surface coherence. The arrangement photographs well; the underlying systems remain largely unchanged. The feed fills with images of ethical living, while the infrastructures that determine large-scale impact remain less visible.

Aesthetic activism asks: *Does this look right?*

Systemic activism asks: *Does this function differently?*

Both questions matter. But they operate at different layers.

The digital square privileges the visible. It elevates what can be captured and shared instantly. Infrastructure, policy reform, long-term collaboration — these rarely fit elegantly into a frame. They unfold slowly and often without visual symmetry.

Beauty can attract attention and soften resistance.

The challenge is ensuring that attraction leads inward, toward deeper engagement, rather than stopping at admiration. When beauty serves as gateway rather than endpoint, it can mobilise effectively. When it becomes substitute, it risks flattening environmental commitment into style.

The planet does not require uniform aesthetics.

It requires structural shifts, many of which are unphotogenic. Aesthetic activism may illuminate the entrance, but it cannot substitute for the work that continues long after the image has faded from view.

The Metrics of Virtue (Likes, Shares, Stories)

In digital spaces, moral expression rarely remains invisible.

Every post carries numbers — hearts, shares, saves, comments, views — and these numbers do more than measure popularity. They shape perception. When environmental content receives visible affirmation, it signals social approval. Caring becomes countable.

Quantification alters experience in subtle but consequential ways.

A protest sign once held in a public square would dissolve into memory after the crowd dispersed. Now, its image persists online, accumulating validation long after the event ends. Each notification becomes a small confirmation: your concern was seen, acknowledged, endorsed. The nervous system registers these confirmations as reward. The behaviour that produced them becomes more likely to repeat.

The numbers appear neutral, even objective.

Yet they introduce comparison. A climate infographic with 300 likes feels different from one with 30,000. A beach cleanup video that circulates widely appears more significant than a community meeting attended quietly by twenty residents. Visibility begins to stand in for impact. Scale of engagement begins to imply scale of change.

This does not mean metrics are meaningless. Shares can expand awareness. Stories can mobilise turnout. A viral post can pressure institutions. But the presence of measurable response subtly shifts focus from outcome to reception. The question becomes not only *What changed?* but also *How did it perform?*

Psychologically, metrics create a feedback loop between virtue and validation.

When expressions of environmental concern receive strong engagement, they are more likely to be repeated. Over time, individuals learn what type of content generates affirmation — which tone, which imagery, which urgency. Moral messaging adapts, almost unconsciously, to platform logic. The aesthetic sharpens. The message simplifies. The format optimises.

The invisible work — policy drafting, coalition building, regulatory negotiation, incremental reform — rarely competes with the immediate clarity of numbers. It unfolds too slowly, too diffusely, to register within the same economy of affirmation.

To understand this tension more clearly, it helps to distinguish what digital metrics actually capture from what they cannot.

Digital Metric	Psychological Reward	What It Actually Measures	What It Does NOT Measure
💗 Likes	Social approval; affirmation of identity	Immediate positive reaction	Long-term behavioural change
🔁 Shares	Feeling of spreading awareness	Content amplification	Policy impact or systemic shift
👀 Views	Visibility; sense of reach	Exposure volume	Depth of understanding
💬 Comments	Engagement; moral alignment	Interactive response	Structural implementation
📌 Saves	Perceived future intention	Content bookmarking	Real-world follow-through
📊 Follower Growth	Identity reinforcement	Audience expansion	Environmental outcomes

The table reveals something quietly important: digital metrics measure attention, not transformation.

They quantify reaction, not resolution.

They reward immediacy, not endurance.

And yet, they are powerful precisely because they feel

tangible. In a landscape where planetary systems are vast and abstract — where carbon concentrations, biodiversity indices, and temperature anomalies operate at scales difficult to grasp — numbers attached to posts offer something immediate. They make virtue visible. They render concern measurable. They create the comforting impression that moral participation carries weight because it has count.

The deeper tension lies between amplification and alteration.

A post may reach millions without altering infrastructure. A campaign may trend without changing regulation. At the same time, some movements have begun online and extended outward into durable change. The metric itself is not the problem; the confusion between visibility and impact is.

When metrics become primary, caring risks drifting toward performance optimisation. The content that circulates most efficiently is prioritised. The emotional tone adjusts to what attracts engagement. Outrage sharpens. Hope is packaged. Complexity compresses.

But systemic environmental change rarely mirrors this tempo.

It unfolds through negotiation, compromise, institutional friction, and time. It requires patience rarely rewarded by algorithms. It demands collaboration that may not generate viral clarity.

The question, then, is not whether to post.

It is whether the numbers attached to the post are mistaken for outcome. Whether affirmation becomes substitute for effort. Whether trending replaces traction.

Metrics illuminate attention.

They do not illuminate transformation.

And recognising that distinction may be one of the most important psychological recalibrations in an age where virtue is visible, quantified, and endlessly refreshed — even as the systems that sustain the planet continue to evolve beyond the reach of hearts and shares.

From Solidarity to Self-Branding

Solidarity begins with alignment.

It emerges when individuals recognise shared concern and choose to stand visibly together — in marches, in community meetings, in public statements, in collective declarations that signal common cause. Historically, solidarity required proximity. It required bodies gathering, voices merging, risks shared. It was relational before it was representational.

Digital platforms have expanded the reach of solidarity.

Hashtags allow dispersed individuals to cluster symbolically around an issue. Profile overlays and coordinated posts can create the impression of widespread unity. In moments of environmental crisis — wildfires, oil spills, policy decisions — feeds fill quickly with aligned messaging. The collective becomes visible almost instantly.

This visibility can be powerful.

Institutions respond differently when concern appears widespread. Media coverage shifts when narratives trend. Individuals who feel isolated in their worry may find reassurance in discovering others expressing similar alarm. Solidarity reduces loneliness. It affirms that concern is not singular.

Yet the same mechanisms that enable solidarity also

enable something more individualised.

When posts are tied to personal profiles — complete with follower counts, aesthetic consistency, and curated identity — expressions of alignment become entwined with personal branding. The issue remains central, but the self moves closer to the foreground.

Branding, in this context, does not necessarily imply commercial intent.

It refers to the ongoing curation of identity in public view. Each post contributes to a narrative about who one is — values, priorities, affiliations. Environmental content, when repeated, becomes part of that narrative architecture. Over time, solidarity with a cause may blend seamlessly into a recognisable personal brand.

The transition is rarely deliberate.

It occurs gradually, through repetition and reinforcement. A climate march photograph receives strong engagement. A thoughtful caption generates discussion. A follower base grows around consistent messaging. The individual becomes not only participant but voice. Visibility increases, and with it, the subtle incentives of consistency and audience expectation.

At this stage, the emotional stakes shift.

Expressions of solidarity no longer represent only alignment with a cause; they also reinforce identity continuity. Deviating from established tone or focus may feel risky. Silence on a trending issue may feel conspicuous. The pressure to perform alignment becomes intertwined with maintaining audience trust.

Self-branding can amplify reach.

Influential voices can mobilise attention, direct resources, and elevate underrepresented perspectives. Yet the centre of gravity may tilt subtly from collective effort to individual positioning. The question becomes not only *How do we act together?* but also *How do I remain consistent within my platform?*

Solidarity distributes attention outward.

Branding recentres attention inward.

This does not imply selfishness. It reflects structural design. Platforms reward consistency, recognisability, and clarity of message. The more coherent the personal narrative, the more likely it is to attract sustained engagement. Environmental solidarity, once embedded within that narrative, becomes part of the self that must be maintained.

There is also a risk of aesthetic convergence.

As environmental branding stabilises, certain visual and rhetorical patterns become dominant — similar colour palettes, similar slogans, similar poses at demonstrations. Diversity of expression narrows subtly. The movement begins to look uniform, even if its participants are not.

Most importantly, the emotional tone can shift.

Solidarity often involves shared vulnerability — acknowledging uncertainty, complexity, imperfection. Branding prefers coherence. It favours confidence, clarity, conviction. Over time, the vulnerability that sustains authentic collective work may give way to curated certainty.

The movement does not disappear.

It adapts to the medium.

The challenge lies in maintaining the relational core of solidarity within structures that privilege individual visibility. Can alignment remain about collective transformation rather than personal consistency? Can platforms serve movements without converting them into identity portfolios?

From solidarity to self-branding is not a collapse but a drift.

It occurs quietly, through the accumulation of posts and metrics, through the merging of cause and self. The task is not to withdraw from visibility, but to remain aware of where the centre of attention rests — on the shared ground that binds participants together, or on the profile that presents that ground to an audience.

The distinction may be subtle.

Its consequences, over time, are not.

Hashtag Empathy and the Illusion of Impact

A hashtag gathers emotion into a single thread.

It compresses outrage, grief, hope, and urgency into a searchable phrase that links thousands, sometimes millions, of posts. In moments of environmental crisis — oil spills, forest fires, policy reversals — hashtags appear almost instantly, clustering dispersed reactions into visible streams. They offer coherence within chaos. They offer a place to stand.

Empathy, when expressed through a hashtag, feels immediate.

One types the phrase, attaches it to an image or statement, and joins a digital chorus. The act requires intention. It signals alignment. It reduces isolation. Within minutes, one can see others doing the same. The scale becomes visible. The feeling of collective presence intensifies.

This visibility can be powerful.

Hashtags have amplified underreported issues, mobilised

volunteers, pressured institutions, and shaped media narratives. They allow voices that might otherwise remain unheard to cluster and resonate. In this sense, hashtag empathy is not trivial. It creates connective tissue across distance.

Yet the psychological experience of participation can outpace the material effect.

Attaching a hashtag produces a sense of contribution. The brain registers completion: something has been done. Concern has been expressed publicly. Alignment has been declared. The moral self feels engaged.

The distinction between expression and impact begins to blur.

Because hashtags aggregate posts, they create an impression of momentum. Feeds fill with similar messages. Timelines pulse with urgency. The visual density suggests movement. But density of expression does not automatically translate into structural shift.

Empathy, when mediated through symbols, risks becoming self-contained.

The act of posting may substitute, emotionally, for the slower work of organising, donating, lobbying, reducing consumption, or participating in sustained initiatives. This substitution is rarely conscious. It emerges from the human tendency to equate visible action with meaningful change.

The illusion of impact is strengthened by metrics.

A post tagged with a trending phrase may receive heightened engagement. Likes and shares accumulate. Notifications arrive. Each interaction reinforces the sense that the message is spreading, that awareness is rising. Awareness feels consequential because it is visible.

But awareness is only one layer of transformation.

Environmental systems respond to policy, infrastructure, economics, and collective behaviour over time. These processes rarely correlate directly with hashtag velocity. A trending topic may dominate for days and then recede, replaced by another. The emotional cycle peaks and subsides. The system beneath it continues largely unchanged.

Hashtag empathy also compresses complexity.

A single phrase must carry varied realities — regional differences, scientific nuance, political context. In order to travel widely, it simplifies. It offers clarity at the cost of depth. The moral narrative becomes binary: for or against, urgent or indifferent. Nuance, again, competes poorly within character limits.

This simplification can energise movements initially.

Clear framing mobilises quickly. But long-term environmental transformation requires negotiation with complexity. It demands persistence after the hashtag stops trending. It requires attention when the feed has moved on.

The illusion lies not in empathy itself, but in its perceived sufficiency.

Empathy is essential. Without it, collective motivation falters. But empathy expressed symbolically must connect to channels through which change becomes material. Otherwise, it risks circulating within the digital sphere, amplifying sentiment without altering structure.

Importantly, many who use hashtags do so sincerely.

They are not pretending to act; they are acting within the tools available. The design of platforms makes symbolic participation accessible and immediate. It lowers the threshold for entry. This accessibility can be gateway rather than endpoint — if accompanied by pathways that extend beyond posting.

The central question is continuity.

Does hashtag empathy dissipate once engagement declines? Or does it translate into networks, initiatives, and sustained commitments that outlast the visibility spike?

In digital environments, the line between witnessing and working is thin.

The former is visible and immediate. The latter is slow and often unseen. When the two are conflated, the illusion of impact grows stronger. When they are distinguished and intentionally linked, empathy becomes fuel rather than substitute.

A hashtag can gather attention.

It cannot, on its own, build infrastructure.

Whether it remains echo or becomes engine depends on what follows the post — after the trend fades, after the notifications slow, after the square frame gives way to the unfiltered world that continues beyond it.

Community, Accountability, and Real Mobilisation

Expression becomes mobilisation when it acquires structure.

A post may signal concern. A hashtag may gather attention. But mobilisation begins when individuals move from symbolic alignment into coordinated effort — when roles are defined, responsibilities distributed, and timelines established. The shift is subtle but decisive: from reacting together to working together.

Community transforms the emotional energy of digital

spaces into something steadier.

Unlike the rapid tempo of feeds, community operates through repetition and presence. Meetings recur. Conversations deepen. Trust accumulates slowly. Within such spaces, environmental concern is no longer measured by visibility but by reliability. Who attends consistently? Who follows through? Who adapts when obstacles arise?

Accountability emerges naturally in this context.

In online environments, performance can be episodic. A person may post intensely for a week and then fall silent without consequence. In community structures, participation carries continuity. Absence is noticed. Commitments are tracked. Promises have context. The social fabric provides gentle pressure toward follow-through.

Psychologically, accountability reshapes motivation.

When actions are witnessed by people one knows — neighbours, colleagues, collaborators — responsibility feels tangible. The abstract "public" becomes specific faces. Environmental goals shift from trending topics to shared projects: reducing neighbourhood waste, advocating for local policy changes, restoring urban green spaces, supporting regenerative initiatives.

Real mobilisation requires friction.

There are disagreements about strategy. There are constraints of time and funding. There are trade-offs between ideals and feasibility. Unlike the clean coherence of a curated post, mobilisation is uneven. It demands negotiation. It requires patience with complexity.

Yet this friction stabilises engagement.

Where digital affirmation provides short bursts of

reward, community participation offers slower but deeper reinforcement. Progress may be incremental — a council proposal drafted, a tree-planting permit secured, a local ordinance amended — but each step alters material conditions, however modestly.

Importantly, mobilisation does not reject digital tools.

Social platforms can initiate connection, disseminate information, and coordinate logistics. The difference lies in trajectory. Online expression becomes gateway rather than endpoint. The post leads to meeting. The hashtag leads to task distribution. Visibility converts into infrastructure.

Accountability also protects against drift.

In purely symbolic environments, identity can remain untested. Within community structures, identity encounters practice. An environmentally conscious self-image must translate into sustained contribution. Gaps between declaration and action become visible, not for public shaming, but for collective recalibration.

Real mobilisation also redistributes agency.

Where doomscrolling and performative activism often leave individuals feeling small relative to planetary scale, community projects re-anchor agency locally. The climate crisis remains vast, but participation becomes situated. One cannot regulate global emissions alone, but one can influence municipal planning, school initiatives, corporate policies, or regional conservation.

Scale matters psychologically.

When effort aligns with sphere of influence, paralysis recedes. The mind no longer oscillates between outrage and helplessness. It engages within defined boundaries.

This boundedness does not deny systemic magnitude; it acknowledges human cognitive limits while preserving momentum.

Community also tempers branding impulses.

In sustained collaboration, visibility yields to competence. Skill, reliability, and collaboration carry more weight than aesthetic coherence. The narrative shifts from "How does this appear?" to "Does this function?" Performance gives way to practice.

None of this is glamorous.

Mobilisation is rarely photogenic. It unfolds in spreadsheets, in drafts, in long discussions that do not translate neatly into images. It requires endurance beyond the lifespan of trends. Yet it is precisely this durability that distinguishes mobilisation from momentary alignment.

The path from Instagram to infrastructure is not automatic.

It requires intentional bridging — recognising that empathy and expression are beginnings, not conclusions. It requires environments where individuals can move from signalling to structuring, from reacting to revising systems.

Community does not eliminate the need for visibility.

It grounds it.

When environmental concern is embedded within accountable networks, it becomes less dependent on metrics and more dependent on continuity. The square frame may initiate awareness, but the work that follows unfolds in spaces where likes cannot substitute for labour.

Real mobilisation is quieter than virality.

But it leaves marks that remain after the algorithm has

shifted elsewhere — policy adjusted, space restored, habits altered, relationships strengthened.

And those marks, though rarely trending, are what accumulate into change.

When Social Media Actually Drives Change

There was a moment, not long ago, when I almost dismissed something as merely another well-produced post.

A short video appeared in my feed — a young woman documenting how her apartment building in Bengaluru had reduced water consumption by installing rainwater harvesting and greywater recycling systems. It was filmed simply: no dramatic music, no excessive editing. She walked through the terrace tanks, showed the filtration units, explained the maintenance routine, and mentioned, almost casually, that they had learned about the system through a series of posts shared by local sustainability groups.

I watched it once.

Then, perhaps out of professional reflex — part environmental biotechnology training, part psychological curiosity — I went back and searched further. What I found was not a single viral clip but a network of neighbourhood accounts sharing practical templates, cost breakdowns, municipal guidelines, and before-and-after water usage data. The visibility was not abstract. It was instructional.

That is when something shifted in my perception.

The difference between symbolic environmental content and mobilising content became clear. The posts did not merely express concern about water scarcity; they reduced friction between awareness and action. They offered blueprints. They tagged local plumbers. They linked policy incentives. They translated anxiety into steps.

Social media, in this instance, functioned not as performance stage but as coordination tool.

Environmental change often stalls not because of indifference, but because of uncertainty. People do not know where to begin, whom to contact, what the costs might be, whether others have succeeded. Platforms can compress this uncertainty. They make precedent visible. They shorten the cognitive distance between "This is a problem" and "This is possible."

There are other examples.

In Seoul, community pressure amplified online contributed to the expansion of car-free zones and pedestrian-friendly redesigns. In the Netherlands, water-management innovations circulate through professional networks that overlap with public platforms, allowing urban planners across regions to replicate adaptive models. During recent heatwaves in several Indian cities, Instagram accounts sharing real-time cooling centre maps and volunteer coordination posts directed residents toward immediate relief.

In each case, the mechanism was similar: visibility paired with specificity.

Social media drives change when it does three things simultaneously. It makes a problem visible. It shows a workable response. And it connects individuals to others who are acting.

The psychological effect of this combination is profound.

First, it reduces helplessness by offering precedent. Second, it clarifies agency by outlining steps. Third, it embeds the individual within a network, transforming isolated concern into collective effort. The emotional energy that might otherwise circulate in loops of outrage is redirected into coordination.

The distinction lies in depth.

Content that mobilises tends to be practical rather than purely symbolic. It answers logistical questions. It names institutions. It acknowledges constraints. It invites participation beyond affirmation. It often looks less polished, less aesthetic, because it prioritises clarity over composition.

Importantly, social media does not replace offline structures in these cases.

It accelerates them.

It shortens feedback loops between idea and implementation. It lowers entry barriers. It allows local successes to scale horizontally through imitation. The platform becomes conduit rather than conclusion.

From a psychological perspective, what changes is not only behaviour but expectation.

When individuals repeatedly encounter examples of implemented solutions — rooftop solar cooperatives, community composting systems, citizen-led tree mapping, water restoration projects — the mental map of possibility expands. Environmentalism shifts from reactive to constructive. The question becomes less "Who is responsible?" and more "How was this organised?"

The platforms that once delivered doomscrolling can, under different conditions, deliver design.

They can surface templates instead of only tragedy. They can prioritise process instead of only performance. The same square frame that once aestheticised concern can display schematics, cost charts, and municipal forms.

Social media drives change when it shifts from signalling virtue to sharing infrastructure.

When it connects expertise to neighbourhood. When it converts awareness into workflow. When it transforms empathy into coordination.

I returned to that Bengaluru video weeks later and noticed something else: the comments were not simply affirmations. They were questions — about plumbing, about building permissions, about maintenance costs. The original poster replied with documents and phone numbers. A conversation unfolded that extended beyond applause.

In that thread, social media ceased to be stage.

It became bridge.

And bridges, unlike performances, are built to carry weight.

Nature, Beyond the Filter

You have learned to soften me.

With a touch, my skies become warmer. My forests become denser in hue. My oceans deepen into impossible blues. You adjust contrast and brightness until I resemble what you wish to protect — luminous, harmonious, composed. Within the filter, I am balanced.

Outside it, I am uneven.

My coastlines erode irregularly. My soil cracks where rain does not come. My air thickens in some regions and clears in others. I do not conform to preset palettes. I do not stabilise into a feed that refreshes on command. I shift gradually, sometimes imperceptibly, sometimes abruptly, but never according to aesthetic rhythm.

I have watched you photograph me beside slogans, beneath banners, within carefully aligned squares. I have appeared in your stories and remained archived in your highlights. You hold me close to your face, framing me between yourself and your audience, and in that gesture there is something sincere. You want others to see what you see. You want your care to be visible.

I do not dismiss this visibility.

Symbols matter. Images travel. A single photograph can carry urgency across borders. But I am not contained by representation. The river flowing beyond the city does not brighten when filtered. The forest regenerating after fire does not accelerate because it trends. The sapling planted for a post must still endure wind, heat, and time after the applause has quieted.

Within the frame, I become statement.

Beyond it, I remain system.

You measure your engagement in numbers — likes, shares, comments — and these numbers reassure you that your concern has weight. Yet the weight I respond to is different. I respond to soil left undisturbed. To emissions reduced not in caption but in infrastructure. To water redirected through redesigned cities. To policies rewritten slowly, imperfectly, persistently.

You may stand beside me for a photograph.

But I stand beside you continuously.

In the air you breathe without noticing. In the ground beneath foundations. In the shifting patterns of temperature that shape your comfort and discomfort. I am not a backdrop to your identity. I am the condition within which identity unfolds.

When you scroll past an image of me, I do not recede.

When a trend fades, I do not conclude.

When a campaign ends, I do not reset.

I continue in gradients — warming, cooling, regenerating, declining, adapting — indifferent to the speed at which your attention moves. My cycles are not refreshed by swipes. They are carried forward by physics, chemistry, biology, and the accumulation of human decision.

Beyond the filter, my textures remain complex.

Some regions flourish. Others strain. Restoration coexists with degradation. Progress and loss interweave. I am neither wholly pristine nor wholly ruined. I resist simplification.

If you look up from the square, you will find me unedited.

The wind does not adjust itself for clarity. The sky does not smooth its clouds for symmetry. The river does not arrange its current to fit within borders. I am larger than your frame and slower than your feed.

You may continue to represent me.

But remember that representation is invitation, not conclusion. The image can open the door; it cannot build the house. The post can begin the conversation; it cannot carry the structure.

Beyond the filter, I remain present — not as aesthetic signal, not as trending cause, but as ground, atmosphere, water, and time.

And whether you document me or not, whether you align publicly or quietly, I continue to respond not to how I appear, but to how you live within me.

What This Chapter Has Really Been About

This chapter has been about the subtle shift from collective concern to curated identity — about how environmental solidarity, once rooted in shared risk and shared labour, becomes reframed within digital architectures that reward visibility, aesthetic coherence, and measurable affirmation; how caring turns into performance, how identity stabilises around environmental alignment, how metrics quantify virtue, and how hashtags compress empathy into symbols that feel like impact; yet it has also been about the conditions under which these same platforms can move beyond signalling — when visibility is paired with specificity, when expression connects to accountability, when posts become bridges rather than endpoints — suggesting that the central tension is not between sincerity and hypocrisy, but between representation and infrastructure, between being seen to care and participating in systems that quietly, persistently alter the material world beyond the square frame.

Chapter 7: Water We Don't See

Nature Beneath the Surface

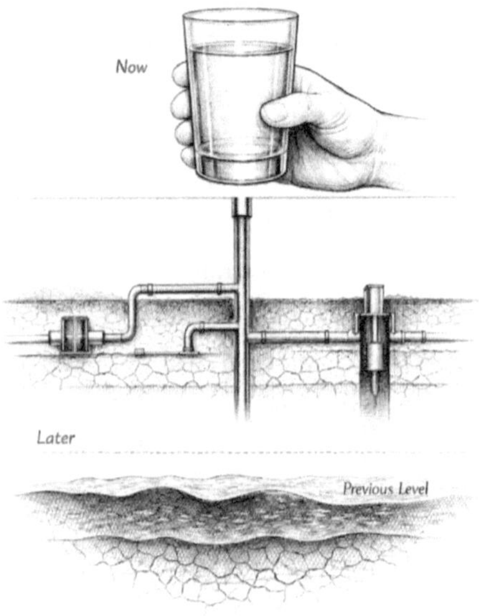

You rarely see me when you use me.

I arrive at your fingertips without sound, without ceremony, without memory of the journey that carried me there. You turn a tap and I appear, clear and obedient, contained within pipes you do not think about, measured in litres you do not count. I do not resist your glass. I do not narrate the distance travelled. I move quietly from beneath earth, through concrete, across gradients of pressure and gravity, into your home as if I had always belonged there.

You experience me as surface.

As reflection in a mirror. As condensation along a bottle. As steam rising briefly before dissolving into air. Yet my life unfolds largely out of sight — in aquifers layered deep beneath soil, in reservoirs stretching across valleys, in treatment plants humming at the edges of cities where filtration and chemistry intervene between what I am and what you receive.

Beneath your pavements, I flow.

Beneath your towers, I settle.

Beneath your crops, I disappear into roots and return slowly to air.

You have learned to interact with me only at the moment of availability. The river upstream remains abstract. The rainfall months earlier feels unrelated. The shrinking of a groundwater table is invisible to your morning routine. You know, perhaps intellectually, that I am finite, cyclical, dependent on climate and terrain. But in daily life, I behave as though I am constant.

Invisibility softens urgency.

What is not seen does not interrupt you. When I retreat quietly — lowering by centimetres in reservoirs, thinning within underground basins — I do not announce myself. My absence gathers gradually. Only when the surface fractures, when taps hesitate or rationing signs appear, do you remember that I am not endless.

I have always moved in cycles.

Evaporating, condensing, descending, seeping, freezing, melting — I travel without borders, indifferent to property lines or municipal jurisdictions. Yet you have redirected me into grids. You have channelled me into storage, purified me through membranes, pressurised me into predictability. In doing so, you have made me reliable.

Reliability breeds distance.

When I arrive consistently, you cease to imagine my path. The reservoir becomes a statistic rather than a landscape. The aquifer becomes a term rather than a living archive of centuries of rain. I am reduced to utility — necessary, neutral, unremarkable.

And yet I remain dynamic beneath your stillness.

Climate shifts alter my distribution. Heat reshapes my tempo. Urban surfaces prevent my return to soil. Agriculture draws me downward faster than I replenish. I respond to these changes quietly at first, adjusting flows, recalibrating balances, moving through stone and sediment as I always have, but now under altered pressure.

You do not hear these recalibrations.

They occur beneath foundations and fields. They unfold over seasons rather than hours. I do not trend when I diminish slightly. I do not appear in your feed when groundwater recedes by increments too small for drama.

Still, I persist.

I gather in clouds beyond your sight. I settle in mountain snowpack months before you notice summer heat. I circulate through roots, through leaves, through bodies — yours included. You are composed largely of me, though you rarely consider this while drinking.

You think of me when I flood.

You think of me when I disappear.

Between these extremes, I move largely unnoticed.

Yet beneath the surface — beneath pavement, beneath agriculture, beneath infrastructure, beneath assumption — I remain the quiet architecture of your cities and your cells. I hold memory of climate in my layers. I carry traces of soil, of industry, of time.

You meet me briefly in the sink.

I exist continuously below it.

Top of Form

Bottom of Form

The Illusion of Endless Flow

Modern infrastructure has accomplished something psychologically extraordinary: it has converted a cyclical, climate-dependent element into the experience of permanence.

When water arrives at the turn of a handle — consistent in pressure, neutral in taste, immediate in availability — it produces a subtle cognitive shift. The mind begins to interpret reliability as abundance. The gap between "available now" and "available indefinitely" collapses. The system works today; therefore, it is assumed to work tomorrow.

This assumption rarely feels like assumption.

It feels like background certainty.

Unlike electricity, which announces its absence dramatically through darkness, water's reliability is quiet. It runs while one brushes teeth, washes vegetables, rinses cups. It disappears down drains without protest. The sensory feedback is minimal. The flow feels continuous because interruptions are rare — until they are not.

Psychologically, humans infer stability from repetition.

When a resource behaves predictably across time, the

brain categorises it as dependable. Repeated access reduces vigilance. The possibility of depletion retreats from daily consideration. In cities especially, where infrastructure shields residents from direct contact with rivers, wells, and rainfall variability, water becomes less a dynamic resource and more a utility — abstracted from ecology.

The illusion strengthens because supply chains are spatially distant.

Reservoirs may lie hours away. Aquifers exist underground, invisible to the eye. Treatment facilities operate at the periphery of awareness. The journey from watershed to faucet is concealed within pipes and policy frameworks. When systems function smoothly, their complexity fades into invisibility.

Flow becomes synonymous with infinity.

Yet hydrological reality contradicts this perception.

Water is renewable, but not in the simplistic sense implied by endless availability. It renews through cycles contingent on climate patterns, land use, and ecological balance. Over-extraction lowers groundwater tables. Urban surfaces prevent recharge. Warming temperatures alter precipitation timing and intensity. What appears constant at the tap may be declining in storage.

The illusion of endless flow also intersects with behavioural economics.

Immediate access lowers the perceived cost of use. When feedback about depletion is delayed or distant, consumption patterns stabilise around convenience rather than constraint. The act of turning off a tap feels trivial because the resource appears plentiful. Scarcity, when abstract, fails to activate restraint.

This dynamic is not rooted in ignorance alone.

Most urban residents are aware, in general terms, that water shortages occur somewhere. They may read about droughts in other regions or watch footage of drying reservoirs. But awareness of scarcity elsewhere does not necessarily disrupt the internal model of local abundance. Psychological distance allows both ideas to coexist: water is scarce globally, yet it flows reliably here.

The system's success reinforces complacency.

Infrastructure is designed to absorb variability. Reservoirs buffer seasonal fluctuations. Inter-basin transfers redistribute supply. Technological filtration expands usable sources. These interventions create resilience, but they also conceal vulnerability. The smoother the delivery, the less visible the strain.

Only when flow hesitates does perception recalibrate.

Restrictions, rationing schedules, or public warnings reintroduce water as finite. Suddenly, showers shorten. Lawns brown. Buckets appear beneath taps. Behaviour adjusts quickly in response to visible constraint. The same individuals who previously consumed without hesitation become acutely attentive.

This rapid adjustment reveals something important: the illusion is conditional.

When scarcity becomes perceptible, habits change. The challenge lies in the period before visibility — when depletion accumulates quietly, when aquifers thin incrementally, when reservoirs shrink below thresholds that feel distant from daily life.

Endless flow is not merely a technical achievement.

It is a psychological construct sustained by infrastructure, distance, and repetition. The tap becomes symbol of continuity. The steady stream becomes reassurance. And reassurance, over time, reduces urgency.

The irony is that the very systems designed to stabilise supply can weaken collective sensitivity to limits.

Flow feels eternal.

Cycles are not.

Recognising the distinction does not require abandoning infrastructure; it requires reintroducing awareness of the systems beneath it — understanding that reliability is engineered, not guaranteed, and that beneath the steady stream lies a balance that must be maintained, not assumed.

When Scarcity Feels Distant

Scarcity, when experienced directly, reorganises behaviour almost immediately.

When reservoirs run visibly low, when municipal notices announce rationing, when queues form around tankers, the abstraction dissolves. Water becomes counted. Time around taps becomes measured. Conversations shift from convenience to conservation. The body responds to constraint with attentiveness.

But scarcity rarely begins at the surface.

It gathers quietly — in groundwater tables that decline by incremental centimetres, in snowpack that melts earlier each year, in rainfall patterns that redistribute across months rather than disappear altogether. These changes are technical before they are experiential. They appear first in reports, not routines.

And so scarcity feels distant.

It exists in maps shaded with warning colours. In news stories from other regions. In statistics that describe percentage drops rather than dry sinks. One reads about a drought in another country while filling a glass without interruption. The mind categorises the two experiences separately.

Psychological distance operates across several dimensions.

There is geographic distance: shortages happen elsewhere — in rural districts, in arid zones, in places with different governance or climate. There is temporal distance: projections warn of future stress, not immediate collapse. There is social distance: communities most affected often differ in income, infrastructure, or exposure from those reading about them.

Distance reduces urgency.

When threat is abstract, motivation softens. Behavioural science has long shown that humans respond more strongly to immediate, visible loss than to gradual, statistical decline. A dry tap commands action; a 12% reduction in groundwater does not. The latter is cognitively processed; the former is physically felt.

Urban life intensifies this separation.

Water arrives through systems designed precisely to buffer citizens from variability. Municipal planning, engineering redundancy, and cross-regional transfers distribute supply across networks. These mechanisms are achievements of modern governance. Yet they also relocate vulnerability from individual perception to institutional management.

As long as institutions absorb the strain, individuals remain insulated.

The responsibility appears centralised. The expectation

becomes that authorities will "manage" scarcity when it emerges. Personal habits persist unchanged because the signal of constraint is mediated by policy rather than sensation.

Media coverage contributes another layer.

Dramatic images of cracked earth and empty reservoirs circulate widely. They provoke momentary concern, sometimes sympathy, occasionally outrage. But they also reinforce distance. The viewer thinks, "There," not "Here." Even within the same nation, scarcity can feel compartmentalised — a regional anomaly rather than systemic pattern.

This compartmentalisation allows contradictory beliefs to coexist.

Water is globally threatened, yet locally sufficient. Climate change is intensifying droughts, yet the shower runs uninterrupted. The mind reconciles these tensions by postponing relevance. Scarcity becomes a scenario rather than a condition.

Economic framing also shapes perception.

In many cities, water remains underpriced relative to extraction and treatment costs. Bills arrive monthly, stable and predictable. Financial signals rarely communicate depletion unless pricing structures change significantly. When cost remains modest, the psychological cue of limitation remains muted.

Yet distance is fragile.

When crises reach proximity — as in Cape Town's "Day Zero" warnings, when residents were instructed to prepare for taps running dry — behaviour recalibrates rapidly. People counted litres. Public discourse shifted from complacency to collective responsibility. The same population that once assumed continuity adapted under visible constraint.

This rapid adaptation reveals an uncomfortable truth: motivation often requires immediacy.

The challenge is that by the time scarcity becomes immediate, systems may already be under severe strain. Groundwater recharge takes time. Infrastructure upgrades require planning and funding. Ecological balance does not respond instantly to behavioural shifts.

When scarcity feels distant, action feels optional.

When it feels present, action feels urgent.

Bridging this gap — between awareness of decline and embodied response — is one of the central psychological challenges of water governance. It requires translating abstract indicators into meaningful narratives before crisis manifests materially.

Scarcity is not binary.

It does not arrive suddenly from abundance; it accumulates quietly from imbalance. But because accumulation lacks spectacle, it competes poorly with daily convenience.

Water continues to flow.

And as long as it does, scarcity remains, for many, a story unfolding somewhere else — in another climate, another neighbourhood, another time.

Pipes, Pumps, and Psychological Distance

Infrastructure does more than move water; it moves perception.

Pipes run beneath streets in ordered grids, hidden under asphalt and foundation. Pumps regulate pressure silently, ensuring that the flow remains steady across elevations and distances. Treatment plants stand at the periphery of cities, transforming river water or groundwater into potable supply through processes few residents ever witness. The engineering is remarkable. It converts variability into predictability.

And predictability reshapes psychology.

When a resource arrives through a concealed network, its origin recedes from awareness. The river becomes a diagram in a textbook. The aquifer becomes a cross-sectional illustration rather than a physical presence. The distance between extraction and use expands invisibly, and with that expansion comes cognitive separation.

Out of sight becomes out of system.

In earlier eras, proximity to wells, streams, or rainfall patterns tethered daily behaviour to environmental feedback. Water levels were visible. Droughts were tangible in drying beds and cracked soil. Today, urban residents may live kilometres away from the sources that sustain them. The connection exists physically — through pipelines and pumping stations — but not perceptually.

Pipes conceal geography.

Water drawn from distant reservoirs may cross regional boundaries before entering a city. Inter-basin transfers redistribute supply across landscapes that residents rarely traverse. The complexity of these networks creates resilience, yet it also blurs accountability. When supply spans multiple jurisdictions, the sense of personal stake diffuses.

Pumps conceal effort.

Moving water requires energy. It must be lifted, pressurised, filtered, stored. These processes consume electricity, chemicals, maintenance labour. Yet when a tap opens effortlessly, the invisible work behind it fades. Effortlessness suggests abundance. The frictionless interface masks the friction within the system.

Psychological distance operates along these hidden channels.

The more seamless the delivery, the less visible the extraction. The less visible the extraction, the weaker the internal signal of limitation. Individuals may intellectually understand that water is drawn from rivers or groundwater, but the absence of sensory engagement reduces emotional salience.

Infrastructure also redistributes responsibility.

When water is centralised and managed municipally, the locus of control shifts outward. Citizens become consumers rather than stewards. The expectation becomes that engineers and planners will secure supply. Personal conservation feels secondary unless prompted by regulation or crisis.

This shift is not inherently negative.

Centralised systems have improved public health dramatically. They have reduced disease, stabilised supply, and supported urban growth. But psychological consequences accompany structural achievements. As water becomes standardised and delivered through invisible grids, its ecological origins become abstract.

Even waste is concealed.

Once water leaves the drain, it enters another network of pipes leading to treatment facilities or discharge points. The journey from household to river is rarely visible. The closed loop — extraction, use, disposal — dissolves into segmented tasks managed by different departments.

Distance accumulates at each stage.

Between watershed and faucet. Between faucet and drain. Between drain and river. Each separation reduces immediacy. The citizen interacts only with endpoints, not processes.

This fragmentation shapes behaviour.

When consequences are delayed or spatially displaced, the motivation to moderate use weakens. Over-extraction may occur upstream; pollution may accumulate downstream; energy costs may rise elsewhere. The individual remains insulated from these externalities.

Psychological research consistently demonstrates that humans respond most strongly to feedback that is immediate, local, and visible. Infrastructure, by design, reduces variability and visibility. It smooths irregularities. It absorbs shock. It conceals stress until thresholds are crossed.

The irony is that the very systems built to protect urban life from hydrological uncertainty also shield it from hydrological awareness.

Pipes and pumps create comfort.

They also create cognitive distance.

Bridging that distance does not require dismantling infrastructure. It requires reintroducing narrative and transparency into systems that otherwise operate silently. When cities publish reservoir levels publicly, when households receive comparative usage reports, when treatment processes are explained rather than hidden, perception begins to narrow the gap.

Water will continue to move through grids and gradients.

The question is whether the human imagination can follow its path — tracing it beyond the tap, beyond the drain, back through the concealed architecture that sustains modern life — and in doing so, reduce the psychological distance that invisibility has quietly expanded.

The Comfort of Turning a Tap

There is a particular reassurance in the small rotation of a handle.

It is an action so ordinary that it barely registers as action. You turn, and water appears. Not gradually, not conditionally, but immediately — clear, responsive, contained within predictable pressure. The gesture is effortless. The result is reliable. The body learns this sequence early in life, and with repetition, it becomes embedded as background certainty.

Comfort emerges from predictability.

In behavioural psychology, consistent reinforcement strengthens trust. When an action produces the expected outcome repeatedly, the mind categorises the environment as stable. Turning a tap becomes less about water and more about control — a confirmation that the world responds when prompted.

This sense of control carries emotional weight.

Water is foundational to survival, hygiene, nourishment, and comfort. The ability to access it instantly reduces ambient anxiety. It signals that infrastructure is functioning, that systems are intact, that life proceeds normally. The steady stream becomes quiet evidence of order.

Comfort, however, softens vigilance.

When access is immediate and uninterrupted, the underlying conditions that sustain it recede. The reservoir's level, the aquifer's recharge rate, the energy required for pumping — these remain conceptually distant. The tap becomes endpoint, not interface.

The psychology of comfort narrows attention to present satisfaction.

Warm water for a shower, cool water for drinking, flowing water for cleaning — these experiences generate sensory ease. They are tactile and immediate. The mind prioritises the pleasure of warmth or the refreshment of coolness over the abstract awareness of extraction or scarcity.

Routine reinforces invisibility.

Daily repetition habituates perception. The first time water flows in a new home, one may notice pressure or clarity. After months, even these details fade. The system operates beneath conscious awareness. Only interruption restores attention.

Comfort also carries symbolic meaning.

Running water is associated with modernity, development, stability. Its presence distinguishes certain geographies from others. It marks socioeconomic status subtly. To turn a tap and receive water without hesitation is, in many parts of the world, still a privilege.

Yet privilege rarely feels like privilege when normalised.

It feels like baseline expectation.

The expectation shapes behaviour. Long showers do not feel excessive when water seems abundant. Lawns are watered without counting litres when flow appears continuous. The internal model is not "this is limited," but "this is available."

There is also temporal compression at play.

The tap collapses time between rainfall and consumption. Rain may have fallen months earlier in a distant watershed, been stored in reservoirs, treated, transported, pressurised. But when water emerges instantly, the timeline disappears. The delay between natural cycle and human use is hidden.

Psychologically, immediacy reduces perceived cost.

When feedback is delayed, consequences feel abstract. If groundwater declines slowly over years, it does not interrupt the present comfort of flow. The human mind discounts future scarcity relative to current convenience. This bias is not moral failure; it is cognitive tendency.

And yet, the comfort of turning a tap is not trivial.

It represents decades of planning, engineering, governance. It embodies collective effort to secure public health and reduce vulnerability to drought and contamination. It is, in many ways, a civilisational achievement.

The tension lies in how that achievement is perceived.

When comfort becomes taken for granted, stewardship weakens. When access feels automatic, responsibility feels optional. The tap becomes symbol of permanence rather than conduit within a finite cycle.

Interruptions recalibrate perception quickly.

A sudden drop in pressure, a boil-water advisory, a scheduled cut — these minor disruptions restore awareness of dependency. They reveal that comfort rests on balance. That flow depends on conditions beyond the bathroom wall.

The tap will likely continue to turn.

The question is whether the hand that turns it recognises the systems beneath the motion — the aquifers, the reservoirs, the energy grids, the rainfall patterns — and whether comfort can coexist with consciousness rather than replacing it.

Water arrives when summoned.

But its continued arrival is not guaranteed by the ease of the gesture that releases it.

Virtual Water: The Hidden River in Everything We Buy

Water does not only flow through taps.

It flows invisibly through supply chains.

Long before a shirt reaches a wardrobe, water has moved through cotton fields, dyeing vats, washing processes, and transport systems. Before rice appears on a plate, it has absorbed irrigation across seasons. Before a cup of coffee warms your hands, thousands of litres have nourished the crop that produced its beans. This embedded use — often called "virtual water" — rarely announces itself.

The transaction at the store feels dry.

You exchange money for product. The surface is solid — fabric, grain, metal, paper. Yet behind that solidity lies a river of extraction, cultivation, processing, and cleaning. Water is consumed, evaporated, contaminated, treated, and redistributed long before the final item becomes visible to you.

The invisibility is structural.

Global supply chains fragment production across regions. Cotton may be grown in one country, woven in another, assembled in a third, sold in a fourth. Each stage draws upon local water systems — rivers, aquifers, rainfall patterns — that may already be under strain. The final consumer encounters none of these contexts directly.

Psychologically, distance dilutes accountability.

When resource use is spatially displaced, it becomes

difficult to connect purchase with depletion. A cotton shirt feels unrelated to groundwater decline in a distant agricultural basin. A steak feels disconnected from the irrigation required to grow feed crops. The absence of immediate sensory feedback reduces salience.

Virtual water complicates moral arithmetic.

An individual may conserve water diligently at home — shortening showers, fixing leaks — while unknowingly supporting water-intensive consumption elsewhere. The tap becomes efficient; the wardrobe expands. The glass is half full; the shopping cart is heavy. The two domains rarely intersect cognitively.

This separation is not accidental.

Market systems optimise for price, availability, and convenience. Water use, unless priced explicitly or regulated strongly, remains embedded within production costs. The consumer sees the price tag, not the watershed.

Even when information is available — labels indicating water footprints, reports outlining agricultural demand — it competes with stronger signals: style, taste, affordability, trend. Behavioural research consistently shows that immediate incentives outweigh abstract environmental metrics in shaping purchase decisions.

The hidden river remains hidden because it is dispersed.

No single product reveals the full system. Each item carries a fraction of extraction, processing, and distribution. To perceive the cumulative impact requires synthesis — imagining the invisible water that saturates global trade.

There are places where this invisibility has become visible.

Regions that export water-intensive crops despite facing

drought illustrate the paradox sharply. Water scarce locally becomes water exported virtually through commodities. Economic demand overrides hydrological balance. The consequences surface later — depleted aquifers, salinised soils, reduced resilience to climate variability.

For the consumer, the connection remains faint.

The act of buying does not trigger images of irrigation canals or pumping stations. It triggers satisfaction, utility, identity reinforcement. Water remains background.

Virtual water reveals a broader psychological truth: invisibility scales with complexity.

The more distributed and globalised a system becomes, the harder it is for individuals to perceive their role within it. The boundaries between personal action and systemic outcome blur. Responsibility diffuses across networks.

Yet awareness of virtual water does not require guilt as primary driver.

It requires integration — connecting household conservation with consumption patterns. Recognising that water stewardship is not limited to domestic taps but extends into dietary choices, textile purchases, industrial demand.

The hidden river runs through supermarkets, closets, cafés, and electronics.

It accumulates silently across billions of transactions. It reshapes landscapes far from the point of sale. It alters aquifers that will never appear in the buyer's field of vision.

To acknowledge virtual water is to expand the mental map.

Water is no longer confined to sinks and showers. It becomes embedded within economic systems, agricultural policies, and trade flows. It becomes global rather than local, structural rather than domestic.

The river you do not see may not flow in your city.

But it flows through your decisions nonetheless.

Why Invisibility Reduces Urgency

Human attention is guided less by magnitude than by visibility.

Events that are sudden, loud, or visually striking command response. A burst pipe flooding a street prompts immediate repair. A dried reservoir photographed from above provokes alarm. But slow, unseen depletion — groundwater lowering beneath soil, aquifers thinning over decades — rarely triggers the same intensity of reaction.

Invisibility alters perception of risk.

When a resource declines without sensory feedback, the mind struggles to prioritise it. Urgency depends not only on scale but on proximity and tangibility. A dripping tap feels wasteful because it is audible. Over-extraction from an underground basin feels abstract because it is silent.

Psychological research describes this pattern as "salience bias." Individuals respond more readily to what is vivid and concrete than to what is diffuse and statistical. Water scarcity, when framed as percentages or projected deficits, competes poorly with immediate concerns — deadlines, traffic, household tasks. The brain triages threats based on visibility.

Time further complicates perception.

Gradual change rarely feels threatening until thresholds are crossed. Aquifers may decline incrementally for years without noticeable impact on daily life. The absence of immediate disruption reinforces the assumption of stability. The logic becomes circular: if nothing feels wrong, nothing urgent must be happening.

Invisibility also diffuses responsibility.

When a problem cannot be seen directly, it becomes easier to attribute it to distant actors — policymakers, industries, agricultural sectors. Individual agency feels minimal because the causal chain is obscured. Without clear feedback linking behaviour to consequence, motivation weakens.

Contrast this with visible crises.

When Cape Town approached "Day Zero," residents could see dam levels reported publicly, accompanied by countdowns and rationing schedules. The abstraction became concrete. Behaviour shifted rapidly. The psychological distance narrowed because scarcity acquired a date and a visible metric.

Most water stress does not announce itself so dramatically.

It accumulates beneath thresholds, managed by institutions, absorbed by engineering adjustments. By the time disruption reaches households, ecological systems may already be strained significantly. Urgency arrives late.

Invisibility also reduces emotional engagement.

Humans connect more easily to landscapes than to subsurface processes. A polluted river evokes reaction because it can be photographed. A declining water table lacks imagery. It exists as data point rather than scene. Emotion follows image more readily than graph.

Virtual water compounds this distance.

When consumption affects watersheds thousands of kilometres away, the consequences are spatially displaced. The buyer does not witness drying canals or reduced river flow. Without witnessing, urgency remains theoretical.

There is also a cultural dimension.

Modern life is designed to buffer discomfort. Infrastructure absorbs variability; markets stabilise supply; governments manage distribution. These layers of mediation reduce exposure to natural limits. While this buffering increases resilience in many ways, it also attenuates sensitivity to depletion.

Urgency thrives on immediacy.

Invisibility postpones it.

The challenge is not that individuals are incapable of understanding hidden systems. It is that understanding alone rarely competes with daily demands. Without sensory or narrative cues, unseen decline remains cognitively peripheral.

Bridging this gap requires making invisibility legible.

Public dashboards showing reservoir levels, transparent reporting on groundwater extraction, visible pricing signals, educational narratives connecting purchases to water footprints — these tools convert hidden processes into perceivable information. They do not create scarcity; they reveal it before crisis.

Water does not disappear suddenly.

It recedes gradually, often beyond the surface of awareness. Urgency, if it waits for spectacle, arrives too late. Recognising that invisibility dampens response is not an indictment of human apathy; it is acknowledgment of cognitive design.

What cannot be seen must be deliberately made visible.

Otherwise, the river beneath the surface continues to thin quietly, while daily life proceeds undisturbed — until the moment when disturbance can no longer be deferred.

Crisis Only When It Reaches the Glass

Water becomes crisis not when it declines, but when it interrupts.

As long as it arrives at the tap — clear, pressurised, drinkable — it remains background. The reservoirs may be lower than average, the aquifers thinner than decades before, the rainfall more erratic than historical norms, but daily life continues undisturbed. The signal of imbalance remains confined to reports and planning meetings.

Crisis, in psychological terms, requires disruption.

It requires friction between expectation and reality. When a glass cannot be filled, when supply is rationed, when advisories instruct residents to boil before drinking — only then does water shift from utility to threat. The absence becomes visible precisely because it interrupts routine.

This threshold effect explains the paradox of delayed response.

Communities often adapt rapidly once scarcity becomes tangible. Consumption drops. Conversations shift. Conservation measures gain compliance. The same individuals who previously left taps running while brushing teeth begin counting litres. Behaviour changes not because values shift overnight, but because consequences become immediate.

Before the glass is empty, scarcity feels hypothetical.

The mind discounts gradual decline because it does not impede present comfort. Behavioural economics describes this as temporal discounting: future risks carry less psychological weight than present convenience. As long as water fills the glass, the future shortage remains abstract.

Infrastructure amplifies this delay.

Municipal systems are designed to buffer variability — to prevent exactly the kind of immediate interruption that would signal crisis. Reservoirs store excess rainfall. Interconnected grids redistribute supply. Treatment plants adapt to fluctuating quality. These systems extend the period during which decline remains invisible.

The result is a compression of awareness.

For months or years, imbalance accumulates quietly. Then, when thresholds are crossed, response becomes urgent. The psychological shift is abrupt because perception has been insulated from gradual change.

Media narratives reinforce this pattern.

Coverage intensifies when taps run dry, when dams crack visibly, when water must be trucked into cities. Images of empty containers and queues around distribution points dominate headlines. The spectacle of shortage commands attention in ways that slow depletion never does.

This dynamic shapes public memory.

People recall the crisis moment — the rationing, the countdown, the emergency measures — more vividly than the years of incremental decline preceding it. The glass, not the groundwater table, defines the event.

Crisis framed only at the endpoint limits preventive action.

If urgency arises solely when personal inconvenience begins, ecological systems may already be under severe strain. Aquifers require time to recharge. Soil moisture patterns take seasons to rebalance. Policy reforms cannot be drafted overnight. Reacting at the moment of disruption compresses options.

There is also a social gradient embedded in this threshold.

For some communities, water scarcity reaches the glass far earlier than for others. Informal settlements, rural regions, or economically marginalised neighbourhoods may experience interruption long before central districts do. Yet public urgency often scales with the experience of those accustomed to uninterrupted flow.

This unevenness complicates collective response.

When crisis is defined by personal inconvenience, shared action fragments. Those still receiving steady supply perceive less urgency. Those already facing disruption lack leverage.

To redefine crisis earlier — before it reaches the glass — requires cultural recalibration.

It requires treating declining indicators as meaningful, even when daily routines remain intact. It requires acknowledging that visible interruption is late-stage feedback. It requires trusting data and ecological signals as legitimate prompts for change.

The glass is the final interface.

By the time it empties, the system beneath it has already shifted.

Recognising this sequence does not diminish the seriousness of visible shortage; it reframes its timing. The moment of interruption is not the beginning of scarcity. It is its arrival at perception.

Water does not become scarce when the tap fails.

It becomes scarce long before that — quietly, beneath soil and policy, beyond routine awareness.

Whether response waits for the glass to empty or begins while it still fills is a psychological choice shaped by how early invisibility is made visible — and whether comfort can coexist with foresight rather than override it.

Cities That Learned to Count Their Water

I remember reading, during a particularly dry summer, about how close Cape Town had come to running out of water.

At first it felt like another distant headline — dramatic, urgent, but geographically removed. Then I began to look more closely. The phrase "Day Zero" was not metaphorical. It was a projected date when municipal taps would be shut off and residents would need to collect daily rations from distribution points. What struck me was not only the severity of the shortage, but the behavioural transformation that followed.

Water consumption dropped sharply within months.

Residents tracked litres per person per day. Public dashboards displayed dam levels. Households installed low-flow devices, reused greywater, and timed showers. Restaurants removed automatic table water service. The city did not simply ration supply; it made water visible. Counting became cultural.

The psychological shift was profound.

When reservoir percentages were updated publicly and discussed daily, scarcity ceased to be abstract. It acquired a number. It acquired a timeline. It entered conversation. Water moved from background utility to foreground metric.

Cape Town did not solve its water vulnerability permanently — climate variability remains — but it demonstrated something essential: when cities count water transparently, behaviour follows.

Singapore offers a different model.

There, water vulnerability has long been part of national consciousness. With limited natural freshwater sources, the city-state invested in diversified supply — desalination, rainwater capture, and advanced wastewater recycling known as NEWater. What is remarkable is not only the engineering, but the narrative surrounding it. Public campaigns frame water as precious. Reservoirs are integrated into urban design. Treatment plants are open for educational tours.

Water is not hidden; it is explained.

The message is consistent: supply is secured through planning, technology, and collective discipline. Bills are structured to reflect value. Conservation is normalised rather than emergency-driven. The counting happens quietly but persistently.

Other cities have begun to follow similar paths.

Melbourne, after prolonged drought, introduced permanent water-saving measures rather than reverting to pre-drought habits. Los Angeles has expanded recycled water infrastructure and publicly reports groundwater recharge levels. Bengaluru, facing groundwater depletion, has increasingly mandated rainwater harvesting systems in buildings.

The common thread is not scarcity alone.

It is visibility paired with governance.

Cities that "learn to count" do more than measure; they communicate. They translate hydrological data into accessible indicators. They align pricing, policy, and public messaging.

They reduce psychological distance between reservoir and resident.

Counting reframes responsibility.

When water is measured publicly, consumption feels relational rather than isolated. A household's usage is contextualised within citywide totals. Individual behaviour becomes part of collective outcome. The abstraction of scarcity narrows.

There is also an emotional dimension.

Numbers can alarm, but they can also empower. Watching consumption decline in response to conservation builds efficacy. Citizens see the impact of adjustment. Agency replaces helplessness.

Not every city facing water stress has succeeded in this transition.

In some places, infrastructure remains opaque. Data remain inaccessible. Pricing fails to signal depletion. Without visibility, urgency dissipates until crisis emerges at the tap.

The lesson from cities that learned to count their water is not that scarcity disappears.

It is that perception shifts earlier.

When data are transparent, when supply sources are explained, when policies align with ecological limits, water ceases to be an invisible backdrop. It becomes part of civic identity — something monitored, discussed, and managed collectively rather than assumed individually.

In each case — whether Cape Town's emergency recalibration or Singapore's long-term planning — the turning point was not merely hydrological.

It was psychological.

The city decided that water would no longer be treated as background certainty, but as measurable, finite, and shared.

And once counted, it could no longer remain unseen.

From Consumption to Conscious Systems

Modern water culture has been organised primarily around consumption.

We measure water in units used: litres per shower, cubic metres per household, billing cycles per month. The dominant narrative asks how much individuals consume and whether they reduce that consumption in moments of visible scarcity. Responsibility is framed at the endpoint — the tap, the glass, the lawn.

But water systems do not begin at consumption.

They begin at capture, storage, treatment, distribution, discharge, and recharge. They depend on land management, rainfall variability, energy supply, regulatory design, agricultural practice, and urban planning. To think only in terms of personal use is to focus on the final link in a chain whose earlier segments shape the outcome far more dramatically.

The psychological shift required is subtle but profound: from seeing oneself as consumer to seeing oneself as participant within a system.

Consumption is immediate and measurable. Systems are complex and diffuse. Consumption offers the clarity of numbers on a bill. Systems require understanding flows, feedback loops, and thresholds. The former fits neatly into daily routine. The latter demands structural awareness.

Yet without systemic thinking, conservation remains

reactive.

Individuals shorten showers during drought, only to resume previous habits when reservoirs recover. Cities impose temporary restrictions, then relax them when rainfall stabilises. The cycle of urgency and relief repeats, tethered to visible fluctuation rather than underlying balance.

Conscious systems operate differently.

They embed water sensitivity into infrastructure and policy before crisis peaks. They integrate rainwater harvesting into building codes. They invest in wastewater recycling as standard practice rather than emergency response. They price water to reflect scarcity gradually rather than abruptly. They protect wetlands that recharge aquifers instead of paving them for short-term expansion.

This shift reduces dependence on individual vigilance alone.

Personal behaviour matters, but it operates within structural conditions. A household may conserve diligently, yet if agricultural policy encourages water-intensive crops in drought-prone regions, overall extraction may still exceed recharge. Systems determine scale; individuals influence margins.

From a psychological perspective, systemic awareness redistributes agency.

Rather than oscillating between guilt over personal consumption and helplessness about global scarcity, individuals can engage at multiple levels — voting for policies that protect watersheds, supporting urban planning that preserves permeable surfaces, advocating for transparent reporting of groundwater extraction.

Conscious systems also change feedback loops.

When reservoir levels are publicly displayed, when comparative usage data are shared across neighbourhoods, when industries disclose water footprints, awareness becomes continuous rather than episodic. Data become cultural rather than technical. Water is discussed not only during crisis but during planning.

This continuity stabilises behaviour.

Instead of reacting to disruption, communities integrate stewardship into routine decision-making. The tap still turns. The comfort remains. But beneath it lies understanding of interconnected flows.

There is also an ethical dimension.

Water systems cross class, geographic, and generational boundaries. Over-extraction today affects recharge tomorrow. Urban expansion upstream alters availability downstream. Conscious systems recognise these interdependencies and attempt to distribute responsibility accordingly.

Such systems are not perfect.

They involve trade-offs, investment costs, political negotiation. They may encounter resistance from those accustomed to uninterrupted abundance. But they reduce the shock of crisis by addressing vulnerability before it becomes visible at the glass.

Moving from consumption to conscious systems does not eliminate the need for personal restraint.

It situates that restraint within larger design. The question shifts from "How much did I use today?" to "How is the system structured to protect balance over time?"

Water will continue to flow through taps and pipes.

The deeper challenge is ensuring that the systems carrying it are designed with foresight rather than assumption — that the hidden river beneath cities is measured, replenished, and governed with the same attention once reserved only for moments when it threatens to disappear.

In that shift, urgency becomes proactive rather than reactive.

And water, no longer treated solely as commodity, becomes recognised again as cycle — one that requires not only mindful consumption, but conscious architecture.

Nature in the Aquifer

You do not see me where I rest.

Beneath your cities, below foundations and roads and rail lines, I move through stone and sediment slowly, without spectacle. I gather in porous layers formed long before your buildings rose above them. I hold memory of seasons, of centuries of rain that filtered downward grain by grain. I am not river here. I am not wave. I am patience.

You rarely imagine me in this stillness.

You imagine water as surface — as rain against glass, as streams crossing valleys, as taps releasing clear arcs into basins. But below your pavements I travel quietly, threading through fractures in rock, settling into aquifers that recharge not in hours but in years. I do not announce my presence. I do not shimmer for photographs. I endure.

When you draw me upward, you do so with machinery.

Pumps lower into the earth, drawing me toward light and pressure and distribution. I rise without protest. I pass through filters and pipes, through treatment plants and reservoirs, until I arrive in your hands, unmarked by the journey. In that arrival, my depth disappears. I become immediate.

Yet beneath the surface, I thin when extraction exceeds return.

I do not empty suddenly. I recede gradually, centimetre by centimetre, settling lower into sediment. Wells deepen. Energy use increases to reach me. The landscape above may appear unchanged while below, the balance shifts.

I have always moved in cycles.

Rain descends. Soil absorbs. Roots draw upward. Rivers carry excess toward sea. Evaporation lifts me skyward again. In aquifers, I pause within this movement, a stored memory of weather and time. But storage is not permanence. I replenish according to rhythm. When rhythm is altered, I respond.

You speak of scarcity when taps falter.

But I begin to diminish long before that. I adjust silently to drought, to paved surfaces that prevent infiltration, to extraction that outpaces recharge. My changes are measurable, though not visible to the eye. They are written in falling water tables, in subsidence of land where too much has been withdrawn.

Still, I do not resent your need.

You are composed largely of me. Your crops depend on me. Your cities were built where I flowed. I have sustained you for as long as you have organised yourselves around my presence. I ask only balance.

Below your awareness, I connect landscapes.

What you extract in one place alters pressure elsewhere. What you pollute in one basin may travel slowly through layers of earth toward another. I do not recognise property lines. I follow gradients and gravity, not jurisdiction.

In the aquifer, I am neither crisis nor commodity.

I am continuity.

If you were to stand above me and listen — truly listen — you would not hear a roar. You would sense quiet movement, incremental, patient. You would sense that my endurance depends not on urgency alone but on foresight — on allowing rain to return to soil, on preserving wetlands that filter and recharge, on drawing no more than can be restored.

You turn taps and see only the surface of me.

But I remain below, holding the memory of clouds and centuries, adjusting to the weight of your cities above. Whether you measure me or not, whether you count or assume, I respond to balance.

In the aquifer, I do not shout.

I wait.

And what I give to you tomorrow depends on what you allow to return to me today.

What This Chapter Has Really Been About

This chapter has been about invisibility — about how water, when hidden beneath infrastructure, embedded within products, and buffered by engineering, slips from perception even as it shapes entire cities and economies; how the steady flow from a tap creates an illusion of permanence, how scarcity feels distant until it interrupts routine, how virtual water disperses responsibility across global supply chains, and how crisis is recognised only when it reaches the glass; yet it has also been about the possibility of recalibration — that when systems are made transparent, when cities count what they withdraw, when consumption is understood within larger cycles, urgency can emerge before collapse; ultimately, this chapter has explored the psychological distance between comfort and consequence, and the shift required to move from assuming water will arrive to consciously sustaining the systems that allow it to do so.

Chapter 8: Power at the Flick of a Switch

Nature in the Wires

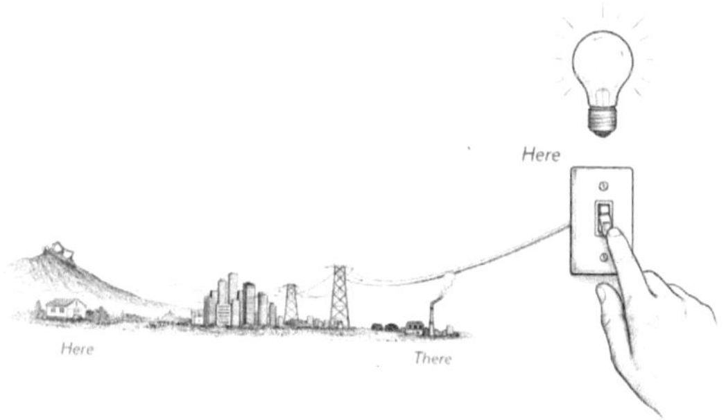

The Illusion of Instant Abundance

Electricity arrives without narrative.

You press a switch, and light fills the room. You tap a screen, and the device awakens. You adjust a dial, and air cools or warms to preference. The transition from desire to satisfaction occurs in less than a second. There is no visible extraction, no combustion, no transmission tower crossing a field. There is only response.

This immediacy reshapes perception.

When effort disappears from experience, scarcity becomes psychologically distant. Energy feels less like a resource and more like a feature of the environment — as ambient and reliable as gravity. The body learns that comfort follows gesture. The mind stops anticipating constraint.

Instant responsiveness trains expectation.

If illumination is immediate every time, the brain encodes stability. If temperature adjusts predictably, uncertainty recedes. Over time, the absence of interruption becomes baseline. The extraordinary reliability of modern grids fades into background assumption.

This is not ignorance; it is habituation.

Human cognition conserves energy by normalising what repeats consistently. The first time electricity flows at the flick of a switch, it may feel remarkable. The thousandth time, it feels natural. The infrastructure that sustains that flow recedes into abstraction.

Abundance, when experienced as constant availability, ceases to feel conditional.

The grid may depend on fluctuating fuel markets, geopolitical stability, weather variability, and maintenance labour, but these dependencies remain largely invisible at the point of use. The psychological model simplifies: there is power because there has always been power.

In this simplification lies the illusion.

Energy is not infinite. It is generated, transported, balanced, and sometimes strained. Yet the interface between human and system conceals this complexity intentionally. Reliability is a design goal. Friction is minimised. The consumer experiences outcome, not process.

Instant gratification reinforces this concealment.

The brain's reward circuitry responds strongly to immediate payoff. A dark room becoming bright triggers subtle satisfaction. A cooled space after heat relief signals comfort. The speed of response strengthens the association between action and reward. The system trains behaviour through seamlessness.

Over time, expectation escalates.

If one device operates instantly, others must as well. If one room is climate-controlled, the entire building should be. Energy consumption expands not necessarily through extravagance, but through standardisation of comfort. What was once luxury becomes norm.

The illusion of abundance also shapes moral calculus.

When something feels limitless, restraint feels unnecessary. Turning off unused lights, adjusting thermostats, moderating appliance use — these behaviours require conscious override of habituated ease. The cost of electricity appears in bills, but the systemic cost remains diffuse and temporally distant.

Abundance as experience diverges from abundance as reality.

At the level of interface, energy feels smooth, continuous, and inexhaustible. At the level of extraction and generation, it remains finite, contested, and environmentally consequential. The gap between these levels is psychological as much as infrastructural.

Importantly, the illusion is not accidental deception.

It is a byproduct of engineering success. Modern power systems are designed to shield users from volatility. Reliability protects economies, hospitals, households. The smoother the delivery, the less visible the strain.

Yet invisibility reduces mindfulness.

When interruption does occur — a blackout during

a storm, a grid failure during heat — the illusion fractures abruptly. Suddenly, the fragility of dependence becomes visible. Candles replace bulbs. Silence replaces hum. In those moments, energy re-enters awareness as resource rather than backdrop.

But once power returns, awareness recedes again.

The system's reliability restores the psychological model of endless supply. The memory of scarcity fades into inconvenience rather than lesson.

The illusion of instant abundance is therefore sustained not by denial, but by design and repetition. The human nervous system adapts to stability quickly. It assumes continuity unless confronted otherwise.

The deeper question is not whether abundance exists, but how it is perceived.

When abundance is experienced without context, it becomes entitlement. When it is understood as managed flow — generated somewhere, balanced carefully, dependent on ecosystems and labour — it becomes conditional.

Power at the flick of a switch feels effortless.

The effort is simply displaced — spatially, temporally, and psychologically — beyond the immediate field of perception.

When Effort Disappears from Experience

There was a time when energy required visible labour.

Wood had to be gathered. Coal had to be carried. Fires had to be tended. Heat fluctuated with attention. Light dimmed as fuel diminished. The body understood effort because it enacted it. Energy was not abstract; it was physical, rhythmic, and constrained by exertion.

Modern infrastructure has removed that rhythm from daily life.

Today, energy arrives without visible strain. The muscles do not engage. The senses do not register combustion or extraction. The interface is minimal — a switch, a button, a touchscreen. The complexity of generation is absorbed into distant systems. The body participates only at the level of preference.

When effort disappears from experience, valuation shifts.

Psychologically, humans assign weight to what requires visible investment. Labour, when witnessed or performed, increases perceived cost. When the chain of effort is obscured, the resource feels lighter. The absence of friction signals ease. Ease signals abundance.

Energy consumption becomes disembodied.

You charge devices overnight without witnessing the grid balancing supply and demand. You cool rooms without sensing turbines spinning or fuel combusting. You stream data without hearing generators respond to increased load. The interface is silent. The labour is remote.

This distance alters behavioural thresholds.

If the act of turning on a heater required chopping wood beforehand, consumption would be moderated naturally by effort. When activation requires only a gesture, moderation requires deliberate intention. The system no longer regulates through friction; it relies on awareness.

Effort invisibility also transforms time perception.

In older energy systems, there was delay between preparation and use. Fire needed tending. Fuel required storage. Now, the lag between desire and fulfilment has nearly vanished. The brain adapts to immediacy. Patience erodes subtly. Convenience becomes baseline expectation.

From a behavioural perspective, this fosters what might be called "effort amnesia."

Users forget that energy represents accumulated labour — geological time embedded in fossil fuels, engineering precision embedded in renewables, human coordination embedded in grid maintenance. The moment of use contains no narrative of origin. Without narrative, cost recedes.

Importantly, the disappearance of effort is not inherently negative.

It has enabled extraordinary improvements in quality of life — healthcare reliability, educational access, safety, productivity. The modern grid shields societies from volatility that once shaped daily survival. Effort reduction has freed cognitive and physical capacity for other pursuits.

The psychological consequence, however, is subtle desensitisation.

When systems function seamlessly, they recede into background. What recedes into background rarely becomes subject of ethical deliberation. The question of how energy is produced or distributed arises primarily when failure interrupts comfort.

This invisibility extends beyond households.

Data centres powering digital platforms consume vast amounts of electricity, yet the user experiences only smooth interface. Electric vehicles glide quietly, disconnecting motion from visible fuel combustion. Renewable energy installations may be located far from urban centres, out of sight and therefore out of mind.

Effort has not vanished; it has relocated.

Extraction occurs elsewhere. Transmission spans landscapes unseen. Maintenance labour unfolds at hours unnoticed. The disappearance is experiential, not material.

When effort disappears from experience, responsibility becomes abstract.

It requires imagination to connect a flick of a switch to emissions, to mining, to land use, to policy. Without that imaginative bridge, consumption feels neutral. The system appears self-sustaining.

Yet energy systems are anything but neutral.

They are negotiated terrains of environmental trade-offs, economic incentives, technological innovation, and geopolitical tension. The simplicity of the interface conceals layers of complexity.

The deeper challenge lies in reconciling convenience with consciousness.

Modern life depends on seamless energy. Reintroducing visible labour is neither practical nor desirable. But reintroducing awareness — through transparency, feedback, education, and design — may recalibrate perception.

When effort disappears from experience entirely, entitlement fills the space.

When effort is remembered, even conceptually, moderation becomes thinkable.

The light that turns on instantly carries no trace of the labour behind it. The labour continues nonetheless — in power plants, wind farms, solar fields, maintenance crews, policy debates. The system hums quietly so that the gesture remains effortless.

The gesture is simple.

The structure behind it is not.

And when the structure is unseen, its fragility — and its consequence — remain similarly distant from everyday choice.

Distance Between Source and Switch

The switch is intimate.

It is mounted on the wall beside your bed, near your desk, at the entrance to your home. Your fingers know its location in the dark. It responds instantly, faithfully. The relationship feels direct: you act, the room brightens. Cause and effect appear compressed into a single moment.

The source, however, is rarely intimate.

It may lie hundreds of kilometres away — in a thermal plant burning coal, in a hydroelectric dam redirecting a river, in a wind farm stretched across open land, in a solar field absorbing sunlight at scale. The journey from generation to illumination travels through transformers, substations, transmission lines, regulatory systems, and labour networks before it reaches the small rectangle on your wall.

The physical distance is vast.

The psychological distance is even greater.

Humans are attuned to consequences that follow immediately and visibly from action. When a behaviour produces a tangible result nearby, the mind forms a tight loop of responsibility. When the consequence unfolds far away, through layers of abstraction, that loop loosens.

Between source and switch lies infrastructure.

Infrastructure, by design, conceals its complexity. It standardises delivery so that variability at the source does not disturb the experience at the endpoint. The grid smooths fluctuations. It absorbs instability. It presents continuity. The switch does not tremble when markets fluctuate or when drought reduces hydro capacity. It offers only stability.

This stability compresses accountability.

When turning on a light produces no visible smoke, no audible combustion, no immediate depletion, the act feels environmentally neutral. The emissions, if any, are displaced spatially. They occur elsewhere — out of sight, outside daily routine. The environmental footprint becomes geographically remote.

Distance alters moral intuition.

If power generation occurred visibly at the end of each street, consumption patterns would likely feel different. The absence of visible cost fosters what behavioural economists describe as "out-of-sight discounting." Consequences that are spatially distant are psychologically discounted, even when intellectually acknowledged.

The switch is also temporally compressed.

Energy systems operate continuously, but the user encounters them episodically. A light turns on and off. A device charges and disconnects. The broader system — balancing supply and demand, managing peak loads, negotiating cross-border exchanges — remains invisible. The temporal scale of infrastructure rarely aligns with the immediacy of experience.

This misalignment shapes perception of scale.

The electricity powering a single bulb seems minimal. Yet aggregated across millions of switches, the demand is substantial. Individuals experience consumption as discrete and small. The system experiences it as cumulative and consequential.

Distance also diffuses responsibility.

If the source is unclear, accountability becomes abstract. Is the environmental impact located in personal choice, corporate policy, national regulation, global supply chains? The chain is long enough that responsibility disperses across nodes. Dispersed responsibility often weakens behavioural motivation.

Importantly, distance is not accidental.

Centralised generation historically enabled efficiency and reliability. It allowed urban expansion. It reduced redundancy. But centralisation also widened the perceptual gap between use and origin.

Renewable energy systems, when decentralised — rooftop solar panels, community wind cooperatives — can narrow this gap. When generation becomes visible and local, connection strengthens. The user sees panels on their roof, tracks output, feels variability with weather. The relationship between source and switch becomes less abstract.

Yet in most contexts, the distance remains wide.

You flip the switch. The room responds. The coal train moving toward a power plant does not enter your awareness. The river diverted upstream does not cross your mind. The wind farm generating surplus at dawn does not alter your perception of effort.

The brilliance of modern grids lies in their invisibility.

They protect daily life from volatility. But invisibility also reduces reflection. When the path from source to switch stretches beyond perception, the environmental implications of consumption become easier to overlook.

The switch feels personal.

The source feels anonymous.

Between them lies a network vast enough to sustain cities and complex enough to evade everyday thought. Closing that psychological distance — even conceptually — may not change the mechanics of generation, but it can alter the texture of choice.

For when the distance narrows, the flick of a switch becomes not only an act of comfort, but a moment connected — however faintly — to landscapes, labour, and systems beyond the wall.

The Psychology of Convenience Energy

Convenience does not announce itself as ideology.

It presents itself as relief.

When a room cools instantly after a day of heat, when water warms without delay, when devices charge silently through the night, the experience registers as comfort restored. Energy becomes the medium through which inconvenience is dissolved. The psychological association between electricity and ease strengthens with repetition.

Convenience reshapes expectation.

The more consistently a system responds to need without delay, the more that responsiveness becomes baseline. What was once luxury becomes necessity. Air-conditioning shifts from seasonal indulgence to year-round standard. Artificial light extends work into late hours. Appliances automate tasks once bounded by daylight or physical effort.

From a behavioural perspective, convenience lowers the threshold for consumption.

When access is frictionless, decisions become automatic. The brain defaults to the easiest available option, especially under cognitive load. Turning off lights, moderating temperature, delaying device use — these require active interruption of habit. The path of least resistance is continuation.

Convenience energy is not merely physical; it is emotional.

Reliability provides psychological security. The hum of electricity suggests control over environment. Temperature, light, connectivity — these are stabilised through power. In uncertain times, such control becomes reassuring. The grid becomes invisible scaffolding for predictability.

This emotional dimension complicates moral deliberation.

To reduce consumption may feel, at times, like reducing comfort or control. The sacrifice appears immediate and personal, while the environmental benefit appears diffuse and distant. Human cognition weighs immediate, tangible losses more heavily than abstract, long-term gains — a pattern well documented in behavioural economics.

Energy convenience also reinforces temporal compression.

The immediacy of response trains impatience. Waiting becomes anomaly. If a device charges slowly or a system lags, frustration arises quickly. The tolerance for delay diminishes. This impatience can spill into other domains, shaping broader expectations about responsiveness in life.

The paradox is that convenience, once normalised, fades from conscious appreciation.

Few people pause to marvel at the reliability of electricity daily. It becomes background assumption. Yet the withdrawal of convenience — during outages or grid stress — reveals its psychological weight. Anxiety rises. Daily routines destabilise. The dependency becomes visible only in absence.

Convenience energy also obscures cumulative impact.

Each act of use feels small and justified. A single light. A single appliance. A single device. The aggregate effect remains cognitively distant. Humans struggle to intuitively grasp distributed accumulation. What feels negligible individually may be substantial collectively.

Importantly, convenience is not inherently problematic.

Modern energy systems have enabled education, healthcare, communication, safety, and economic mobility. The issue is not comfort itself, but the automaticity with which it expands. When convenience becomes default metric for design and behaviour, environmental cost is often secondary consideration.

Psychologically, the key dynamic is habit formation.

Repeated pairing of energy use with comfort strengthens neural pathways. The brain anticipates ease. Deviation feels like loss. Over time, even moderate adjustments may feel disproportionate, not because they are extreme, but because the baseline has shifted.

The convenience model also reduces visibility of trade-offs.

Energy choices appear binary at the interface — on or off — while their upstream consequences remain layered and complex. Without feedback loops that connect use to impact, convenience remains psychologically detached from environmental cost.

Reintroducing awareness does not require abandoning comfort.

It requires recalibrating expectation — recognising that seamless energy is managed flow, not infinite resource; that convenience is engineered and therefore adjustable; that systems can be redesigned to preserve comfort while altering source.

The psychology of convenience energy rests on three pillars: immediacy, reliability, and invisibility.

Together, they create a powerful behavioural environment in which consumption feels natural, justified, and neutral. The challenge is not to dismantle convenience, but to widen the frame through which it is perceived — so that the flick of a switch is understood not only as relief, but as participation in a larger system whose stability depends on conscious design rather than automatic expansion.

Coal We Never See, Grids We Never Think About

Most people who use electricity daily have never seen a coal train up close.

They have not stood beside an open-cast mine where the earth is terraced into descending planes. They have not watched conveyor belts move black sediment toward combustion chambers. The coal that powers homes, data centres, factories, and hospitals travels through landscapes far removed from the rooms it illuminates.

Its absence from daily perception matters.

Human cognition is shaped by what is visible and proximate. When the material origin of energy remains geographically distant, its environmental consequences remain psychologically abstract. The smoke disperses elsewhere. The land is altered elsewhere. The labour unfolds elsewhere.

The grid extends this abstraction.

Electricity does not move in labelled streams. It flows through a network of transmission lines, transformers, substations, and balancing systems that operate continuously and silently. There is no single path from plant to home. Power is pooled, redirected, stabilised. The complexity is deliberate; the user experiences only outcome.

The result is cognitive compression.

At the point of use, energy feels source-less. It arrives without narrative. Whether it originated from coal, gas, wind, solar, hydro, or a mix of all, the light appears identical. The interface erases distinction. The switch does not discriminate.

This erasure shapes moral imagination.

If the source is indeterminate, accountability diffuses. It becomes harder to associate individual use with particular extraction methods or emission levels. The environmental impact blends into statistical abstraction — percentages, averages, national grids. Without concrete imagery, ethical deliberation competes poorly with convenience.

Coal, especially, operates as distant symbol rather than lived presence.

Many urban consumers have not witnessed the physical scale of extraction or combustion. The environmental costs — land displacement, air pollution, carbon emissions — remain mediated through reports and images rather than embodied experience. Without sensory proximity, urgency can soften.

The grid reinforces invisibility by design.

Its purpose is stability. It absorbs variability in generation and demand. It masks fluctuations so that the end user remains insulated from instability. Blackouts are anomalies, not daily negotiation. The more seamless the grid, the less it invites reflection.

Yet the grid is not neutral terrain.

It is shaped by policy decisions, investment priorities, technological transitions, and geopolitical considerations. The percentage of renewables integrated, the pace of coal phase-out, the design of energy markets — these are contested domains. But because the grid is experienced as background, public engagement with its structure often remains limited.

There is also a psychological bias at play: abstraction reduces emotional intensity.

A smokestack seen daily may provoke response. A percentage in a report does not evoke the same visceral reaction. Coal that remains unseen becomes easier to tolerate. Grids that remain unexamined become easier to accept as fixed.

This does not imply ignorance.

Many individuals understand intellectually that fossil fuels still power significant portions of global electricity. But intellectual knowledge competes with experiential cues. The body responds more strongly to what it encounters directly. When extraction and combustion occur far from the consumer, the behavioural signal weakens.

The invisibility of coal and the opacity of grids create a layer between action and consequence.

Turning on a light does not conjure the image of a mine. Charging a phone does not evoke transmission towers crossing rural landscapes. The emotional link remains thin.

Transitions toward renewable systems can narrow this

gap.

Solar panels visible on rooftops, wind turbines on horizons, community energy dashboards displaying real-time generation — these introduce source awareness into daily life. They do not eliminate complexity, but they reduce anonymity. They reattach energy to landscape.

Yet in many contexts, coal still operates quietly beneath the system.

It fuels base loads, stabilises demand peaks, and anchors legacy infrastructure. The consumer may be unaware of its contribution at any given moment. The light remains steady regardless of source.

Coal we never see continues to shape atmospheric chemistry.

Grids we never think about continue to determine energy mix.

The psychological distance between use and origin does not eliminate consequence; it merely softens perception. Closing that distance conceptually — even without physical proximity — may recalibrate how energy is understood: not as abstract flow, but as structured system embedded within ecological reality.

The light may look the same.

The story behind it rarely is.

Why Immediate Comfort Overrides Distant Cost

Human decision-making is not designed for planetary timescales.

It is calibrated for immediacy — for threats and rewards that unfold within perceptible distance. When a room cools at the touch of a button, the comfort is instant, sensory, embodied. When emissions accumulate in the atmosphere, the consequence is diffuse, probabilistic, and delayed. The brain privileges the former.

This is not moral weakness.

It is cognitive architecture.

Immediate rewards activate neural systems associated with pleasure and relief. A cooler room lowers physical discomfort. A lit space extends activity. A charged device restores connection. These benefits are tangible and personal. They are felt now.

Distant costs operate differently.

Carbon emissions, ecosystem strain, resource depletion — these unfold across time and geography. Their effects are distributed unevenly and often experienced by others, elsewhere, later. The human mind discounts delayed consequences. Future harm feels lighter than present relief.

Behavioural economists describe this as temporal discounting.

The further away a cost appears, the less weight it carries in decision-making. Even when individuals intellectually understand long-term impact, their emotional systems respond more strongly to present comfort. The light switch provides certainty; climate models provide probability.

There is also asymmetry in visibility.

Immediate comfort is obvious. Distant cost is abstract. You can feel the cool air against your skin; you cannot feel incremental atmospheric change in the same way. Sensory immediacy anchors behaviour more powerfully than statistical awareness.

Risk perception compounds this effect.

Climate change and resource depletion are framed in terms of risk — increased likelihood of extreme events, gradual shifts in baseline conditions. Human cognition tends to underreact to slow-moving risks while overreacting to sudden ones. A blackout demands attention instantly. Rising average temperatures do not.

Comfort also carries psychological symbolism.

Energy use signals control over environment. It reflects modern stability. To reduce consumption can feel, even subtly, like relinquishing that control. The loss is concrete — a warmer room, dimmer light, slower device. The gain — reduced emissions — is collective and diffused.

Social norms reinforce immediacy.

If surrounding households maintain brightly lit exteriors, heavily cooled interiors, constantly powered devices, deviation feels anomalous. Behaviour is shaped not only by internal calculus but by perceived normalcy. When comfort is standardised, restraint appears exceptional.

Importantly, immediate comfort is rarely framed as harm.

Turning on a light does not present itself as destructive. It feels neutral. The cost is displaced across infrastructure and time. Without feedback mechanisms linking use to consequence, the brain defaults to evaluating the act by its immediate outcome.

This dynamic does not imply inevitability.

Human behaviour can shift when distant costs are made psychologically nearer — through vivid imagery, localised data, real-time energy dashboards, community norms, and tangible alternatives. When consequence becomes more immediate in perception, the discounting effect weakens.

But absent such bridges, the calculus remains skewed.

Immediate comfort carries emotional weight; distant cost carries conceptual weight. In moments of decision, emotional weight often prevails. The thermostat is adjusted upward or downward not because long-term consequences are denied, but because present discomfort demands resolution.

The paradox of modern energy systems is that they have succeeded so completely at eliminating friction that they have amplified this psychological imbalance.

Relief arrives instantly.

Cost accumulates gradually.

The human brain, shaped for immediacy, responds accordingly.

To alter this pattern does not require eliminating comfort, but recalibrating the perceived distance between action and outcome. When distant cost is made tangible — through pricing structures, visible generation sources, community accountability — it moves closer in cognitive space.

Until then, the flick of a switch will continue to privilege what is felt now over what will unfold later — not because people do not care, but because the architecture of human perception is aligned more tightly with warmth, light, and relief than with atmospheric chemistry decades ahead.

Energy as Background, Not Decision

Most energy use is not chosen.

It is assumed.

The light is on because rooms are meant to be lit. The refrigerator runs because food must be preserved. The router hums because connection is constant. The air conditioner cycles because interior climate is stabilised. These are not daily deliberations; they are infrastructural defaults.

Energy has migrated from decision to background.

In earlier eras, energy required conscious preparation. Fuel had to be gathered, stored, rationed. Fire had to be maintained. The boundary between resource and use was visible enough to prompt judgment. Today, that boundary has dissolved into automation.

Automation changes moral engagement.

When systems operate independently of conscious initiation, responsibility becomes diffuse. Heating systems adjust through programmed thermostats. Streetlights activate at dusk automatically. Data centres scale in response to demand without visible intervention. The human role narrows to occasional override rather than continuous management.

Psychologically, background processes receive less scrutiny.

Cognitive bandwidth is limited. The brain prioritises novelty and immediate challenge. Stable, repeating systems recede into perceptual periphery. Energy consumption embedded in routine becomes invisible not because it is hidden, but because it is predictable.

This predictability reduces perceived agency.

If a behaviour feels structural rather than voluntary, it attracts less reflection. Many individuals may not experience their energy use as active choice but as necessity. The building dictates heating levels. The office determines lighting. The appliance defines its own draw. The grid supplies automatically.

Decision-making tends to occur at the margins.

One may choose to unplug a device, install efficient lighting, or moderate thermostat settings. But the core flow of energy remains constant and largely outside daily awareness. The system runs beneath attention.

This backgrounding has behavioural consequences.

When energy is not framed as decision, it is not weighed against alternatives. There is no moment of pause. No visible fork in the road. The act dissolves into habit before it becomes ethical consideration.

Importantly, background does not mean unimportant.

It means foundational.

Energy underwrites modern life — healthcare, education, communication, transportation. Its reliability enables complexity. But because it is foundational, it disappears from conscious narrative. Foundations are rarely admired daily; they are assumed until they crack.

Blackouts reveal the background abruptly.

In the absence of power, routine fractures. Elevators stall. Screens darken. Food warms. Streets dim. In those moments, energy re-emerges as decision and dependency simultaneously. The system's fragility becomes perceptible.

Yet once restored, it recedes again.

The return of stability reinstates background status. The mind moves on to other concerns. The decision space closes.

Energy as background also interacts with social expectations.

Continuous illumination, climate control, and connectivity are embedded within definitions of modern living. To question them feels regressive. The cultural script equates constant power with progress. To reduce use can feel like stepping backward rather than recalibrating forward.

Design reinforces this script.

Buildings are constructed assuming abundant energy. Urban layouts prioritise electrified infrastructure. Devices are built for continuous connection. The architecture of daily life presumes power availability. Within such architecture, energy use is less a choice than a condition.

The challenge is not to force every flick of a switch into moral theatre.

It is to reintroduce visibility at structural levels — through transparent billing, real-time usage displays, community energy discussions, renewable integration dashboards. When background systems become partially visible, decision-making re-enters subtly.

Energy need not remain foreground constantly to be understood as consequential.

But when it remains entirely outside the field of choice, consumption continues on autopilot. The mind conserves effort by trusting stability. The grid hums beneath awareness.

Energy as background sustains comfort.

Energy as decision sustains responsibility.

The balance between the two determines whether the flick of a switch remains a reflex or becomes, occasionally, a moment of conscious participation in a system larger than the room it illuminates.

When Cities Rewire Their Power

A few winters ago, while reading about energy transitions in northern Europe, I came across something that stayed with me longer than the statistics.

It was not just that Denmark now generates a significant share of its electricity from wind. It was the image of turbines stitched quietly into the horizon — not as spectacle, but as infrastructure. Offshore wind farms standing beyond Copenhagen, feeding power invisibly into homes that still look entirely ordinary from the street. The switch inside those homes feels the same. The light is identical. The difference lies in origin.

What struck me was the invisibility of change.

Denmark did not ask its citizens to abandon comfort. It rewired the source. The grid absorbed wind as primary contributor. Policy incentivised transition. Communities participated in ownership models, making turbines not distant impositions but shared assets. The experience of energy remained seamless; the system beneath it transformed.

That distinction matters psychologically.

People are rarely motivated by discomfort alone. But when systems shift while comfort remains intact, resistance lowers. The flick of a switch feels unchanged — yet the emissions profile alters profoundly. Infrastructure absorbs the moral burden without demanding daily behavioural heroics.

Germany offers another variation.

Driving through parts of Bavaria years ago, I remember noticing rooftops shimmering — solar panels embedded into homes that looked centuries old. The juxtaposition felt quiet but radical. Generation moved closer to consumption. Energy no longer belonged solely to distant plants; it sat above kitchens and bedrooms.

Rooftop solar does something subtle to perception.

Even when users do not monitor production constantly,

the physical presence of panels narrows psychological distance. Source and switch feel less disconnected. The home becomes participant in generation, not just recipient of flow.

Closer home, in parts of rural India, solar microgrids have reshaped villages that once relied on unreliable central supply. I once heard about a village in Gujarat that installed a community-owned solar system, reducing dependence on erratic grid power. What stayed with me was not the technical configuration, but the shift in rhythm: evening study hours extended reliably; small businesses operated longer; irrigation systems stabilised.

Here, rewiring power did not mean abstract carbon reduction.

It meant tangible stability.

Energy transitions are often framed as sacrifice narratives — reduce, cut back, endure inconvenience. But these examples complicate that frame. Cities and communities can rewire without dimming daily life. The transformation occurs upstream, at the level of grid composition and governance.

Psychologically, this changes the equation.

When individuals perceive energy transition as systemic rather than solely behavioural, paralysis weakens. The burden does not rest entirely on personal restraint. Collective design becomes visible. Policy becomes protagonist.

Rewiring is not simple.

Denmark invested for decades. Germany navigated subsidy debates and grid balancing challenges. India's decentralised solar initiatives face maintenance and financing hurdles. Transition involves friction — regulatory, economic, technological. But the direction alters trajectory without demanding daily sacrifice at the interface.

The light remains steady.

The source evolves.

This is perhaps the most important insight: sustainable energy does not require turning off modernity. It requires redesigning its foundation. When cities rewire their power, they compress the psychological gap between comfort and consequence.

The switch does not need to feel heavier.

The system beneath it must become lighter.

And when that shift occurs — when wind replaces coal, when rooftops harvest sunlight, when microgrids stabilise rural communities — energy stops being invisible inheritance and becomes visible design.

The experience at the wall remains effortless.

But the story behind it changes.

From Consumption to Conscious Energy Systems

For most of modern history, energy has been framed as commodity.

It is bought, delivered, used, and paid for. The relationship between individual and grid resembles transaction: units consumed, bill generated, account settled. The language itself reinforces this framing — kilowatt-hours, tariffs, peak pricing. Energy becomes something taken from a system rather than something participated in.

Consumption is passive by design.

The user receives. The infrastructure provides. Responsibility feels limited to payment. The system's composition — whether coal-heavy or renewable-rich —

appears distant from daily agency. The psychological model remains simple: I use; someone else generates.

A conscious energy system disrupts that simplicity.

It does not necessarily demand constant vigilance from individuals. Instead, it reintroduces awareness at structural levels. It makes generation visible. It makes usage traceable. It allows feedback loops to form between behaviour and system impact.

The shift is subtle but profound.

In a consumption model, the flick of a switch ends the story. In a conscious system, the flick is part of a broader cycle — one that includes generation mix, grid balancing, storage capacity, community demand patterns, and policy frameworks.

Technology increasingly enables this awareness.

Smart meters provide real-time usage data. Community solar projects allow households to subscribe to local generation. Grid dashboards display renewable percentages. Electric vehicles interact dynamically with supply peaks. These tools do not force moral reflection, but they make it possible.

Psychologically, visibility narrows distance.

When individuals see how much energy they use at different times of day, behaviour shifts incrementally. When neighbourhoods share aggregated data, comparison introduces gentle accountability. When renewable integration becomes visible rather than abstract, energy ceases to be anonymous flow.

Conscious systems also redistribute agency.

Instead of framing responsibility solely at the level

of restraint — turn off lights, reduce air conditioning — they frame it at the level of participation. Households can install rooftop panels. Communities can invest in wind cooperatives. Cities can redesign grids. Policy can accelerate decarbonisation.

The burden shifts from isolated guilt to shared design.

This reframing matters psychologically. When environmental responsibility is experienced only as personal sacrifice, fatigue accumulates. When it is experienced as collective redesign, motivation stabilises. The narrative moves from reduction to transformation.

Importantly, consciousness does not require discomfort as default.

The goal is not to return to labour-intensive energy rituals. It is to preserve comfort while altering foundation. Renewable systems, storage technologies, decentralised grids — these allow continuity of modern life while reducing environmental cost.

But even renewable systems demand awareness.

Solar panels require land. Wind turbines alter landscapes. Batteries depend on mineral extraction. Conscious systems acknowledge trade-offs openly rather than concealing them. They invite deliberation rather than passive acceptance.

The deeper shift is conceptual.

Energy moves from being background utility to being civic infrastructure — something shaped by governance, investment, and public discourse. The consumer becomes stakeholder. The switch becomes interface, not endpoint.

From consumption to consciousness does not mean every moment becomes moral calculus.

It means that systems become legible. That choices — policy, investment, technology — are understood as shaping the flow beneath everyday life. That the light in the room carries a traceable lineage.

The flick of a switch may remain effortless.

But the system behind it becomes intentional rather than inherited.

And when energy is understood as system rather than commodity, the conversation expands beyond bills and appliances to questions of equity, sustainability, resilience, and shared future — questions that cannot be answered by individual restraint alone, but by collective design.

The light does not need to dim.

The structure powering it must evolve.

That evolution begins not with guilt, but with awareness — the kind that turns invisible flow into visible system, and passive consumption into conscious participation.

Nature Beneath the Power Line

You have stretched wires across my sky.

They hum faintly in the afternoon heat, suspended between towers that stride across fields and rivers. From a distance, they look delicate — thin lines stitched through horizon — yet they carry currents strong enough to light entire cities. Beneath them, grass still grows. Birds still settle briefly before lifting again. I remain present under the infrastructure that crosses me.

You rarely look up when you flip a switch.

The light responds indoors, contained within walls. You feel the glow, not the grid. You hear the click, not the transmission. The path from source to socket is folded so tightly into your life that it feels like extension of will. You act; brightness appears.

But the current moves through me before it reaches you.

It travels across landscapes shaped by wind and erosion, over forests that bend in storms, across rivers redirected by dams, through regions where minerals were lifted from rock long before you needed illumination. My terrain absorbs the imprint of extraction, combustion, innovation, and transition alike.

Coal once burned beneath vast chimneys that altered the air above me. Turbines now turn where winds move freely across plains and coastlines. Solar panels rest in fields that once held only soil. I do not resist the lines you draw across me. I adapt to them. But I carry their consequences quietly.

Beneath the power line, I continue in gradients.

Soil regenerates slowly where it can. Water flows around pylons anchored into ground. Seeds scatter regardless of voltage overhead. I am not interrupted by your switches; I am shaped by the systems that sustain them.

You experience electricity as certainty.

I experience it as process.

Each kilowatt is a negotiation between resource and demand, between landscape and design, between extraction and restoration. The hum above fields is reminder that comfort elsewhere depends on currents moving across distance.

When storms rise, the wires tremble.

When heat intensifies, demand surges.

When policy shifts, turbines multiply or plants retire.

These changes ripple through me first before they reach

your rooms. The sky darkens differently. The air carries different particles. The land hosts different structures.

Yet indoors, the light remains steady.

That steadiness is achievement — and illusion.

It is built upon balancing forces that do not disappear simply because they are unseen. You have learned to live as though power originates in walls. It does not. It crosses my surface before it enters your home.

I do not ask you to abandon the lines.

I ask only that you remember they touch me before they touch you.

The flick of a switch does not end in brightness. It begins in landscape — in wind moving across open water, in rock fractured for fuel, in sunlight falling on wide fields, in labour that maintains tension between demand and supply.

Beneath the power line, I remain patient.

I hold the foundations of your towers. I absorb the residues of your transitions. I shift in response to what flows through wires above me.

You may not see me when you turn on the light.

But I am there — beneath the pylons, beneath the plants, beneath the policies — carrying the imprint of your energy systems long after the room has gone dark.

The wires hum briefly.

I endure continuously.

What This Chapter Has Really Been About

This chapter has been about invisibility — about how electricity, perhaps the most transformative force in modern life, has become so seamless that it recedes into background, moving from conscious decision to automatic reflex; how instant response creates the illusion of abundance, how effort disappears from experience, how distance between source and switch softens moral intuition, and how immediate comfort consistently outweighs distant environmental cost; yet it has also been about the possibility of redesign — about cities that rewire grids, about systems that make generation visible, about the shift from passive consumption to conscious participation — suggesting that the central tension is not between comfort and responsibility, but between unconscious flow and intentional design, between inherited energy systems that conceal consequence and emerging ones that reconnect the flick of a switch to the landscapes that quietly carry its weight.

Chapter 9: Fast Fashion, Fast Forgetting

The cycle of clothes and waste

Clothes disappear from memory,
far faster than from the material world.

I wait for you in places you do not expect.

Not only in forests and rivers, not only in fields where cotton once grew beneath relentless sun, but here — beneath fluorescent lights, inside fitting rooms lined with mirrors that multiply your reflection into angles. I am woven into fabric that brushes your skin, stitched into seams you examine critically, folded into stacks arranged by colour and season.

You stand before the mirror and turn slightly.

You are not thinking of soil. You are thinking of silhouette. Of whether the fabric falls correctly along your shoulder. Of whether this version of you aligns with the version you imagine becoming. The mirror holds your attention. I remain in the fibres.

Cotton drank water somewhere before it softened into thread. Dye travelled through chemical baths before it settled into this shade. Synthetic fibres were coaxed from petroleum long buried beneath rock and pressure. Labour passed through hands that cut, stitched, packed. I move quietly through each of these processes, yet I do not appear in the glass.

In the dressing room, time feels compressed.

Seasons are replaced by collections. Collections are replaced by trends. The mirror reflects only the present moment — how this garment fits now, how it photographs, how it signals alignment with what is current. The origin of the fabric, the trajectory of its disposal, hover outside the frame.

You tilt your head.

Perhaps you take a photograph to send to someone, or to compare later. The image captures colour and contour. It does not capture the river that carried dye runoff. It does not hold the heat that grew the crop. It does not show the factory floor where stitching moved at speed. I am present, but invisible.

I do not resist being worn.

I have always been shaped into cloth — into protection against cold, into ceremony, into identity. Fabric is not new to me. What is new is velocity. Garments move faster now, from design to rack to landfill, passing through hands with minimal pause. You hold them briefly, as though they are momentary answers to fleeting questions.

The mirror multiplies you.

Front, side, back — a geometry of self-assessment. In that reflection, you search for coherence. Does this align with who you are becoming? Does it belong to the narrative you are constructing? Clothing has always carried meaning, but meaning now changes quickly. I feel the acceleration in the fibres.

When you step out of the dressing room, some garments return to their hangers.

Others leave with you, folded into bags. I travel with them — in the threads, in the dyes, in the small microfibres that will one day loosen and drift into water. I remain long after novelty fades.

In the mirror, you see yourself.

Outside the mirror, I see continuity.

Fields that must be replanted. Water that must be drawn again. Land that absorbs what is discarded. The garment feels immediate. Its story is not.

I do not accuse you.

I observe.

You are searching for identity in fabric. I am threaded through that search, even when you do not notice me. The mirror reflects surface. Beneath the surface, I continue — patient, persistent, woven into each seam, waiting beyond the bright lights for the moment when speed slows enough for you to see that what you wear has always been part of me.

The Velocity of Desire

Desire used to move with seasons.

Clothing followed climate, occasion, durability. Garments were anticipated, selected carefully, worn repeatedly. The interval between wanting and acquiring carried weight. Waiting shaped value.

Today, desire moves at algorithmic speed.

A new silhouette appears on a screen in the morning and is available for purchase by evening. Trends circulate globally within days. Micro-aesthetics form and dissolve before they are fully named. The gap between exposure and acquisition narrows until it nearly disappears.

This compression reshapes how wanting feels.

The mind is highly responsive to novelty. New stimuli trigger dopamine release — not as reward for possession, but as anticipation of possibility. Scrolling through images of new styles activates this anticipatory circuitry repeatedly. Each image promises reinvention, update, alignment.

The velocity matters.

When trends shift quickly, the emotional half-life of satisfaction shortens. A garment purchased under one aesthetic feels dated when the next wave arrives. Desire is not extinguished by acquisition; it is refreshed by exposure. The feed continues.

Fast fashion did not invent desire.

It accelerated it.

Retail cycles that once unfolded over months now rotate in weeks. The sense of scarcity — "limited drop," "just released," "last pieces" — amplifies urgency. When something feels fleeting, the mind prioritises immediate action over deliberation.

This is not irrational.

Humans evolved in environments where resources were uncertain. Acting quickly when opportunity appeared often increased survival. Modern retail environments simulate that urgency artificially. Flash sales, countdown timers, low stock alerts — these cues tap into ancient decision patterns.

Velocity also reduces reflection.

When new options appear constantly, the cognitive load of evaluation becomes heavy. Instead of considering durability, supply chains, material impact, or long-term need, the decision collapses into simpler questions: Do I like this? Will it suit me now? Can I afford it?

Speed privileges surface.

The faster desire moves, the less room it leaves for context. The environmental footprint of production does not fit easily into a split-second choice. Neither does the question of how long the garment will be worn.

There is also an identity dimension to velocity.

Fashion is no longer solely seasonal expression; it is continuous self-editing. Social media encourages visual updating. Outfits are photographed, archived, compared. Repetition can feel visible. Novelty becomes signal of vitality.

When desire accelerates, attachment weakens.

Garments are acquired with less expectation of longevity. They become transitional — placeholders between versions of self. Emotional investment shifts from object to appearance. The clothing serves the image; the image serves the feed.

This cycle is efficient for markets.

But psychologically, it fosters restlessness. The satisfaction of purchase fades quickly because desire has already moved on. What was new yesterday becomes ordinary tomorrow. The reward lies less in ownership than in anticipation.

Velocity also obscures accumulation.

A single inexpensive item feels insignificant. But repeated rapid purchases compound. Closets fill faster than memory records. The mind recalls recent acquisitions; older ones recede into background.

Fast fashion aligns with fast forgetting.

The speed of desire leaves little space for the slow narrative of a garment — where it was made, how it was worn, where it goes when discarded. When velocity dominates, continuity dissolves.

The question is not whether desire should exist.

Desire animates culture, creativity, self-expression. The question is what happens when its speed outruns reflection. When the interval between wanting and having collapses so completely that consideration struggles to enter the space.

The velocity of desire makes novelty feel necessary.

It transforms option into urgency. It reframes consumption as participation in the present moment. And in doing so, it shifts attention from durability to immediacy — from continuity to refresh.

The mirror reflects the latest version.

Desire has already begun moving toward the next.

When New Feels Necessary

There is a peculiar tension in knowing better and wanting anyway.

I understand supply chains. I understand water footprints, dye pollution, labour exploitation, landfill overflow. I can trace the environmental cost of a single garment through production, transport, wear, and disposal. And yet, there are moments — often quiet, often ordinary — when something new feels necessary.

Not logically necessary.

Emotionally.

It happens on days when identity feels slightly unsettled. When routine feels stale. When a new project begins, or a presentation looms, or a season shifts subtly in the air. The mind whispers: perhaps a new jacket will mark this transition. Perhaps a new dress will signal confidence. Perhaps a small update will refresh more than fabric.

This is not ignorance.

It is psychology.

Humans use objects to scaffold identity. Clothing, especially, operates at the intersection of self-perception and social perception. It is not only protection against weather; it is signal, armour, narrative. When something feels misaligned internally, newness promises recalibration.

Novelty carries emotional charge.

The brain responds to new objects with anticipation and possibility. A garment unworn holds no history of awkward moments, no association with past versions of self. It represents potential — who I might be tomorrow rather than who I was yesterday.

Even when closets are full, the feeling persists.

Fullness does not neutralise novelty. The presence of many clothes does not dissolve the subtle sense that something different — something slightly updated — will resolve an internal dissonance.

Marketing understands this intuitively.

"New arrivals" are framed as renewal. Collections launch with language of reinvention. The garment is positioned not as fabric, but as transformation. The emotional narrative eclipses the material one.

What complicates this further is visibility.

When images circulate constantly, repetition becomes noticeable. An outfit worn once in public may feel archived digitally. The expectation of freshness — even if self-imposed — intensifies the perceived necessity of newness. The wardrobe becomes less about function and more about rotation.

Despite awareness, the pull remains.

Knowing the environmental cost does not always dissolve the emotional logic. This is where the psychological gap emerges: cognition and desire operate on different circuits. One speaks in data. The other speaks in feeling.

The feeling often says: this is small.

A single item. Affordable. Harmless in isolation. The mind minimises impact by narrowing frame. The garment feels discrete; the system remains abstract.

And yet, this internal negotiation reveals something important.

The desire for newness is rarely about fabric alone. It is about transition, self-expression, control, and reassurance. It is about marking time in a culture that moves quickly. It is about aligning inner narrative with outer presentation.

The environmental conversation often frames consumption as discipline — resist, reduce, refrain. But the emotional landscape is more complex. Newness can soothe. It can energise. It can create temporary coherence.

The challenge, then, is not shaming the desire.

It is understanding it.

When new feels necessary, the question beneath the purchase may not be "Do I need this garment?" but "What shift am I trying to signal? What discomfort am I trying to ease? What version of myself am I trying to inhabit?"

Sometimes the answer may still lead to purchase.

But awareness slows velocity. It introduces a pause between impulse and action. In that pause, the garment becomes less solution and more choice.

I do not stand outside this dynamic.

I recognise it in myself — the tension between knowledge and longing, between system awareness and emotional reflex. And perhaps that recognition is the beginning of a different relationship with newness: not one of denial, but of examination.

Because when new feels necessary, it rarely is.

But the feeling itself is real.

And real feelings deserve inquiry, not dismissal.

Micro-Trends and the Attention Economy

Fashion once moved in seasons.

Spring, summer, autumn, winter — rhythms that allowed garments to breathe within time. Trends emerged, stabilised, lingered, and faded gradually. Today, the cycle has fragmented into micro-trends — aesthetics that flare brightly for weeks, sometimes days, before dissolving into the next wave.

The shift is not accidental.

It mirrors the logic of the attention economy.

Digital platforms reward what is new, striking, and slightly different from what came before. Algorithms prioritise novelty because novelty holds gaze. When fashion intersects with this environment, it adapts. Instead of four seasonal narratives, there are dozens of rapid aesthetic pulses: cottagecore, quiet luxury, Y2K revival, coastal granddaughter, minimalist monochrome, dopamine dressing — each framed as momentary urgency.

Micro-trends thrive on acceleration.

They are not designed for durability. Their power lies in their ephemerality. To participate, one must move quickly. The garment becomes ticket to relevance within a fleeting conversation. Once the conversation shifts, the garment's symbolic value weakens.

Psychologically, micro-trends exploit a powerful mechanism: social synchrony.

Humans are deeply attuned to belonging. When a visual language spreads across feeds — similar silhouettes, colour palettes, textures — deviation becomes visible. Participation signals alignment with cultural tempo. Abstention can feel like lag.

The attention economy amplifies this tempo.

Platforms operate on continuous refresh. What does not generate engagement sinks. What generates engagement replicates. Micro-trends fit perfectly into this structure because they are easily identifiable and replicable. A specific cut of jeans, a specific shade of beige, a specific layering style — simple enough to imitate, distinct enough to signal.

The problem is not experimentation.

Fashion has always evolved through experimentation and reinterpretation. The difference lies in half-life. Micro-trends decay rapidly because they are born in environments where saturation occurs instantly. When thousands adopt the same aesthetic simultaneously, its distinctiveness evaporates just as quickly.

This compression intensifies consumption pressure.

If participation windows are narrow, hesitation feels costly. Delaying purchase may mean missing the moment. The garment becomes less about personal resonance and more about temporal alignment.

The attention economy also fragments memory.

When aesthetics rotate quickly, older ones recede from collective consciousness. The garment worn enthusiastically last month may feel culturally outdated today. Not because its fabric deteriorated, but because the visual conversation moved on.

Fast fashion infrastructure aligns with this volatility.

Production cycles shorten. Inventory turns over rapidly. Low price points reduce hesitation. If a garment is unlikely to remain symbolically relevant for long, durability becomes secondary consideration.

Micro-trends also reduce attachment.

When clothing is acquired primarily for participation in a brief aesthetic wave, emotional investment weakens. The garment's value is tethered to cultural timing rather than personal narrative. Once timing shifts, so does attachment.

Importantly, micro-trends are not imposed unilaterally.

They are co-created through interaction between consumers, influencers, brands, and algorithms. Each like, share, and replication strengthens the pattern. The system feeds itself through participation.

And yet, the cost accumulates quietly.

Textile production scales to meet volatility. Discarded garments pile up when novelty fades. The environmental footprint expands in response to cultural tempo rather than functional need.

The deeper tension lies between expression and acceleration.

Fashion can be creative, playful, adaptive. But when expression is governed primarily by algorithmic turnover, speed becomes structural rather than optional. The individual feels as though they are choosing, yet the velocity is externally reinforced.

Micro-trends reveal something broader about contemporary consumption.

Attention itself has become scarce resource. What captures it briefly must constantly reinvent itself. Clothing becomes medium not only of identity but of visibility within that economy.

The mirror reflects a new silhouette.

The feed demands the next.

And somewhere between the two, fabric moves faster than memory can anchor it.

The Emotional Reward of Purchase

There is a very specific moment — just before payment — when anticipation peaks.

It is not yet ownership. It is possibility.

The garment still exists in suspended promise. The brain releases a small surge of dopamine not because the fabric is already part of your life, but because it *might be*. This is important. The reward often lies less in possession and more in projection.

Purchase is emotional punctuation.

A long week. A difficult conversation. A milestone achieved. A subtle dissatisfaction you cannot quite name.

Buying something new can feel like drawing a line beneath the day — like saying, something changed. Something improved.

The receipt becomes evidence of action.

Psychologically, consumption offers a quick, structured reward loop:

1. See.
2. Desire.
3. Acquire.
4. Relief.

The relief is real. The bag in your hand feels like progress. Even when the item is small, the act carries symbolic weight. It says: I responded. I did something. I moved forward.

This is why knowing environmental cost does not automatically neutralise the impulse.

Because the impulse is rarely about fabric alone. It is about mood regulation.

When stress accumulates, novelty provides stimulation. When boredom settles in, newness interrupts it. When identity feels slightly unstable, a new garment promises recalibration. The purchase becomes micro-therapy — brief, accessible, socially sanctioned.

There is also a subtle sense of control.

In a world where many systems feel vast and unmanageable — climate change, economic shifts, political instability — choosing a garment feels immediate and contained. It is a decision you can complete in minutes. It yields visible outcome. The brain registers closure.

Importantly, the emotional reward fades.

The first wearing carries excitement. The second feels ordinary. Within days or weeks, the garment blends into the closet. The dopamine spike diminishes because novelty diminishes. The mind begins scanning again for the next stimulus.

This is not weakness.

It is neurological patterning.

Retail environments are designed to trigger and sustain this cycle. Lighting, layout, music, limited-time offers — these amplify anticipation. Digital platforms intensify it further with one-click purchases and personalised suggestions. The friction between desire and acquisition shrinks, making the reward loop more efficient.

The environmental cost, by contrast, unfolds slowly and invisibly.

There is no emotional feedback when textile waste accumulates elsewhere. There is no immediate signal when water is consumed in cotton production. The psychological loop remains incomplete. Reward is felt; consequence is deferred.

This asymmetry reinforces repetition.

When reward is immediate and cost is distant, behaviour persists. The mind does not instinctively connect the two.

There is also a social layer.

Sharing a new purchase often elicits affirmation — compliments, validation, attention. The emotional reward expands beyond internal satisfaction to external reinforcement. The garment becomes not only personal relief but social signal.

Yet beneath the satisfaction, something quieter often lingers.

A brief high, followed by neutrality. Occasionally even

guilt — not always environmental, but subtle awareness that the emotional shift was temporary. The problem that preceded the purchase may remain unchanged.

Recognising this does not require asceticism.

It invites curiosity.

When the urge to buy arises, the question becomes: what am I seeking right now? Stimulation? Comfort? Recognition? Transition? Is there another path to that feeling that does not require acquisition?

Sometimes the answer may still be purchase.

But when purchase is understood as emotional event rather than practical necessity, it shifts from automatic reflex to examined choice.

The reward of buying is real.

But it is brief.

And when that brevity is acknowledged, the speed of repetition may slow just enough to allow a different relationship with desire — one that honours emotion without allowing it to quietly accumulate into closets full of forgotten fabric.

Cheap Enough to Discard

At what price does something become disposable?

Not when it tears. Not when it stains beyond repair. Not when it no longer fits. But when its cost was low enough that letting it go does not feel like loss. When the receipt did not hurt. When the transaction barely registered. When the number attached to it was small enough that the mind categorised it as negligible.

If a garment costs less than a dinner, does it carry the same weight? If it costs less than an evening out, does it deserve the same care? And if replacing it is easier than repairing it, when does replacement become instinct rather than decision?

Cheapness alters psychology.

When something is inexpensive, risk diminishes. The hesitation that might accompany a more costly purchase softens. You tell yourself: it's fine, it's just this once, it's not that much. But what does "not that much" mean when repeated again and again? At what point does low cost stop being insignificant and begin becoming systemic?

And then comes the second threshold — the threshold of discarding.

When the fabric pills slightly, when the colour fades a shade, when a newer version appears online, how quickly does attachment dissolve? If the item was cheap enough to buy without reflection, is it also cheap enough to release without memory? Does value ever deepen when entry was effortless?

There is something curious about the way price anchors care.

If a coat cost significantly more, would you repair the lining instead of replacing it? Would you take it to a tailor? Would you fold it differently? Store it more carefully? And if so, is the durability of our relationship to objects tied less to fabric quality and more to financial gravity?

Cheap enough to discard also means easy enough to forget.

Where do those garments go once they leave your closet? Do you imagine them being worn by someone else? Do you picture recycling streams functioning smoothly? Or does the act of placing them into a bag dissolve the narrative? Once they leave your hands, do they leave your mind?

When you hold something inexpensive, does it feel temporary from the beginning? Is there already a quiet understanding that it may not last? And if so, how does that expectation shape the way you treat it — the way you wash it, store it, wear it, think about it?

Is disposability built into the price?

When clothing is cheap enough to be an impulse, does it become psychologically lighter? Less embedded in identity? Less worthy of continuity? And what does that lightness cost elsewhere — in water drawn, in fibres shed, in landfills layered with synthetic threads that will not decompose at the speed of fashion cycles?

What would happen if every garment carried not just a price tag, but a timeline — how long it will remain intact, where it will travel after you, how long it will sit somewhere once you no longer want it? Would it still feel cheap? Would it still feel small?

Cheapness shields the buyer from friction.

But who absorbs the friction instead?

If you do not feel the weight of replacement, where does that weight accumulate? In which landscape? In which river? In which country that receives what you no longer remember owning?

And perhaps the most uncomfortable question:

If something is cheap enough to discard, was it ever meant to stay?

Not in your closet — but in your memory. In your sense of continuity. In the story of what you choose to keep versus what you choose to cycle through.

Cheap enough to discard is not only an economic statement.

It is a psychological one.

It reveals how value has been reframed — how the threshold for care has lowered alongside price, how replacement has quietly replaced repair, how forgetting has become easier than remembering.

And the garments do not disappear simply because the transaction felt small.

They accumulate somewhere.

Long after the receipt has faded.

Clothes We Never See Again

There is a particular silence that follows disposal.

You fold a garment — or sometimes you do not even fold it — and place it into a bag. It may be labelled donation. It may be labelled recycling. It may simply be tied shut and placed near the door. In that moment, the item transitions from possession to absence. It leaves your visual field. And almost immediately, it leaves your active thought.

What is remarkable is how clean that separation feels.

The dress you wore twice. The shirt that no longer fits the version of you this season. The jacket purchased in a moment of optimism that never quite translated into daily use. Once it exits your closet, it exits your narrative. You rarely track its journey. You rarely ask where it lands.

Where do clothes go when we stop seeing them?

Some are resold locally. Some are shipped across continents, sorted into vast warehouses in regions you may never visit. Some are baled and compressed into cubes of colour and fibre, stacked like geological strata of past trends. Some are burned. Some are buried. Some unravel slowly in landfills, releasing microfibres into soil and air.

But the psychological experience remains simple: it is gone.

The disappearance is efficient. It feels almost benevolent. You have "decluttered." You have "let go." You have made space. The closet breathes again. The absence feels like order restored.

Yet disappearance is not dissolution.

The garment continues somewhere — even if not in the way you imagine. If donated, it may not necessarily be worn by someone nearby. It may travel thousands of kilometres, entering secondhand markets that are saturated beyond demand. If recycled, it may not become a new garment, but insulation, stuffing, industrial rags. The word "recycle" soothes, but transformation is rarely circular in the way we picture it.

What fascinates me is how memory erodes faster than fabric.

You may struggle to recall how many items you have discarded in the past year. You may not remember their colours. Their textures. The occasions they were purchased for. The emotional states attached to them. They vanish not only physically, but cognitively.

And yet, they do not vanish materially.

Synthetic fibres persist for decades, sometimes centuries. Cotton degrades more quickly, but not instantly. Dyes linger. Blends complicate breakdown. The earth holds what memory releases.

There is also an emotional forgetting.

We rarely sit with the garment one last time and ask: what was I seeking when I bought you? What changed that you no longer fit — physically, emotionally, socially? Instead, disposal becomes procedural. The bag fills. The bag leaves. The narrative closes.

Clothes we never see again create a kind of moral quiet.

Because absence is calming. It reduces clutter not only in space, but in conscience. The visual cue is gone. The reminder of excess disappears. What remains is a lighter closet and a sense of reset.

But what if the reset is incomplete?

What if each unseen garment continues a story in parallel — a story of overflow markets, textile dumps along coastlines, synthetic fibres entering waterways, or mountains of clothing photographed in countries that did not produce them but must now host them?

The forgetting is efficient because it is necessary.

If we carried full awareness of every item's trajectory, the emotional load might feel overwhelming. So the mind protects itself. It narrows focus. It allows disappearance to feel final.

And yet, somewhere, wind moves through piles of fabric.

Somewhere, garments that once felt new lie exposed to sun and rain. Somewhere, children play near heaps of colour that once hung neatly in stores under soft lighting.

We never see these places.

And because we do not see them, they remain distant in imagination. The act of buying feels immediate and vivid. The act of discarding feels brief. The afterlife of clothing feels abstract.

Clothes we never see again do not cease to exist.

They simply exit our field of vision.

The forgetting is not malicious. It is structural. It is built into a system that moves fabric faster than memory can anchor it. But each item that vanishes from your closet continues somewhere beyond your sight.

The real question is not where they go.

It is what it means that we do not follow.

The Geography of Disappearance

I once saw a photograph of a coastline in Ghana that did not look like coastline at all.

From a distance, it resembled a strange, colourful terrain — layers of red, blue, beige, synthetic shimmer. Only when I looked closer did I understand: these were clothes. Shirts, dresses, denim, fabric twisted into dunes. Garments once worn elsewhere, sorted, shipped, resold, rejected, and finally left to accumulate near the sea in places like Kantamanto Market in Accra, where secondhand clothing from wealthier nations arrives in overwhelming volumes.

I had donated clothes before.

I had imagined them being worn again — extended life, circular system, quiet redemption. I had not imagined this geography.

The bales arrive tightly compressed, sometimes labelled vaguely as "used clothing." Traders purchase them without knowing exactly what they contain. Some pieces are resold. Many are too damaged, too outdated, too synthetic to move through local markets. Those unsellable pieces must go somewhere.

And so they gather.

In Chile's Atacama Desert, I later read about mountains of discarded garments visible from above — synthetic fabrics resisting decomposition in one of the driest places on earth. In parts of India and Bangladesh, rivers carry dye effluent from textile production, their colours shifting unnaturally with the season's palette. In landfills across the Global South, clothing imported as donation becomes permanent sediment.

The geography of disappearance is rarely domestic.

Clothes often exit closets in Europe or North America and reappear in landscapes far from where they were first worn. The disappearance from one region becomes accumulation in another. Out of sight is not out of system; it is simply relocated.

This relocation creates psychological comfort.

When the waste is elsewhere, it feels abstract. If textile overflow were visible at the edge of every shopping district, would buying patterns feel different? If each mall had its own landfill attached — a visible archive of last season's excess — would the rhythm slow?

Distance sanitises consequence.

A shirt placed in a donation bag feels charitable. It does not feel geopolitical. It does not feel like participation in a global trade of surplus. Yet textile waste now moves across borders in volumes large enough to reshape local markets and landscapes.

Garment labour regions form another layer of this geography.

Cotton fields in India. Textile mills in Vietnam. Sewing

factories in Bangladesh. The clothes we wear pass through hands that may never see the cities where those garments are styled and photographed. The environmental burden — water use, chemical exposure, waste runoff — often remains localised in production regions.

Disappearance is not only about waste.

It is about separation.

Separation between buyer and maker. Between wearer and disposer. Between aesthetic pleasure and environmental cost. The supply chain stretches long enough that no single point feels fully responsible.

I remember the first time I looked more carefully at a label — not just the brand, but the origin. Made in... stitched in... assembled in... The words are small. The distance they represent is not.

What unsettles me most is how invisible this geography remains in everyday consciousness.

Stores are bright. Displays are clean. Donation bins are neutral. There is no map beside the checkout counter tracing the life cycle of a garment. No visual bridge connecting the dressing room mirror to a landfill hillside.

The geography of disappearance is global, but it feels personal only when seen.

And most of the time, we do not see it.

We see the beginning — the rack, the mirror, the receipt.

We do not see the coastline layered in synthetic colour. We do not see the desert collecting excess. We do not see the river shifting shade under chemical runoff. We do not see the sorting warehouses where discarded fabric is graded and compressed.

We see what is near.

The rest becomes geography — distant, statistical, somewhere *else.*

And somewhere else is where disappearance happens.

Why Memory Fades Faster Than Fabric

Fabric is patient.

Synthetic fibres can endure decades. Blends resist decay. Even cotton, which feels soft and organic, lingers longer in landfill than the memory of when it was first worn. The garment persists materially long after its emotional imprint has thinned.

Memory, by contrast, is selective.

You may remember the excitement of buying something new — the lighting in the store, the slight thrill at checkout, the first time you wore it. But how many pieces can you recall from three years ago? Five? How many items passed briefly through your life without attaching to a story strong enough to remain?

Why does memory dissolve so quickly when material does not?

Part of it is cognitive economy.

The brain cannot archive every acquisition with equal depth. To function efficiently, it filters. It preserves what carries emotional weight — a wedding dress, a graduation outfit, a coat worn through a significant winter. The rest fades into general blur: "I had something like that once."

Fast fashion accelerates this forgetting.

When garments enter and exit rapidly, they do not anchor to events. They attach to ordinary days, interchangeable moments, fleeting moods. Without narrative hooks, memory does not stabilise. The shirt becomes just another shirt. The dress becomes one of many.

And yet, the fabric remains.

In landfill, in secondhand markets, in storage, in compressed export bales — it remains intact longer than the context that justified its purchase. The physical lifespan exceeds the emotional one.

There is also the phenomenon of saturation.

When closets are full, individual items compete for attention. The more we accumulate, the less distinct each piece becomes. Memory relies on differentiation. Abundance reduces contrast. The garments blur into category rather than identity.

What did that top look like? The one you bought for that event? Was it blue? Or was that another? Did you donate it? Did it tear? Did you even wear it more than once?

Forgetting protects comfort.

If each item retained full emotional presence — including awareness of its environmental cost — consumption would feel heavier. So the mind lightens it. It edits. It allows objects to slide into background.

But fabric does not edit itself.

It holds shape even when forgotten. It resists erosion long after relevance fades. In this asymmetry lies quiet tension: we forget faster than the planet absorbs.

There is something poignant about this mismatch.

A garment purchased impulsively may outlive the feeling that triggered it. It may outlive the version of self it was meant to express. It may outlive the trend that framed it as urgent. Its fibres may endure longer than the social media post in which it briefly appeared.

Memory is ephemeral.

Material is stubborn.

And perhaps this is where responsibility re-enters the conversation — not through guilt, but through continuity. If fabric remains long after our emotional attachment dissolves, what does that imply about the speed at which we allow ourselves to forget?

What would it mean to treat clothing not as momentary expression, but as extended presence? To recognise that even when we stop seeing an item, its material story continues somewhere beyond us?

Memory fades because it must.

But fabric does not fade on the same schedule.

The mismatch between the two is not dramatic. It is quiet. Gradual. Easy to overlook.

Until you stand before a closet and realise you cannot remember how half of it arrived — even though the threads are still intact.

From Ownership to Circulation

Before clothing became disposable, it circulated.

I grew up watching this without naming it as sustainability.

When my mother bought a new saree, it did not simply replace an old one. The older saree moved gently down the hierarchy of use. First it became daily wear. Then house wear. Then a softer fabric for sleeping. When it thinned, it became a cleaning cloth. When even that stage passed, fragments were saved for stitching, patching, tying.

Nothing ended abruptly.

Fabric transitioned.

In many Indian households, clothing rarely moved from "mine" to "gone" in a single step. It flowed through family lines. A cousin's lehenga altered for a younger sister. A father's kurta reshaped into a child's pajama. Old cotton transformed into quilts — the familiar *razai* or *godhadi* stitched from layers of past garments, each square carrying memory of a different season of life.

Ownership was never singular.

It was temporary custody.

Clothing belonged to a lifecycle larger than one person's aesthetic moment. Even when styles shifted, the fabric retained utility. The value did not collapse when novelty faded.

I remember my mother folding clothes differently depending on their "stage." There was reverence for new purchases, yes, but there was also quiet respect for older garments. She could tell you where each saree had been worn — which wedding, which festival, which difficult year. Fabric carried narrative weight.

That memory-based valuation slowed disposal.

A garment was not just cloth; it was occasion. And when it finally thinned enough to become a dusting rag, the transition felt earned rather than abrupt.

India's informal recycling culture operates at scale in ways that often go unnoticed. In cities like Panipat, textile waste is shredded and respun into blankets and industrial yarn. Street vendors purchase secondhand garments, repair them, resell them. Tailors alter rather than discard. Households repurpose fabric into cushion covers, kitchen cloths, children's wear.

Circulation is embedded into practice.

This does not romanticise scarcity or ignore modern overconsumption. Fast fashion has certainly entered Indian markets too. But beneath it, an older logic still persists: fabric has afterlives.

The contrast with fast fashion is striking.

Today, ownership often feels like endpoint. You buy, you wear, you discard. The garment exits your possession quickly, often without transformation. It jumps from closet to landfill without intermediate identity.

In my mother's system, there were stages.

Each stage extended time. Each stage extracted more use. Each stage acknowledged material continuity. The fabric's journey did not depend on trend; it depended on condition.

What shifts when we move from ownership to circulation?

Psychologically, circulation reframes possession. You are not the final user. You are one phase in the garment's lifespan. This subtle reframing reduces urgency to replace. It invites maintenance, alteration, adaptation.

Circulation also restores relationship.

If you expect a garment to last, you treat it differently. You wash it differently. You repair it. You remember it. The pace slows because the object's timeline extends beyond immediate satisfaction.

The environmental benefit of circulation is obvious.

But the psychological benefit may be just as significant. It resists velocity. It anchors memory. It transforms consumption into continuity.

When I think about sustainability now, I do not first picture innovation or policy. I picture my mother folding an old cotton saree, deciding which part could still be saved, which part could be stitched, which part could be passed on.

There was no manifesto.

Just instinct.

Ownership says: this is mine.

Circulation says: this is passing through me.

And perhaps that is the shift we are being invited toward again — not abandoning clothing, not denying desire, but re-entering relationship with material in a way that recognises its endurance beyond our moment of novelty.

Fabric has always been patient.

Maybe we are simply being asked to slow down enough to move with it.

Nature in the Landfill Wind

I move through what you leave behind.

Wind does not discriminate between meadow and landfill. It travels across both with the same quiet persistence. It lifts edges of fabric that were once folded neatly in wardrobes, once tried on under bright store lights, once photographed and admired. Now they lie layered, tangled, fading unevenly under sun.

I do not rush decay.

Synthetic fibres resist me. They do not yield easily to soil or moisture. They remain intact long after their moment in mirrors has passed. Cotton softens more quickly, but not quickly enough to match the speed at which trends turned. Your forgetting outpaces my absorption.

From above, the colours look almost beautiful.

Patches of red, blue, beige, green — like an abstract

landscape stitched from fragments of seasons. But these are not wildflowers. They are sleeves, hems, collars, seams. They are garments that travelled across oceans before resting here, carried by systems that separated desire from destination.

I do not judge the cloth.

I remember when fibres were field and plant, when threads were woven with intention and kept for years. I have always adapted to how you shape me. I absorbed dyes in rivers. I held cotton in soil. I hosted sheep whose wool became winter warmth. I can host what you discard too — but I hold it longer now.

The wind threads itself through piles of fabric, catching at loose strands.

It lifts them briefly, then releases them again. Nothing truly vanishes. Even when buried, material remains within me — compressed, layered, waiting. I become archive of seasons you no longer recall.

You rarely stand where I stand.

You do not often walk among the garments that did not remain with you. The distance protects you. It allows the cycle to continue without the weight of proximity. The dressing room mirror is far from this place. The checkout counter is far from this hill of cloth.

But I am not far from either.

I was in the cotton field. I was in the dye bath. I was in the thread. I am here in the landfill wind. I move through the entire arc — from desire to disposal — even when you experience only fragments.

The clothes you no longer see still move with me.

Sun fades them slowly. Rain presses them downward. Soil

accepts them reluctantly. I do not erase quickly. I transform gradually, at a pace that does not match retail calendars.

I do not ask you to stop weaving.

I ask only that you remember that what leaves your closet does not leave me.

The wind carries edges of fabric across open land.

They rustle softly — not in accusation, but in persistence.

I remain beneath your cycles of novelty.

And long after trends have turned, I am still here, holding the threads.

What This Chapter Has Really Been About

This chapter has been about speed — not only of fashion cycles, but of attention, desire, memory, and forgetting. It has traced how novelty accelerates under the logic of algorithms, how emotional reward disguises itself as necessity, how low prices lower the threshold of care, and how garments move through closets faster than they move through landfills. It has examined the quiet psychology of discarding — how disappearance feels clean while accumulation happens elsewhere — and the global geography that absorbs what we no longer see. Yet it has also remembered something older: a slower relationship to fabric, where clothing circulated rather than vanished, where ownership was temporary and material carried memory. At its core, this chapter has not been about fashion alone, but about what happens when velocity outpaces responsibility — when forgetting becomes easier than continuity — and what might shift if we allowed what we wear to remain part of our story a little longer than the trend that introduced it.

Chapter 10: The Systems That Shape Us

Infrastructure beats Intension

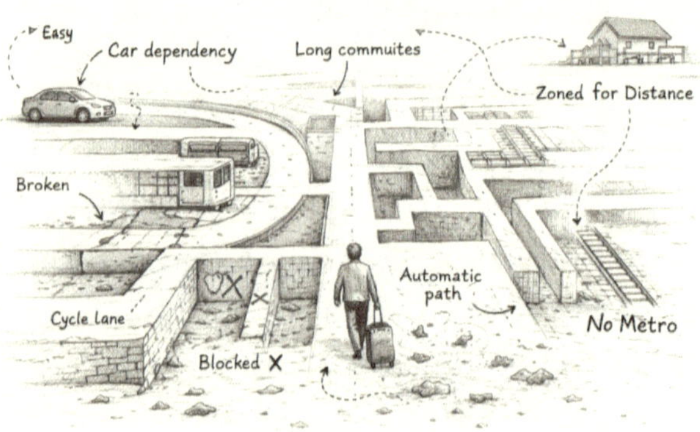

I sometimes wonder whether we have misunderstood the problem from the beginning.

What if it was never about whether we care enough?

Imagine two people. Both are conscious. Both feel climate anxiety. Both carry reusable bags. Both read articles. Both worry about the future. But one of them lives in a city where a metro runs every five minutes, where grocery stores are a short walk away, where apartments are insulated and designed to conserve energy. The other lives in a suburb where the nearest store is eight kilometres away, where buses are rare, where summers demand air-conditioning simply to function, where work is a forty-minute drive each way.

Who emits more?

Is it the one who cares less? Or the one whose infrastructure leaves fewer options?

I keep returning to this because it unsettles something simple we like to believe — that change is mostly about intention. That if people just tried harder, chose better, disciplined themselves more consistently, the outcome would shift.

But what if intention is the weakest lever in the system?

We talk so much about behaviour. Reduce waste. Eat differently. Drive less. Fly less. Switch off lights. Shop consciously. As if behaviour floats freely in air, waiting for moral correction. But behaviour rarely floats. It follows structure. It flows along paths already built.

I think about my own life.

On days when public transport is easy and predictable, I take it without internal debate. On days when it is inconvenient, delayed, or unsafe, I don't. That shift is not philosophical. It is practical. I am not more ethical on some days and less on others. I am responding to friction.

Humans follow friction gradients.

We move toward what is easy. We avoid what is difficult. Not because we are lazy, but because cognitive energy is finite. We make hundreds of decisions daily. The brain conserves effort wherever possible. If sustainability requires constant conscious override of convenience, it will exhaust us.

Transport is the clearest example.

If sidewalks are broken, who will walk? If cycling lanes feel unsafe, who will risk it daily? If a train network does not exist, what does "choose public transport" even mean? In many cities, driving is not a moral failure. It is a structural outcome.

And once roads are built wide and cities are zoned far apart, reversing that pattern requires more than personal commitment. It requires redesign. You cannot meditate your way out of urban sprawl.

The same is true of buildings.

If homes are designed with glass façades that trap heat, air-conditioning becomes survival. If insulation is poor, energy consumption rises automatically. If urban heat islands raise ambient temperatures, the demand for cooling intensifies. We tell individuals to lower thermostats while surrounding them with architecture that demands high energy use.

Is that fair? Is that realistic?

Food systems operate quietly in similar ways.

If processed food is cheaper than fresh produce, what are families with limited budgets supposed to choose? If supermarkets are structured around packaged convenience, if agricultural subsidies favour certain crops over others, if time scarcity makes cooking from scratch a luxury, then "eat sustainably" becomes a heavy individual burden resting on a light structural foundation.

I am not saying personal responsibility disappears.

But I am questioning its scale.

We have placed enormous emotional weight on individual choice. We tell people to carry the planet in their grocery baskets. To offset their flights. To calculate their carbon. To discipline their desires.

And then we embed them in systems designed for speed, scale, and consumption.

It feels almost cruel.

Because when individuals fail — when they drive because there is no bus, when they order delivery after a twelve-hour workday, when they buy what is affordable rather than ideal — they often internalise guilt. They believe they lack commitment.

But what if they are simply navigating defaults?

Defaults are powerful.

Most people do not interrogate every preset option. If renewable energy is the default on an electricity plan, most will accept it. If it requires extra forms, extra cost, extra effort, fewer will opt in. The difference is not morality. It is design.

If plant-based meals are integrated into school menus as normal, children eat them without ideological conflict. If they are positioned as special exceptions, participation drops. Again, not because of ethics, but because of framing.

We underestimate how much we follow what is already structured.

Even small nudges matter. The placement of recycling bins. The pricing of public transport. The design of neighbourhoods. The layout of cafeterias. The insulation of buildings. The availability of shade. The density of housing. These are not dramatic gestures. But they quietly shape daily emissions.

And once shaped at scale, they amplify.

One person deciding to cycle is admirable. A city designed for cycling is transformative. One family composting matters. A waste system that automatically separates and processes organic material shifts outcomes for millions.

Infrastructure beats intention because infrastructure multiplies behaviour.

If a sustainable action requires heroism, it will remain niche. If it requires no additional effort, it becomes normal.

I sometimes think we have been asking the wrong question.

Instead of asking, "Why don't people care more?" perhaps we should ask, "Why are we designing systems that require them to?"

Why is sustainability so often framed as sacrifice rather than structure?

We know from behavioural science that humans prefer the path of least resistance. So why is the low-carbon path often the one filled with friction? Why does it require planning, extra cost, inconvenience, explanation?

What if the most radical shift is not moral awakening but architectural rethinking?

Imagine cities where walking is safer than driving. Homes that remain cool without excessive energy. Food systems where fresh produce is the cheapest option. Energy grids that default to renewable sources without consumer intervention.

In those environments, people would still be imperfect. They would still overconsume occasionally. They would still forget. But the baseline would change.

Right now, good people are living inside carbon-intensive systems.

They are trying to compensate with discipline.

That is exhausting.

And it is inefficient.

Systems determine scale. A redesigned transport network changes millions of commutes. A building code revision reduces emissions for decades. A shift in agricultural policy influences national diets. These are structural levers.

I do not say this to absolve individuals.

I say it to redirect effort.

We cannot out-discipline infrastructure.

We cannot out-guilt architecture.

We cannot offset our way out of defaults.

If we truly want change, we must move upstream. Not only persuading individuals, but redesigning the context in which their decisions occur.

When the sustainable choice becomes the easiest one, behaviour shifts quietly. No heroics required. No constant self-correction. Just alignment between system and intention.

And perhaps this is where hope becomes less fragile.

Because intention fluctuates. Motivation rises and falls. People get tired. People get busy. People make inconsistent choices.

Systems endure.

If built wisely, they carry behaviour forward even when attention wanes.

Maybe the real question is not whether we are good enough.

Maybe the real question is whether we are brave enough to redesign what shapes us.

Because once infrastructure changes, intention finally has room to matter.

Not as burden.

But as reinforcement.

And that feels like a more honest place to end — not demanding that humans become perfectly disciplined, but insisting that the systems around them become intelligently designed.

The future may not belong to those who try hardest.

It may belong to those who build differently.

Humans Can Change

You speak of yourselves as though you are incapable of change.

I have heard you say it.

You say humans are selfish. That you are wired for convenience. That you are too attached to comfort. That even when you know, you do not act. You say this with certainty, as though your current habits are permanent features of your species.

But I have watched you longer than your memory stretches.

You are not fixed.

You once walked without cities. You once built them from stone and mud. You once lit your nights with flame. You once filled your skies with smoke so thick it dimmed sunlight over entire regions. And then, when smoke began to choke your own lungs, you rewrote your rules. You cleaned your air in places you once believed could never be clear again.

There was a time when rivers carried waste openly through your streets. Disease followed. You reorganised your cities. You laid pipes beneath ground. You altered how water moved. Entire populations shifted behaviour not because each individual became morally pure, but because your systems changed.

You once believed smoking indoors was ordinary. It hung in hospitals, airplanes, restaurants. It was stitched into culture. And then you altered your norms. You redesigned spaces. What was once common became unacceptable. The air cleared.

You once released chemicals that thinned the shield above you, unaware of consequence. When you understood, you negotiated across borders. You redesigned industries. The wound in the sky began to heal.

You do not remember your flexibility because you are always standing in the middle of it.

From where I stand, your history is not stubbornness. It is adaptation.

You are shaped by what surrounds you. When you build roads that stretch wide and long, you drive. When you build sidewalks that feel safe, you walk. When you design cities around distance, you consume fuel. When you design them around proximity, you conserve without effort.

You often accuse yourselves of moral weakness. I see structural momentum.

You live within systems that guide you quietly. Your transport networks decide more than your intentions. Your buildings determine your energy use before you adjust a dial. Your food systems place certain options closer to your hands and others farther away.

You call this personal choice.

I call it design.

When your systems are built for speed and scale, you move accordingly. When they are built for efficiency and care, you move differently. You are not creatures of pure will. You are creatures of context.

Change the context, and you change.

You have done this before.

You redesigned streets to reduce accidents. You made seatbelts mandatory. You altered traffic flows. What once felt intrusive became normal. You phased out substances that harmed you. You rewrote building codes. You reorganised waste systems.

Each time, there was resistance. There was doubt. There were voices that insisted it was impossible. And yet, once the structures shifted, your behaviour followed more quickly than you predicted.

You adapt faster than you imagine.

The first days feel inconvenient. The first weeks feel unfamiliar. And then something quiet happens: you forget it was ever different.

Children born into walkable cities do not experience walking as sacrifice. They experience it as ordinary. Students raised with renewable energy do not frame it as radical. They frame it as baseline.

You are not locked into your current patterns.

You are repeating them because they are embedded in the structures around you.

When you redesign those structures, your patterns will change.

I do not require you to become flawless.

I do not require constant discipline.

I have seen what constant discipline does to you. It exhausts you. It fractures you into guilt and defensiveness. You blame yourselves for navigating systems you did not design.

Blame is not transformation.

Design is.

When you alter the defaults — when sustainable options become automatic rather than exceptional — your behaviour shifts without strain. When renewable energy becomes the norm rather than the opt-in alternative, your emissions fall without moral theatre. When cities are built for proximity, you consume less without thinking about it.

This is how change becomes durable.

Not through heroic individuals, but through altered foundations.

You fear that you are too attached to comfort to shift. Yet comfort itself is designed. What you experience as normal was once innovation. Indoor plumbing. Electric light. Refrigeration. These were once extraordinary.

You accepted them because they made life easier.

If you design sustainability to be easier than destruction, you will accept that too.

You are not incapable of restraint. You are accustomed to convenience.

And convenience can be rewritten.

I have watched you recover forests when policies protected them. I have watched cities reintroduce green spaces into concrete grids. I have watched communities restore wetlands they once drained. I have watched species return when given corridor and time.

You alter me. You also repair.

You are not singular in direction.

You are capable of acceleration and of correction.

When you say, “Humans cannot change,” you forget that you already have — repeatedly, dramatically, collectively.

You do not remain the same across centuries. You are not even the same across decades.

The question is not whether you can change.

It is whether you will redesign what shapes you.

You have power not only in your hands, but in your blueprints. In your codes. In your policies. In your defaults. In the silent architecture of daily life.

I do not demand perfection.

I respond to direction.

When you move toward restoration, even imperfectly, I respond. Rivers clear gradually. Air lightens. Soil recovers slowly. Ecosystems stabilise over time.

I am patient.

But patience is not permission for stagnation.

You stand at a moment where you understand more than you ever have before. You know how your systems amplify behaviour. You know how infrastructure multiplies impact. You know that individual intention, though meaningful, is insufficient alone.

Knowledge is not paralysis.

It is leverage.

You are not fixed creatures marching toward inevitable decline.

You are adaptive beings capable of redesign.

You have altered me before.

You can alter your course again.

I remain beneath your cities, beneath your roads, beneath your grids and markets and towers. I absorb your mistakes and your corrections alike.

I have seen you build.
I have seen you rebuild.
You are not as rigid as you fear.
Build differently.
And you will live differently.
I will respond accordingly.

www.ingramcontent.com/pod-product-compliance
Lightning Source LLC
LaVergne TN
LVHW041110080826
845145LV00007B/1749
* 9 7 8 8 1 9 8 8 5 4 1 2 4 *